PITCHING UP AGAIN!

Camping Chaos in the Cotswolds

Deborah Aubrey

ISBN-13: 9798829789947
ISBN-10: 1477123456

Cover design by: Art Painter
Library of Congress Control Number: 2018675309
Printed in the United States of America
July 2023

DEDICATION

For campers everywhere.
Enjoy!

CHAPTER 1

Day 1: Friday

With teeth gritted and his face set like stone, Brian turned left into the car park of the Woodsman Pub. His eyes immediately widened and he made a little sound of surprise at the back of his throat. Beside him, an equally stony-faced Faye also sucked in air. The sight before them was nothing short of a miracle.

The Woodsman Pub was hardly recognisable from the place it had been the year before, when they'd last camped here. Gone were the dead vegetation in pots, the rotting wooden benches and the overall sense of neglect. Instead, a veritable garden display of flowers bloomed in hanging baskets and ceramic planters. The tables were new, sprouting giant umbrellas, under which sat a crowd of people, all chatting and laughing in the sunshine.

"Blimey," Brian gasped.

Faye wanted to say, 'Oh it's lovely,' but she tightly pursed her lips together instead. She wasn't talking. It was killing her.

The car park itself had been levelled and re-gravelled, so now wasn't a boing-fest for cars and caravans. The area next to the pub had been cleared of bushes to allow for more tables on the newly laid paving slabs down the side of the building. As they drew up level with it, they could just about make out a couple of wooden benches at the back. It all looked very neat and tidy, and welcoming.

"Wow," said Faye, despite herself, then glanced at Brian and huffed. She hadn't meant to speak out loud, hadn't, in fact, spoken at all since … well, she couldn't remember now, it seemed like a very long time ago. It was both frustrating and lonely, but he had started it, she couldn't cave in now.

As they admired the sunny, happy vista before them, they once again became aware of the incessant droning sound coming from the back seat of the car, and they both pursed their lips.

Brian drove up to the reception hut, now a much larger, more substantial building standing on the left side of the wooden gate that let onto the camping field beyond. He heaved himself out of the driver's seat - a man tall of stature and wide of shoulders, with a big, bushy beard - and slammed the door hard behind him. And there it was; blissful, peaceful silence. He stood motionless for a moment, savouring the sound of birds and the distant murmur of people chattering away.

Inside, the reception hut was much bigger than before, with more shelves of food, bigger fridges and freezers, and stacks of camping equipment for sale or hire. The counter was new and shiny. Behind it stood an enthusiastic young girl, who threw up her hands when she saw him and cried, "Are you one of our special guests?"

"I believe we are."

"Oh, you're our first!" Brian couldn't remember the last time someone had seemed so happy to see him. The girl, very chirpy looking and super excited, handed him some papers. On the top, a cardboard tag with their name, car registration and pitch number. She paused and took a deep breath before saying, as if from well-rehearsed memory, "Welcome to the Woodsman Caravan and Camping site, we're very happy to have you. We'd be grateful if you could take a few moments to fill in various short surveys throughout the duration of your stay, giving your honest opinions of our new, improved facilities. We'd also be grateful if you didn't mention to other campers that your stay here is free of charge, in exchange for your valuable views. Your pitch is just through the gates, second caravan area on the left. You probably already know where it is," she finished with a breathy giggle, "You've been here before."

"We have." Brian looked around, "It's improved quite a bit since our last visit."

"We hope you enjoy your stay," she said.

Brian went back to the car, smiling, despite himself. By the driver's door he braced himself, took a final peaceful breath, and opened the door. The droning noise from the back seat bore into his head like fingernails down a blackboard as he clambered in behind the wheel. He sat and waited, letting the noise envelope him in a tight grip once more. Faye looked straight ahead, also waiting. Then Brian said, "Do you want to do t'gate or shall I?"

Faye huffed and jumped out, opening it in a huffy, stompy kind of way. Brian drove through, and suddenly there it was, the campsite. Like the pub and the reception hut, it looked very different now; 'primped' was the word that popped into his head. The vast field looked neat and tidy, and half filled with various tents and campervans. There were two caravan areas on his left, each with six hardstanding pitches, the first one already full. He drove slowly over the gravel driveway to the second, where a familiar grey motorhome and a rather battered caravan sat in the far corners. He could see Mark under the awning, next to a table with a mug of tea and a packet of biscuits, a book in his hands. He raised a hand in welcome, and Brian waved back, feeling a brief surge of excitement, until Faye's annoyed face appeared at his open driver's window. "Forget me?" she snapped.

"No, I thought you could manage t'last bit on foot to stretch your legs and enjoy a brief but exquisite moment of silence."

She huffed. He drove into the caravan area, turned right onto an empty pitch, then reversed back. Faye stood there and watched with her arms tightly crossed, not offering any help, for which Brian was infinitely grateful. What he was not grateful for was the continuous, endless noise coming from the back seat. He pulled on the handbrake and turned off the engine.

They had arrived.

* * *

Mark leapt out of his chair and hurried over. "Brian!" he boomed, "You made it okay then?"

They greeted each other in the comfortable way that friends do, shaking hands and bumping shoulders. Brian's smile was wide and genuine behind his beard, as was Mark's. "It's been ages!" Mark laughed.

"It's got to be …" Brian sucked in air. "At least a month. How are you?"

"Good, good."

"Have you seen her yet?"

"No, not since we all got together at Christmas."

"Excited?"

"Mostly terrified, if I'm honest. Well, if I'm *totally* honest, I haven't eaten, I have a headache from all the thinking, and I can't stop shaking." He held his trembling hands out in front of him. "I'm a wreck, Bri."

"Have you had any indications?"

"None, just some texts, you know, that she sends to us all, and we've been out for a drink a couple of times when she's been here, but nothing … personal, just friends."

"I'm sure it'll be fine, lad."

Faye came running over to him for a big hug. "You're looking really well, Mark!"

"It's the unmarried life, it seems to suit me."

"It does!"

Behind them, the back door of their car creaked open. Brian stiffened, staring over Mark's shoulder into the woods that surrounded the campsite. "Brace yourself," he breathed, and Faye glared up at him. Mark wondered what was going on.

"This is my sister," Faye said, as a small, chunky woman leapt down from the back of the Sedona, landing on her feet with a small 'oomph', "Florence."

"Call me Flo," said Flo, coming to stand with them and holding the back of her hand out to Mark, who briefly wondered if he was supposed to bend and kiss it. "Fan*tas*tic to meet you, Mark, I've heard such a lot about you, about all of you really, and I was so excited to get together with you and the others. Isn't it a fan*tas*tic campsite? I love the Cotswolds, don't you? Of course you do," she laughed, "That's why you're here, and you have a garden centre nearby as well, don't you? Can't wait to come and see it, I love shopping for garden stuff. You do too, don't you, Faye, couple of rampant shoppers we are, can't be trusted around …"

"Kill me," Brian breathed out of the side of his mouth, "Kill me now."

Mark laughed, but stopped when he saw the desperation in Brian's eyes. Flo was still talking in a thick Brummie accent, very fast and very high pitched. There didn't seem to be any 'inflow', only a constant outpouring of words. "Run," Brian whispered, "Save yourself, there's nothing that can be done for us, we're doomed, but there's still hope for you if you just run, run *now*."

"You okay, Bri?"

"And I said to Faye, didn't I, Faye," Flo continued, "I said, 'Faye, it would be fan*tas*tic to meet all these marvellous people you've told me so much about,' and here we are, meeting at last on this really fan*tas*tic campsite. It's lovely, isn't it, so much space and fresh air and all these fan*tas*tic trees and …"

"Setting up camp now," Brian suddenly boomed, turning to unhitch the car. "You'll help with the ceremonious landing of the coolbox, won't you, Mark?"

"Yes, of – "

"… middle of the Cotswolds," Flo was saying, cutting him off, "Been before, of course, oh, a long time ago now, but it's still the same, isn't it, the countryside never changes, unless they build on it, of course, but they won't build on the Cotswolds, will they, it's got to be protected or something …"

Faye was gently guiding her into the caravan. "I haven't

put the stabilisers down yet!" Brian bawled. Faye ignored him.

Mark thought there was definitely something strange going on.

* * *

Just as Mark was helping Brian to pull the awning bags from the back of the car, a beige Mini with a Union Jack on the roof drove through the entrance gates. Mark's heart immediately started racing and he felt overwhelmed with relief and excitement and absolute terror. It had been a long time. They had made a pact, an agreement, set a time limit, but that time was now over. A year, a whole year. It had seemed like forever, but the wait was finally at an end. He wasn't sure what would happen next, he just knew he felt happy to see that little car and its driver again.

"Olivia!" Brian cried.

"Liv?" shouted Faye, jumping out of the caravan, "Is she here?"

The little car drove into their caravan area and the engine had barely turned off before Olivia, all smiles and wild, curly hair, leapt out. "OH!" she screamed, racing up to them with open arms, "You're here!" She wrapped Faye in a warm embrace. "*Lovely* to see you, darling. And Brian, handsome as ever." She glanced fleetingly at Mark, standing stock still a couple of feet away.

"You're looking exceptionally well, lass!" Brian said, taking in her glowing face and wide, bright eyes, "World travel is clearly your thing."

"Oh my God, it is!" she squealed, glancing again at Mark, who took a tentative step forward with a nervous smile. "I've been everywhere, done everything, just like Sophie said. It's been *amazing*!"

"It's been *ages* since we last saw you," Faye cried, "When did you get back from your trip?"

"Last week. America was … eye-opening."

"All those WhatsApp pictures were lovely, especially the African safari, I was well jeal."

"I've got so much to tell you!"

"I can't wait!"

Flo burst out of the caravan at that moment with her arms already open in anticipation of her own hug. "You must be Olivia!" she cried, latching onto her.

"It's Liv now," she said, "Liv by name, live by nature, a whole new – "

"Fan*tas*tic to meet you. I'm Flo, Faye's sister, she might have mentioned me? We're very close, complete opposites but we rub along quite well together, don't we, Faye?"

Faye opened her mouth to answer but she wasn't quick enough. "Lost my poor cat a few weeks ago," Flo continued, "Faye was kind enough to let me stay at her house for a bit to recover."

"*Her* house?" said Brian.

"Oh, it was such a shock, I was completely devastated. Old she was, my cat, twelve years, which is a good age for a cat, and ..."

Olivia's smile had dimmed a little from this sudden verbal onslaught, until she turned to give Mark her full attention and the wattage went up again. "Mark," she breathed, stepping forward to give him a genuine but slightly awkward hug.

"Looking lovely as ever, Liv." There was some fumbled cheek kissing and then they both took a step back, glancing furtively at each other. Flo was still talking about her cat.

"You didn't drive the motorhome here, did you?" Brian looked first at the grey beast, now parked across the back of the pitch instead of its length, and then at the tiny car.

"No, I store the van here now, come down whenever I get the chance, which admittedly isn't as oft-"

"To see each other?" Flo interjected, nodding at her and Mark.

"Oh no," Olivia giggled, "Just for a break, you know, but

we sometimes get together for a catch-up, when I'm here."

"Are you two together?" Flo asked.

"No, no," they both said, shaking their heads and smiling awkwardly.

"You look as if you're together. Such a nice-looking couple. I'm usually quite good at sensing if the vibe is right between two people, but I guess my vibey senses must be off today after all that travelling – "

"Ninety minutes," Brian sighed, "Ninety long, torturous, unsilent minutes. It seemed a lot longer."

" – cooped up in the back of a car throws my chakras right out – "

"A seven-seater Kia Sedona is hardly cramped cond-"

" – but I must say, you do make a fan*tas*tic couple. Have you considered getting together?"

"No, no, we're just … friends," Mark said.

"Oh, shame. Never mind, there's always time, and my intuition on these things is hardly ever wrong, you mark my words. Oh, 'mark' my words!" Flo cackled loudly and continued her monologue about vibes and chakras. With a pained expression, Olivia lifted her head and struggled to speak over her to Faye. "Sophie's just called, she can't get away tonight but she'll be here first thing in the morning."

"What about Tel?"

"He's not coming. Sophie's going to bunk up with me in the motorhome."

"… followed me everywhere, she did, the little darling. Fan*tas*tic cat, she was my shadow, I'm quite bereft without her …"

"Tel's not coming?" Faye repeated.

"No."

"They didn't break up, did they?"

"… loved her milk, and mackerel, which is unusual for a cat because of the smell, but she couldn't get enough …"

"I'm not sure," Olivia said, "She was a bit vague about the whole thing."

"Oh, I was looking forward to having some sophisticated eye candy wandering around the place."

"Me too," Olivia giggled.

"I am here, you know," said Brian, deadpan.

"I'm allowed to notice young and handsome when I see it, Bri. I'm married, not dead."

"It's the drooling that's so embarrassing."

"I don't drool!"

"Don't you have enough to drool over already?" Brian stood tall, with his hands on hips and chin in the air like a Marvel superhero. Faye huffed loudly, but a tiny smile struggled to escape the corner of her mouth. Brian looked down at Mark and breathed, "I've still got it. Woman can't resist me."

"I can," she said, brushing past him, "And I am."

"I'm aware. I'm hoping you'll stop resisting soon."

"Don't hold your breath."

Flo was still yakking on about her cat, and Brian's superhero stance slumped, deflated.

Faye touched Olivia's arm, saying, "We'll have a catch-up when we've set up camp, I want to hear all about your adventures."

"I can't wait."

Flo followed her sister into the caravan, taking the ceaseless monologue with her.

"How long has Flo been staying with you?" Mark asked.

"Four weeks, three days, fifteen hours and –" He glanced at his watch. " – thirty-seven minutes."

"Oh."

"Oh, indeed. It's a constant droning sound, like tinnitus or an irritating fly buzzing around your head. It never goes away, it never … *stops!*"

"Brian!" Faye yelled from inside the caravan.

"Yes, my love?"

"Caravan's wobbling."

"That'll be because I haven't put the stabilisers down

yet."

"Are you going to put them down or shall we just wobble around all week?"

"Coming, light of my life."

"I've got to put my shopping away," Olivia said, heading back to her car.

"And I've got to ..." Mark shrugged. "I'll help with the awning, Bri."

"Good man."

Mark glanced back at the Mini as it parked next to the motorhome and watched as Olivia unloaded her bags of shopping. He smiled.

"Good to see you're so happy to help me with the awning," Brian teased. He looked back at Oliva too. She raised a bagged hand and gave them a cute, overbite smile. "Happy with something, anyway, eh?"

* * *

As they set up camp, with Flo flittering between them all, talking the whole time, Brian glanced over at the first caravan area as he plugged in the electric supply. The two sites were separated by a waist-high line of shrubs, and he could see a man lounging beneath a canopy outside the caravan behind theirs. The man raised a hand and said, "Afternoon."

"Afternoon."

"Nice day for it."

"It is."

"Have you been here before?"

"Once, last year. Looked different then."

"Yes, they've apparently done a lot of work on it. Name's Bill, by the way."

"Brian."

Bill stood up and they reached over the hedge to shake hands. "I'm camping for the first time on my own actually. My other half died last year, but I couldn't bear to part with the caravan, we had so much fun in it, so I've just started to use it again."

"I'm sorry to hear that."

"Really good times," he said wistfully. "Don't hesitate to stop for a chat at any time. I've told everyone." A woman outside a caravan across the way raised her hand at that moment and yelled, "Y'okay, Bill?" He raised a thumb high in the air. "Friendly lot," he said.

"Yes, it was a good atmosphere last time we came." Brian suddenly remembered the man in black stalking their caravans, Olivia's presumably now ex-husband being a pain in the posterior, and the yummy-mummies vomiting all over the place. "Had a good time," he said.

"I'm an old hand at this caravan lark, so feel free to ask for advice, always happy to help."

"Cheers, appreciate it."

Bill nodded and wandered off with his hands clasped behind his back, sergeant major style. The new caravan area was identical to theirs and seemed quite lively, with adults and kids milling about, even a couple of tethered dogs panting in the sunshine. Someone had already started up a barbecue, and a couple of kids were playing badminton on the driveway running down the middle. Brian smiled, thinking, as he always did, that this was going to be a good holiday - until the droning sound coming from the caravan reminded him that he'd be lucky to survive the next seven days with his sanity intact.

Sighing, he dragged the Aquaroll to the water tap next to Mark's caravan. He left the tap running into the container and went and sat with him at the table outside.

"Cuppa?" Mark asked.

"I could do with something stronger."

"So early?"

"So needed."

"Trouble at pit, lad?" Mark laughed.

"Pit's caved in."

"Caved in? How do you mean?"

"Foundations are unstable, they could go at any minute."

"What?" Mark sat up straight in his chair. "Are you and Faye in trouble?"

"Aye."

"Oh God, Bri! Is it Flo?"

Brian sighed. "There's never any silence, there's just this constant flow of Flo. It's doing my head in, Mark. I'm convinced she's afraid of silence, like she might get sucked into a vacuum of nothingness if she stops talking. I'm thinking of moving onto hard liquor, purely for mental health reasons."

This was terrible. Brian and Faye were the 'golden couple' who had the kind of relationship every one of them aspired to. "Just ask her to leave."

Brian turned his bearded face towards him, his eyes heavy with despair. "You think I haven't tried? Faye won't let me, says Flo needs her and we should be supportive, but I'm losing my mind. Even sitting here I can hear her voice boring into my brain. It's like a form of torture."

They both looked over at the caravan, where Flo was following Faye around, nattering constantly but not actually doing anything.

"How's Faye taking it?"

"She's used to it, the yakking doesn't seem to affect her at all."

Mark noticed that Faye seemed a bit huffy, constantly having to walk around Flo, who simply did not stop talking and was contributing nothing at all to the setting up of the camp except for getting in the way. "Are you sure about that?" he asked.

"The only time we get to be alone is in bed, but by then we're too exhausted to speak and just lie there, staring at the ceiling, listening to Flo talking to friends on her phone downstairs or in her bedroom, right next to ours. There's no getting away from it, she talks from the minute she opens her eyes until she closes them at night. She even talks in her sleep, I can hear her through the wall, and of course sex is completely out of the question, can barely remember the last time we had any, it's just a distant memory!"

Mark wasn't sure what to say, so he just said, "It's a bit early, and Faye will probably beat me to a pulp, but do you want a beer?"

"I do, I really do."

"Follow me," Mark winked, getting up, "There's something I want to show you inside the caravan."

"Now there's an offer I can't refuse. No, wait, that sounded weird. I'm losing it, Mark."

"I have just the cure."

The caravan door closed shut. Seconds later came the muffled hiss of can tabs.

* * *

"BRIAN!"

"WHAT?"

Faye opened the door to Mark's caravan and peered inside. They were both lying on opposite sofas, resting cans of lager on their bellies.

"Are you drinking, Bri?" she snapped.

"I might be."

"You are, aren't you!"

"I reserve the right to remain silent. Wait!" he gasped, sitting up quickly, "Talking of silence, where is she?"

"Don't be so dramatic, Bri, she's just gone to the toilet."

"Here's to whole minutes of peace and quiet," he said, raising his can and clashing it against Mark's. "Listen to it! Nothing! I feel quite giddy with joy!"

"Brian!"

"Yes, my love?"

"The Aquaroll is flooding the campsite."

"Oh … *merde!*"

Mark laughed as Faye tutted and wandered off. "Merde, Bri?"

"French, you know."

"I did know. I didn't know you knew."

"Oh, I'm a man of many talents, me. I look them up on my phone whenever I get the chance, swear words in different languages. That way I can toss expletives around like confetti and the women remain oblivious. It's very satisfying."

"I'll bet."

"BRIAN!"

"WHAT?"

"THE FLOOD!"

"TURN THE TAP OFF THEN!"

"IT'S NOT MY JOB!"

"Oh *merde, merde, merde*!"

Brian stood up and quickly gulped down the remainder of his can.

* * *

The erection of the awning was quite a jovial affair, as Brian and Mark quenched their hard-working thirst with fresh cans of beer, much to the consternation of Faye, who couldn't say anything because they Weren't Officially Speaking. Flo said a lot though, about how they should lay out the poles, how they should thread the canvas into the side of the caravan more efficiently and how they should lift up the awning with less effort.

"Done much caravanning, have you?" Mark asked, as Flo stood pointing at a pole on the ground.

"No," she said. "But even I know that pole should be on the other side."

"It's the left-hand pole for the left-hand side of the awning," Brian retorted.

"It's the right-hand pole, and you've obviously been doing it wrong all this time."

"It doesn't fit together any other way!"

"Suit yourself," Flo said, wandering off to talk to Faye, who was sitting on the hitch at the front of the caravan having a brief moment to herself.

The men sipped their cans as they laid out and lifted the awning without any bickering at all.

"See!" Brian cried, "It can be done!"

"Man power," Mark laughed, flexing his biceps.

Afterwards, as the women, mostly Faye, lay down the groundsheet and set out the table and chairs, the cushions and blankets, the Teriyaki grill and halogen oven, and the small coolbox on the other table, there came the ceremonious Lifting of the Coolbox from the back of Brian's car. "Still the best thing I ever bought," said Brian, dragging it into the awning, "Although I am considering purchasing a set of industrial earplugs. Oh, did I say that out loud?"

"You did," Mark laughed.

"You did!" snapped Faye.

"I thought you weren't speaking to me, wife."

"I'm not!"

"Yet there you are, speaking to me. Is our little spat over now then?"

"We're not having a spat," Faye spat, "We're having a …" She couldn't think of the right word to describe what they were doing. Silent disagreement? Non-verbal warfare?

"Breakdown?" Brian suggested, chugging on his can. "Clash of wills? No, wait, I've got it, we're having a parting of the ways, or will do if this carries on for much longer."

"Don't say that!" Mark winced.

"Brian!"

"Again, I apologise for speaking out of turn," he said, throwing himself into his favourite chair before Flo could. "It's just that I have all these thoughts in my head, none of which I can articulate without being withered with a look from the wife, and occasionally they just spill out of their own accord." He finished off his can.

"Are you drunk, Bri?"

"Not yet, but I'm working on it, drinking to kill the pain of my battered eardrums and my sad, broken, lonely heart."

Faye stopped what she was doing and stared at him.

"I miss you," he said.

"Oh Brian."

"Are we eating soon?" Flo asked, cutting through the moment, "Only I'm getting a bit hungry and don't want to leave it too late because it sets off my acid reflux and I'll be up half the night and ..."

Brian sighed. Faye sighed and stepped up into the caravan, with Flo right behind her. Mark sighed too and swigged on his can.

Olivia wandered over. "Are we going to the pub?" she asked.

"Why not." Brian heaved himself out of his chair. "Let us savour the dubious delights of the Woodsman pub. They do food now, don't they?"

"Oh yes," Olivia grinned, "They have a new chef and a whole new menu."

"Then off to the pub it is!"

* * *

The Woodsman was packed, *heaving* with people outside at the front tables in the sunshine and inside. Brian, three cans down on an empty stomach, exploded through the doors and inhaled deeply. "Oh!" he boomed, "The delicious smell of home cooking."

"Keep it down, Bri," Faye hissed, "You're being very loud. Have you got your hearing aids in?"

"No."

"Then put them in."

Brian ignored her and sniffed at the air again. "The sign of a good pub is the number of people in it, the atmosphere, and the warm smell of food." He sighed out loud, making his way through the crowd with the others following in his substantial wake.

"We'll never find a table," Faye said, as Flo dashed off to the toilets.

"Over here." Olivia was pointing at the one where they all used to sit.

"It's reserved, Liv."

"Yes, for us. I rang ahead and booked it."

"Olivia!" Brian bawled, pulling out a chair and throwing himself into it, "You're a star."

She giggled, briefly touching the star earrings she was wearing, a gift from Sophie and Tel the previous year - her little talismans.

"Name your poison," Mark said, as they all settled down. They called out their drinks and Mark went up to the bar.

Faye picked up a laminated menu and glanced at the list for 'Friday'. "Ooh, posh nosh. Reasonable prices though. Oh look!" she cried, "They've got beef bourguignon! We had that on our first day last year, do you remember?"

"Courtesy of our cook extraordinaire," Mark said.

"Oh stop," Olivia giggled, waving her hands in front of her.

"Saved my life," Brian sighed, "I was on the brink of famishment, about to expire, and there came this vision with a casserole dish."

"Good times," Faye said.

"I think this is going to be a very good holiday, we can eat here every day."

"And it's all free," Olivia said, "It said so in the email."

"Oh yes!"

"I've never had anything for free before!" Faye said.

Brian coughed loudly.

"You're not free, you're hard work."

"Am I?"

Faye hesitated, then threw her eyes back on the menu. "Are we having starters? I'm not sure what to have, it's all so tempting. And the puddings sound lovely too. What are you having, Bri?"

Brian gave a little grin. She was cracking, she wouldn't be able to hold out for much longer. He really did miss her. What he didn't miss was the sister. "Where's Flo?" he dared to ask.

"She just popped to the loo."

"Again? Is she ill?"

"No, I told you, she's upset about her cat and goes off to have a cry."

"Oh. Well let's enjoy the brief moment of peace while we can."

"Don't be so horrible!"

"You're spoiling my brief moment of silence, woman!"

"We're in the middle of a busy pub, *Brian*, there is no silence!"

"Silence from that certain pitch of endless bloody yakking!"

"You could be a bit more understanding!"

"I've *been* understanding, *and* patient, *and* tolerant. Now I'm just frustrated and exhausted."

"Hey," Mark said, returning with a tray of drinks, "You're supposed to be our role models, not a walking advert for Marriage Guidance counselling."

"We're just going through a bad patch," Faye said.

"A bad patch which started four weeks, three days, sixteen hours and – " Brian glanced at his watch. " – fifty-eight minutes ago."

"Brian!"

"Stop saying *Brian*!"

"Stop being horrible about my sister then!"

"I will, the instant she *goes home*!"

"Oi!" Mark snapped. "We're here to enjoy ourselves, so enjoy yourselves and *stop fighting*!"

"He started it," Faye mumbled.

"Did not!"

"Special guests!" cried a tiny, red-haired woman

approaching their table. "So glad you could make it! I'm Chelsea, I'm the Manager, and I'm here to make your stay here as pleasant as possible. If you need anything, come to me. Something you don't like, come to me. Something you would like, come to me. You're our guinea pigs for the next few days and we want to know exactly what you think of the place, so don't hold back." She lowered her head and whispered, "All food and drink are free, so just help yourselves, but we would like your honest opinions in return, so we'll be handing out short survey sheets, if you wouldn't mind just filling them in, that would be awesome." She stood back up, sparking with enthusiasm. "We've got lots of things for you to try out for us, so just enjoy yourselves, basically, and give us your feedback. Gotta dash, we're incredibly busy, but you know where I am if you want me."

And she was gone. They all grinned at each other, excited, then lowered their heads and were lost in silent, glorious appraisal of the menu.

"This is a vast improvement on last year," Brian said, "All the pub grub classics, plus a few chef specialities." He suddenly exploded with a burst of laughter. "Look what they have, light of my life."

Faye scoured the menu.

"Number three, under 'snacks'. Your favourite." He turned to the others, adding, "Faye loves them but can't order them herself, I have to do it for her. Tell them what number three is, Faye."

"No."

"Go on."

"No!"

"Makes her tongue vibrate up and down uncontrollably," Brian told them. "Go on, Faye, tell them what number three is."

Faye hesitated, rolled her eyes, sighed, and then said, "Falafalel."

Brian pounded the table with amusement. Several

people standing around them turned to look. Faye went crimson. Olivia and Mark struggled not to laugh.

"Is that what you're having?" Brian howled. "I can order it for you in English, if you want?"

"Shut up. And yes, thank you."

"You're welcome. So," he said, changing the subject and turning to Mark, "Ant sold the pub, then?"

"Well, his parents insisted because he was so rubbish at running it."

"Who bought it, some big conglomerate?"

"No, it's still a free house."

Flo came from the toilets, red-eyed and sniffing, and threw herself down in a chair next to Faye. "I'm back!" she cried dramatically, "Did you miss me?"

Brian took a breath, oomphing it out when Faye briskly elbowed him in the ribs.

"So, what you all talking about?" Flo continued, "Anything interesting? Anything juicy? Are we having a drink? I'm parched after all that work setting up camp, it's quite exhausting, isn't it."

Brian breathed in, ready to mention that Flo hadn't actually done anything to help set up camp, but noticed Faye's elbow set at a strategic angle towards him and breathed out again.

"So, are we having a drink?" Flo continued. "I must say, I don't normally drink this early, do I, Faye, but it's different when you're on holiday, isn't it, you can do what you like, when you like."

Brian made a noise at the back of his throat and pursed his lips tightly.

Flo glanced at the menu and cried, "Oh, mackerel! My cat loved her mackerel, which is unusual for a cat because - "

The pub door burst open at that moment, and Jim walked in.

CHAPTER 2

"Watcha!" Jim cried, spotting them at the table and bounding over. "How you all doing?"

"Jim!" Olivia cried, "So glad you could make it!"

They hugged across the table before Jim threw himself down on a chair and raised a finger at the girl behind the bar, who nodded. Mark quickly shook hands, Brian engulfed his digits, and Faye leaned sideways to kiss his cheek. "You look well," she said.

"It's married life, it seems to suit me."

"You got back with your wife then?"

"He did," Mark laughed, "Surprisingly."

"Took some doing," Jim said, oozing cheeky-chappy charm, "But I managed to win her round in the end."

"Wore her down, you mean."

"Yeah, that too."

"Is your wife with you?" Olivia asked.

"She's out with her mates tonight, but she might pop in tomorrow."

"Be lovely to meet her."

Jim rubbed his hands together. "Nice to see the old gang back together again, how are you all hanging?"

"We is hanging well," Faye laughed, and Brian realised he hadn't heard her laugh in a long time.

"You must be Jim," Flo said.

"Clue in the name we all cried out when he walked in, was it?" Brian said, earning him a side-eyed look from Faye.

"I'm Flo, Faye's sister."

"Yes, you look similar," Jim said, "Older or younger sister?"

Flo giggled, and Brian realised he hadn't heard her

giggle in a while either. "Guess," she said.

"Twins?"

"Good one," said Mark.

"Beth taught me the difficult art of diplomacy, amongst other things."

"Like monogamy?"

"Oh don't start, I just got here!"

"Go on," urged Flo, "Guess who's the eldest."

"Careful, lad," Brian rumbled, "It's a trap, you know what these women are like."

"I couldn't possibly say, it's too close to call."

"Me!" cried Flo, "I'm the eldest, but only by a couple of years."

"Five," Faye said.

"Well, four a bit."

"Four years and eleven months."

"Ten and a half months."

"Both fabulous women."

"Beth has been working on you, hasn't she!" Mark said.

"The woman is a saint."

"She'd have to be to put up with you."

Jim leaned forward across the table and said, "Mark, do you think you could cut out the crap? We've known each other for a long time and I know you've never liked me, but I'm a changed man now."

Mark leaned forward and said, "I'll believe it when I see it."

"You're looking at it, mate."

The girl behind the bar came and placed a pint in front of Jim, giving him a wink before rushing off again.

"So, changed man, how come the barmaid knows what you drink?"

"She used to work at the pub down the road from me."

"And the wink?"

Jim raised his hands. "I can't help being irresistible, can I?"

"Jim!" Flo suddenly cried, breaking off from her one-sided conversation with Faye about birthdays, "I must tell you about my cat, Kat."

There was a sudden silence around the table.

"Your cat was called Kat?"

Brian was slowly nodding his head.

"Katty Purry," Flo said, "Kat for short."

"That is the best pet name I've ever heard!" Jim howled, and Flo looked rather pleased with herself.

"Dead now, I'm totally bereft without her."

"Oh, I'm sorry."

Brian started slowing shaking his head at Jim, his eyes wide with warning.

"Fan*tas*tic cat she was, there wasn't a mean bone in her body, until it came to mackerel. She absolutely loved mackerel, loved the smell, very unusual for a cat to like mackerel but Kat did. It was expected, of course, her death, she was old, twelve years, which is a good age for a ..."

Brian watched as Jim's eyes slowly glazed over and that 'trapped' expression appeared on his face. Fortunately, the waitress came for their orders and they all busied themselves with the menu.

"What did you say you wanted for starters, Faye?"

She glared at him across the table. He ordered for her.

* * *

The meal was delicious, despite it being accompanied by Flo's endless yakking about her cat, about the food, about her friends' cats and the neighbours' cats. To counteract the constant flow of Flo, Brian loudly nom-nommed his way through all three courses. "My compliments to the chef," he said, when the waitress came for their empty dessert plates.

"I'm too full to set up camp up now," Jim sighed, rubbing his belly.

"Are you in the van again?"

"No, I borrowed a mate's caravan. It's out there."

They all turned their heads to look out of the window. On the car park sat Jim's small white Transit, attached to a very old caravan with an aged, green hue to it.

"That's older than ours," Brian laughed, "And that's saying something."

"Old, but in perfect working order. It's got a motor mover and everything."

"Is it ... is it *listing* on this side a bit?" Faye asked.

"A bit."

"I'm assuming the green marks all down the side are the remains of the Cotswolds countryside as you ploughed down narrow lanes in a listy manner?" Mark laughed.

"Shut up and show me how to park it."

They all groaned with fullness again, but roused themselves from the table and left the pub. Jim went into the reception hut for his papers, the women chatted by the gate, or rather, listened to Flo, while Mark and Brian gave the green caravan a once-over.

"Bloody pongs," Mark said, holding his nose.

"It's a death-trap. The tyres are flat, and bald."

"I'm surprised he managed to get it here in one piece."

"Out there somewhere is a picturesque lane with no leaves down one side."

"Good job he didn't have to come far then."

"What do you think of it?" Jim asked, coming back.

"It's ... okay."

"I might clean it while I'm here, get some of that moss off."

"You could risk pumping the tyres to see if they crack or not," Brian suggested.

"Mate said they're the original ones."

"So that makes them, what, at least 20 years old?"

Mark sucked in air. Jim said, "They made them to last in those days, didn't they."

"I think we just found our entertainment for the week,"

Brian grinned behind his beard, "Watching Jim camp for the first time and waiting to see if the caravan will last a full seven days."

* * *

It took three attempts for Jim to get through the wide entrance into the caravan area. The whole campsite watched him make a complete hash of a simple turn. Brian saw one of the tenters open up a folding chair and sit down to watch as he ate a sandwich. Everyone in the other caravan area looked on, enthralled, even Bill. The gang tried to offer advice and guide him, mostly Flo, who leaned in his driver's window, looked back and screeched, "LEFT A BIT! A BIT MORE! Have you never reversed before?" Mark stood behind and tried to guide him in with exaggerated arm movements, but Jim obviously wasn't in the habit of looking in his mirrors and nearly run him over. Brian stood in front and gave hand signals, "Turn the wheel right a bit. No, the other right. Not that much. No, too much. Now left, left, *left*. Are you turning the wheel *at all*?" It quickly became clear that he had a very poor grasp of spatial awareness.

After four failed attempts Jim gave up, turned off his van in the middle of the driveway, and got out.

"Let me do it," Brian offered, but Jim shook his head. "I have a cunning plan."

He unlocked the caravan door and a wall of stench instantly poured out. The women screamed and waved their hands in front of their faces, except for Faye, who had no sense of smell and wondered what was wrong with everyone. The door creaked open unwillingly and Jim reached in for a remote-control device.

"Shut the bloody door before we suffocate!" Flo yelled.

Jim slammed it shut, held up the remote control and cried, "Back away, let the man with the motor mover do his work." He pressed a button. Nothing happened.

"If I might suggest you unhitch it from the van first," Brian said.

"Ah." Jim went to the hitching area and stared at it a while.

"Lower the jockey wheel to raise the caravan."

"Jockey wheel?"

"It's that little wheel at the front."

"It's already lowered."

Brian went over to look. "You've had the jockey wheel down all the way here?"

"Mate said it was ready to go. He was at work when I picked it up, but he left the keys under the back wheel. Took me ages to lift it high enough to get it hooked onto the bobbly thing on the back of the van."

Brian was speechless for a long moment. Mark stifled his amusement. The women had long since lost interest and were now sitting on chairs on the grass between Brian and Faye's caravan and Olivia's motorhome, idly watching and sipping from tall glasses, as they listened to Flo's running commentary on what Jim was doing wrong and how he should be doing it and what the dreadful smell could be.

"What's so funny?" Jim asked.

Brian shook his head and talked him through the process of unhitching the caravan from the van. "It's a lot easier to take off than put on," Jim noted, as he raised the caravan with the jockey wheel and unplugged the cables

"Try it now," Mark said.

Jim pressed buttons on the remote control, but still nothing happened.

"Your battery's probably flat," Bill shouted through the hedge, "That's most likely the problem, happens all the time, people put it into storage for months and then expect the battery to be raring to go at a moment's notice."

Jim opened the remote control. "They could be flat," he said. Faye was up in an instant, sprinting across the grass to the caravan and coming back out with a selection of carded batteries for him to choose from, fanning them out like a pack of cards.

"Not those batteries," Bill shouted, "The leisure battery."

"Leisure battery?"

Faye shrugged. She was pretty certain she didn't have one of those.

"Give me strength," Brian breathed. "It does have a battery in it, doesn't it?"

"I dunno, never even heard of one till a few seconds ago."

Brian opened the caravan door and the women instantly started screaming about the smell again. He held his nose and hauled himself inside, closing the door behind him and instantly regretting it on his first breath. Inside smelt damper than damp, it was almost pond-like, and everything was dark and dingy and in disarray.

Jim jumped in, accompanied by a high-pitched chorus of complaints from the women. "Doesn't use it much then, your mate?" Brian asked.

"No, not for a while. Is it supposed to stink like this?"

"It is not."

"Yours doesn't smell like this."

"That's because we clean ours. I wouldn't be surprised if there were new species growing in here. Try not to breathe in too much."

A shaft of light and a bout of screaming heralded Mark's presence in the caravan. "Christ!" he gasped, "Did something die in here?"

Brian gingerly made his way through the moist debris scattered on the floor to the sofas at the front, and lifted up a damp, suspiciously green cushion. He stood there, looking down, not moving, not speaking.

"You okay, Bri?" Mark asked. "Not been overcome with fumes or anything?"

"Don't say anything to the girls, but Jim's brought along a few pets."

"Pets?" Jim moved next to him and suddenly clutched at Brian's huge arm. "WHAT THE HELL ARE *THEY*?"

"Rats, Jim, they're dried up rat carcasses with some kind of fungus growing on them."

"Oh my God!" Mark gasped, "There's bloody loads!"

Brian shook off Jim's horrified grip and turned to lift up the other sofa cushion. "There's more under here."

"OH MY BLOODY GOD!"

"Keep your voice down, unless you want to see a shrieking stampede of women."

"What are we going to do?" Jim cried.

"We?"

"Yes, what are we going to do, Bri?"

"*We* ain't doing anything. *You* are going to clear them out, quickly and discretely. You don't want to be sleeping above dozens of dried-up husks, it's not healthy, and Faye will throw a fit if she finds out we're parked next to a rodent graveyard. At least you have a battery in situ, we just have to plug it in."

Brian pulled out a huge roll of cable from under one sofa and went to plug in the electrics. Mark left because he couldn't stand the smell, and because he didn't want to get involved in the carcass removal. Jim stared at the mess beneath the cushions, then screamed out loud when Brian's big face suddenly appeared in the window in front of him and boomed, "There's masks, gloves and bin bags in the back of my car." He lifted the massive coil of cabling up to the window and added, "Longest extension lead I've ever seen, there's got to be at least thirty metres of it!"

By the time Jim had opened Brian's boot and located the carcass disposal items, Brian had returned to the green lump on wheels with the remote control in his hands. Jim felt a bit miffed as he'd wanted to play with it like a giant remote-controlled car. Brian pressed a button. Nothing happened.

"Have you turned the switch on for the motor?" Bill shouted over.

"Switch?" Jim shrugged.

"You're like a parrot," Mark said, "You just keep repeating what people say."

"That's because they're all *new words!*"

"It'll be on the inside of the caravan somewhere," Bill yelled. "The new ones have compartments on the outside, but yours looks a bit old. It'll be in there somewhere, a red key you have to turn to connect the electricity to the motor mover."

"Go find it and turn it on, Jim."

"Why me?"

"Why do you think?" Jim looked clueless. "Because it's your caravan!"

Jim stomped off, bags, gloves and masks in hand. They heard some banging, some swearing, some cries of, "It bloody stinks in here!" and then, "Found it! It's on!"

Brian pressed some buttons on the remote just as Jim came running back, desperate to have a go. Nothing happened.

"You need to connect the motor to the wheels," shouted Bill.

"How do we do that?"

Bill stood up and squeezed through the hedge. Mark winced. He'd planted that hedge, all the hedges.

"Is it listing?" Bill asked, staring at the green-hued caravan.

"A bit," Jim said.

"More than a bit, I'd say. And those tyres don't look too good either. Are you sure it's roadworthy?"

"Of course."

"It's a manual motor," Bill said, bending to look underneath. "There should be a metal pole in one of the compartments."

"Compartments?" Jim said.

Mark huffed. "I'm not sure camping's your thing, mate."

"Give us a chance, it's my first time!"

"Compartments," Bill said, "There's one at the front and one at the back."

"Front and back of …?"

"The caravan, you idiot," Mark hissed. "Have you had brain surgery lately, a lobotomy maybe?"

"Shut your face."

"The pole?" Bill sighed.

Jim moved to the front of his caravan and ran his fingers over the flush compartment door. "How do I open it?"

"You'll need a key," Bill said, looking at the other two with questioning eyes. They both shook their heads.

Jim searched in his jeans pocket, pulled out a bunch of keys and tried four before finding the right one. "What does the pole look like?" he asked.

"Well," Bill drawled, as the other two squeaked with barely restrained laughter, "It'll look a bit like a metal pole. I don't know how else to explain a pole. It's very pole-like, a bit like a wheel wrench."

"This?" Jim said, holding one up.

"Well done. Now, what you have to do is stick this end into that hole there. That's it. Now, pull the long bit of the pole towards the wheel until you hear a – " There was a heavy clunk as the motor clamped onto the wheel, and Jim beamed with pride. Bits of 'stuff' fell from underneath the caravan and onto the gravel driveway.

"That's it," Bill said. "Now take the pole and do the same on the other side."

Jim raced round, clunked, and came racing back again, as enthusiastic as a puppy who'd learned a new trick and was now expecting a treat.

Bill turned and took the remote from Brian, who was a bit miffed as he'd wanted to play with it like a giant remote-controlled car. "Lift the jockey wheel."

Jim stood at the hitching point, waving his hands around helplessly. Mark lost patience and lifted the wheel himself. He straightened up again and, with a deadpan expression, gave Jim an excellent Khaby Lame impression with his hands.

"Yeah, yeah, you were a newbie once too."

"Haven't you parked that caravan yet?" Faye shouted over. "I could have pushed it in faster with one hand tied behind my back by now."

"I could have pulled it in with my teeth," Olivia giggled, sipping tipsily at her drink.

"My Kat could have done it with less fuss," squealed Flo.

Mark noticed a small group of children had squeezed their way through the hedge at the top of the caravan area and were now huddled together, watching, their eyes rivetted to the remote control.

Bill showed them how to work it, and suddenly, as if by magic, the caravan started moving backwards, very slowly. Three men watched, itching to get their hands on the remote, but instead had to make do with Bill's running commentary as he very neatly reversed the caravan onto its hardstanding pitch. There was a short burst of applause from the campsite and somebody shouted, "Well done!" Bill grinned and gave a low bow.

"Thanks very much," Jim said, taking the control from Bill as casually as he could. "Could just do with a bit more straightening, I think." He pushed a button and the caravan trundled off its pitch at a sharp angle. He got flustered and started pressing all the buttons, and the caravan started zigzagging left and right down the gravel driveway. Brian snatched the remote off him before the caravan disappeared into the surrounding trees and managed to stop it. He was just about to play with the reverse buttons himself, when Bill reached out and took it from him, once more parking it neatly on the pitch.

"Boys," Faye tutted, "Love their toys. Come and have a drink with us, Bill, we're much more fun."

Bill put the remote down on the hitch head and hurried over, throwing himself down on the grass and reclining like a male model in a vintage Premier Man catalogue. Faye handed him a glass from a box of glasses, and Olivia unsteadily topped it up.

"Get those carcasses sorted," Brian hissed at Jim, hurrying to his coolbox with Mark close behind.

Can in hand, Brian tried to recline like Bill on the grass, except Bill was a lot slimmer and obviously more agile, and he couldn't get comfortable without looking and feeling like a beached whale. Eventually he gave up and dragged a chair over.

Mark lay on his back next to Olivia's chair, staring up at the perfect blue sky, feeling happy. They all listened to Flo, occasionally getting the odd word in here and there, but mostly Flo did all the talking. The endless barrage of words washed over Brian, stupefying him. Could the woman breathe through her ears? She didn't seem to inhale at all. And how could she find so much to talk about without pausing for thought for one ... single ... second?

Then a miracle happened. Bill started to speak about his partner, who'd sadly passed away, and Flo, identifying another grieving person, stopped talking and started listening, nodding intently. Brian was aghast, this had never happened before. Other conversations started up around them that *weren't* about cats, and Olivia managed to regale them with some tales from her trips.

Meanwhile, back in the green van, Jim was using a dustpan and brush to clear out the dried-up rats from underneath the sofa, gagging and swearing under his breath. He did a quick job of it, desperate for a drink, despite not having brought any provisions himself. He left the caravan with two full bin bags and plonked them on the grass outside. He went over to the others, parched from the heat and the dust and looking forward to one of Brian's cold cans of beer. When Brian saw him he said, "Did you take it over to the bins?"

Jim sighed and spun round, snatched the bags up and plodded off towards the 'recycling' area.

"And wash your hands!" Brian called after him, "Thoroughly!"

By the time he got back he was sweating buckets. He threw himself down on the grass next to the chattering group and waited. And waited. "Thirsty work pitching up, isn't it," he hinted.

"It is."

"Nice can of cold beer would go down a treat."

Brian lifted up his can and said, "It does."

"Haven't had a chance to stock up yet."

"Haven't you?"

"No."

"Oh."

"Stop tormenting him," Faye said. "Help yourself to a beer, Jim."

"Or I've brought champagne," Olivia said, lifting up a bottle, "Would you like a glass?"

"No thanks, Olivia."

"It's Liv, Liv by name, live by nature."

"Very kind, Liv, but I'd rather have a beer." He leapt up and rushed to the coolbox under the awning.

"Get me one, too," Mark shouted, and Brian sighed.

* * *

"I remember what Sophie told me, she said, 'Try everything, do everything', so I did and I have. It was like my mantra, my raison d'être, 'Try everything, do everything'. Mummy and I went to Lanzarote first, it was the first thing that came up when we searched 'get us out of here' on Google." Olivia giggled. "We had to get away, daddy and Dick were being just horrible. We kicked them both out of the houses and they weren't the least bit happy about it. They were so used to being in control, and now they weren't and it made them very angry. Daddy was apoplectic with rage, I'd never seen him like that before and we were both a bit scared. So we decided to escape and let the lawyers deal with everything, but just packing our bags made us nervous and we had to have a couple of brandies to actually get on the plane. We were literally like rabbits caught in the headlights of an oncoming truck, too scared to go anywhere on our own, everything felt so foreign and dangerous. We stayed in our hotel room for the first two days. Then we hired a DVD from reception, you'll never guess which one."

They all shook their heads.

"Shirley Valentine!"

"No!" Faye gasped.

"I'd never seen it before, Dick didn't like chick flicks so of course I couldn't watch them, but we watched Shirley Valentine and it changed us, this woman who was like us, feeling the way we felt. We took it as a sign that we needed to be braver, we needed to stop being so afraid all the time, of everything. The next day we ventured out to the pool and nothing dreadful happened. Then we caught a bus to a local village and we weren't kidnapped or attacked, we had fun. After that there was no stopping us, we booked every trip we could find, hired water skis, did a wine tour; poor mummy got really sloshed, daddy didn't allow her to drink and I think she made up for lost time!" Another tinkle of laughter. "We felt free, like chickens being let out of the coop first thing in the morning. Mummy was like, 'Let's do this!' and 'Let's do that!', and I was like, 'Yes, let's!' Oh, we had such a good time. Daddy and Dick hassled us, of course, calling our mobiles all the time and sending texts, so many texts, most of them horrible, but we didn't answer, just glanced at them to make sure nobody had died and deleted them.

"Then we were sitting outside a café one afternoon and Dick was sending me text after text after text." She rolled her eyes. They felt her pain. "One of them said, 'I am willing to forgive your little spasm of insanity and come home'. Well, I answered that one! 'Who says insanity is a bad thing anyway?' I put, 'I'm having the time of my life. I'm free and I'm loving it. Stop contacting me.' I threw the phone down on the café table and said to mummy, 'I wish he'd just stop texting me!'

The girl at the next table overhead, she leaned towards us and said, 'Boyfriend?' 'Husband,' I told her. 'Just block him.' I told her I didn't know how, and she picked up my phone, jabbed it a couple of times, handed it back and said, 'Sorted', just like that! We had a much better time after that. I felt guilty, of course I did – "

"You shouldn't," Faye said, "It was the right thing to do."

" – but we were on holiday, you can do what you want on your holiday, can't you."

"That's the theory," said Brian.

"We booked two more holidays on our last day and flew straight from Lanzarote to Mykonos. We did our own Shirley Valentine! It was *marvellous*! Mummy even flirted with a local man who had a boat, can you believe that? Didn't go on it though, we weren't completely without common sense. Then on the spur of the moment we went to Rome to brush up on our Italian."

"Better scratch Italian off your list of expletives," Mark whispered to Brian.

"Duly noted."

"Then we flew to Norway to see the aurora lights, stayed in glass huts in a forest! Didn't see much of the lights though, wrong time of year, apparently, but we'll go back again. We skied and took sled rides and went out for meals and met loads of new people, it was … lovely." Olivia's eyes glazed over at the memory, and she smiled.

"Then what?" Faye asked.

Olivia rolled her eyes. "Came home, we had to really to instruct the lawyers. Daddy and Dick were being very tiresome, were insisting we were *both* going through the menopause and didn't know what we were doing, tried saying we were 'temporarily detached from our faculties' and that they should be given power of attorney. Oh, it's all very boring. We just let the lawyers deal with it, but daddy and Dick were convinced we'd eventually come to our senses again and beg them to come back! No chance of that, we were having too much fun, but they couldn't believe we'd cut them off from all the money, *our* money. Daddy even had to stop going to the golf club because he couldn't afford the fees, he was *outraged*. They wouldn't leave us alone, kept coming to our houses and bombarding us with demands." Brian noticed Mark's hands clenching and a muscle spasming in his jaw. "We had to get injunctions against them in the end to keep them away, that stopped them. Then mummy's friend and her husband, big chap, came with us to Mexico, then the Caribbean."

"Oh wow, Liv!"

"I know, can you believe it, me and mummy jet-setting! We've been to Moscow, which was stunning, then spent three weeks on an African safari, which was *a-ma-zing*. Then we came back for a bit to sign some papers and sort some stuff out, but Richard kept coming to the house late at night, even though he wasn't supposed to, drunk and upset, begging me to let him come back. I did feel sorry for him, but I didn't want him back, I was looking ahead, not backwards, and besides, we had a trip planned to Dubai."

"You certainly took Sophie at her word!"

"I did. I *so* wanted to be like her, cool and confident and sophisticated, but in the end I found myself, just like Shirley Valentine did, and I realised I quite liked myself."

"As do we all, lass."

"Thanks to you," Olivia said. "If I hadn't met you all I'd still be there, with Dick, leading my tiny little life. You showed me there was something else, something better. You showed me what happiness looked like, and I wanted it. Sometimes you have to fight for your happiness, because if you're not happy then what's the point? I fought for mine and won, and nobody's taking that away from me again."

Faye took her hand and squeezed it. "I'm so pleased, you deserve to be happy."

"Marvellous woman," Brian said, "Bloody good cook, too."

Mark raised his hand off the grass and squeezed her

other hand.

"You're all so lovely," Olivia sniffed.

Jim sniffed too, rubbing at his eyes.

"You crying, lad?"

"No, no, just got something in my eyes."

"Rat dust, probably," Mark said, "God, I hope you washed your hands properly after …"

There was a sudden pulse of silence that seemed to last a very long time. Even Flo had fallen silent. Faye glared wide-eyed at Mark and said, "Rat dust?"

Mark sat up, mouth open, brain whirring. "Just an old joke," he spluttered, "We've been mates for a long time haven't we, Jim."

"Yeah, yeah, go way back."

"And 'rat dust' just means … well, it means …" Mark laughed awkwardly. "You know what, I can't even remember what it means, can you, Jim?"

"It means …" He shrugged. "The dust of labour, we call it rat dust, can't remember why now, just summat we made up."

"Odd thing to come up with," Faye said.

"Yeah, we were odd back then."

"One of us still is."

Jim pulled a face. Then he shook his empty can and cried, "Well, would you look at that! My rat dust remedy has all gone!"

Faye nodded towards the coolbox and said, "Help yourself."

"Faye!"

"Brian!"

"It's not a bloody magic box of endless cold beer, you know!"

"How many cans does it hold, Bri?"

"Fifty-six, but – "

"Cheers, Bri."

"Bring me one, too, Jim."

Jim brought two back and handed one to Mark, saying, "You moan at me but you don't moan at him for drinking your beer?"

"That's because he's generous with his stash," Brian said, "You don't even have a stash."

"Not yet, but I'll be stocking up."

"Reception shop is still open."

"Nah," he said, throwing himself down on the grass and pulling back the tab, "I'll go to Sainsbury's tomorrow, cheaper."

Brian made a noise at the back of this throat, then said, "Could have brought me one."

Jim sighed and jumped up again. "Do I have to do everything around here?"

"Everything except buy your own stuff," Mark laughed.

"Bring us a bottle of prosecco, Jim, we're all out of champagne."

Olivia leaned sideways in her chair to check the three empty bottles on the ground next to her and almost toppled over. Mark gripped the arm and held it steady. They smiled at each other.

"So," said Flo, "Are you and Dick divorced now?"

Mark was all ears.

"Not yet, but the decree absolute is imminent. Their lawyers are still fighting with our lawyers over money and marital attributes, that could take a while."

"And your mum?"

"Same, but she's not letting it get her down. In fact, she's backpacking in Thailand at the moment, otherwise she would have been here."

"Backpacking, on her own?"

"No," Olivia giggled, "With her friend, Colin. Nice man, goes to daddy's old golf club, but she met him quite by chance at the theatre."

"Another golfer?" Mark said warily.

"Oh, we had him checked." She gave a naughty giggle. "We hired a private investigator."

"Get you with your private investigator!" Faye laughed. "It'll be private jets and yachts next!"

"Ooh, I hadn't thought of that!" She glanced across the driveway that ran down the middle of the caravan area and said, "Seems strange not to see the super-shiny Airstream there. I hope Sophie makes it tomorrow, would be lovely to see her again."

"And the other pitch," Brian said, "Wonder if they've booked anyone on that one."

"Oh my God," Faye laughed, "Imagine if the yummy-mummies came back!"

Mark instantly gagged at the memory.

"I have some photos of Kat in the caravan, if you want to see them?" Flo said to Bill.

"Love to," he said, sounding as if he meant it.

They wandered into the caravan, and Flo turned to close the door behind them. "Oi!" Brian bellowed, "Leave it open!"

"She's a grown woman," Faye snapped, "She can do what she likes."

"Not in my caravan, she can't."

"Where *is* Flo sleeping?" Mark asked.

"We have a bedroom tent to put up in the awning. Oh, we haven't blown the deluxe, cost an arm and a leg air bed up yet."

"I'll do it," Mark offered, jumping to his feet.

"Good man," Brian said. "Bed and manual pump in the back of the car."

Mark walked over to the black Kia, then stopped dead in his tracks, staring off behind Brian and Faye's caravan.

"You okay, lad?"

Mark turned to face them all. "It's gone," he gasped.

"No, they're definitely in the boot, probably under the –"

"No, not the bed."

"What then?"

"The caravan."

"My caravan?" asked Jim, standing up.

"It's gone."

CHAPTER 3

They all rushed over to the place where Jim's caravan had once stood. The pitch was empty apart from his Transit. There was no sign of the caravan.

"Where is it? Where's it gone?"

"Who would want to steal *that*?"

They looked around, turning on the spot. Brian picked up the electric cable and their eyes followed its length out of the caravan area. It disappeared into the camping field, behind a particularly large tent with four canvas pods coming off it. They could just make out a green roof on the other side. Even as they watched, the green roof moved to the right.

"What the -?"

They hurried towards it en masse. Suddenly they heard a noise and, glancing back, saw the electric plug ping out of its socket, but the caravan continued to move, powered now by the partly charged battery. It was heading straight for a bell tent, the occupants of which were now scrambling frantically through the flaps to safety.

The group rounded the four-podded tent and came face to face with a group of young boys huddled over a remote control.

"What are you doing?" Jim snarled, snatching the remote from one of them, who began to cry as he ran off. Further down the field a woman's voice yelled, "OI, YOU LEAVE 'EM ALONE!" The woman, large, wearing an extremely tight t-shirt and shorts, came stomping up towards them, her massive arms pistoning furiously at her sides. She had a sumo wrestler's face, and the closer it got the angrier it looked. "WHAT YOU DOING, YELLING AT ME KIDS LIKE THAT?"

"They stole my caravan!" Jim argued.

"MY KIDS DON'T STEAL NUFFINK! HOW DARE YOU ACCUSE 'EM OF STEALING!"

"This here caravan," Jim said, patting the green surface and then grimacing at his hand, "Used to stand over there." He pointed back to the caravan area, "And now it's here."

"DON'T MEAN TO SAY MY KIDS DID IT! WHAT PROOF YOU GOT, EH?"

"They were holding the remote control!"

"SHOULDN'T LEAVE IT LYING AROUND THEN, SHOULD YA!"

"She has a point," Mark said, nodding.

"Cheers, *mate*!"

"WHAT'S GOING ON 'ERE?" cried a male sumo wrestler, who could only be the father. "WHAT'S 'APPENING, SHAZZA?"

"THIS MAN'S SHOUTING AT OUR KIDS AND CALLING THEM *FEEVES*, MICK!"

"YOU WHAT?"

"It's just a simple misunderstanding," Jim said, raising his hands, one of them tinged with mould. "Your kids picked up the remote control for the motor mover and ... well, drove my caravan away."

"ARE YOU ACCUSING 'EM OF PINCHING YER CARAVAN, MATE?"

"Not pinching, no, just ... playing with it."

Mick, the sumo man, took a menacing step forward, his face contorted, ready for a fight. Brian, who'd been at the back, also took a step forward. The two men faced each other, one at least eighteen inches shorter than the other but equally as wide. "We'd quite like our caravan back now," Brian said calmly, "The other caravans miss it. Are we done here?"

"I AIN'T 'AVING MY KIDS ACCUSED OF STEALING," shrieked Mrs Sumo.

"Shut up, Shaz!"

"YOU JUST GONNA LET HIM GET AWAY WIV IT, MICK? AIN'T YA GONNA PUNCH HIM OR NUFFINK?"

Mick grabbed hold of Shazza's quite substantial arm and spun her round, pushing her back towards the tent where three young boys stood. "Just leave it, Shaz. I ain't takin' him on, am I, I ain't bloody stupid, y'know."

Jim turned to the others, smiling. Finally, he had the control. He pressed a button. The caravan started moving backwards, and then stopped. "Bugger!"

"Battery's drained," Mark laughed.

"How am I supposed to get it back then?" The others started walking off. "Come on!" he cried, "Lend a bloke a hand in his hour of need!"

"Oh, my back," Brian laughed, rubbing his lower spine.

"My nails!" Olivia giggled.

"My lazyitis," Mark groaned, "Must have caught it from you, Jim."

"I can't push it back on my own, can I!"

"You're not leaving it there," said a man from the Bell tent.

With a sigh, the men turned, lined up behind the caravan, and started pushing. Faye pulled the electric cable out of the caravan and wound it up as the women went back to their tall glasses; this was man's work and they had their soft hands and their nails to consider. As the caravan slowly started to move across the grass there was a dull thump and, looking down, Jim watched one of the motor movers appear from underneath the caravan, freeing itself of all responsibility. "Bugger!"

They managed the ninety-degree turn just past the four-podded tent, and pushed it across the gravel driveway, straight through the entrance to the caravan area.

"Amazing, isn't it," Mark said.

"What is?"

"Three young kids managed to manoeuvre your caravan through this gap with no problem at all, while it took you several attempts."

"Four, it only took four attempts."

"Small children did it in one. What does that tell you, Jim?"

"That the motor mover was very easy to use, and now I don't have one."

With a final effort, the caravan was pushed back onto its pitch. Brian pulled the brake up. "Wind your stabilisers down before any other kids try to make off with it," he said.

Jim shrugged, clueless.

"Leggy things on the corners to stop the caravan wobbling."

"How do I do that, Bri?"

"There'll be a pole in one of the … oh, never mind." He strode over to his car, opened up the boot, and pulled out an electric drill with a large socket attached to it. "Use this, it'll be quicker."

Jim took it from him, looked at it, then at the caravan, then at Brian. Mark laughed, Brian grunted. He snatched back his drill, stomped to the front stabiliser, pushed the socket into the hole on the side of the caravan and checked over his shoulder that Jim was watching. He wasn't, he was staring up at the sky.

"Oi!'" Brian snapped, catching Jim's attention again, "Watch and learn."

He wound down the first leg and pushed the drill into Jim's hands, and strode off towards his own caravan. "Bloody knackered now," he barked, rubbing his lower back. "I think I might go to bed. Wife!"

"WHAT?"

"I'm off to bed."

"Good for you!"

"Are you coming?"

"No."

"Fair enough."

"I wish you and Faye would make it up," Mark said, "I much prefer the way you used to be."

"Before The Sister came." Brian patted Mark on the

shoulder. "She'll come round."

"She won't," shouted Faye.

"She won't be able to resist me for much longer."

"I will!"

Brian lumbered into the caravan. Flo and Bill were still inside, poring over a vast collection of cat photographs on the table. They looked surprised to see him.

"It's my caravan," he said, miffed that they looked miffed.

Flo and Bill made no attempt to move, so Brian pulled off his shirt and started undoing his belt. Flo was up and out in an instant, crying, "Faye! He's pretending to strip off to get rid of me again!"

"If only it was that easy," Brian muttered, nodding at Bill as he left and closing the door behind him.

* * *

Jim didn't sleep well for several reasons. One, the caravan *stank* to high heaven, despite all the windows being open. The sofa bed was lumpy, and so damp it actually felt wet against his skin, and he kept getting flashbacks of all the desiccated bodies that had been underneath, which made him start itching. Also, he hadn't brought any sheets or blankets, so he just lay there, in his clothes, cold, with only a cushion Faye had given him for comfort. Finally, and he'd completely forgotten about this, Brian snored like a blocked drain down a megaphone. He wasn't sure this caravan lark was all it was cracked up to be.

Mark didn't sleep well because he was too excited about seeing Liv again. It had been *weeks* since she'd last come up to stay in her motorhome. He lay on his bed, staring at the ceiling, and smiling to himself, then frowning; did she still want him?

Olivia didn't sleep well because she knew Mark was lying just a few feet away, and because she had a lot of things on her mind; she'd done so much over the last few weeks, she hoped it was enough. She didn't like keeping things from her friends, but she couldn't tell them, not yet, but the deception kept her awake.

Flo didn't sleep very well because she was quite small and the mattress Mark had blown up for her was enormous, like a big, blue bag of air. She literally had to take a running jump at it and launch herself into the air a couple of times before she finally managed to drag herself into the middle of the flocked rectangle. Lying on her front, she felt herself wobbling from side to side as she clutched at the edges, feeling quite seasick. She didn't dare move for fear of setting off the rocking motion, or falling off and breaking her neck, so she lay there, arms and legs outstretched like a starfish, gripping the mattress. Also, she missed her cat, and Brian's snoring was like thunder approaching and receding, and every time he turned over the caravan rocked, which made her seasickness worse.

Faye, drunk on champagne and prosecco, slept like a log.

As did Brian, although he did wake up in the middle of the night for a wee. When he clambered quietly back into bed he lay on his side for a moment, looking down at his wife's face. He really, really missed her. He hoped the standoff would be over soon and they could get back to normal again.

* * *

Day 2: Saturday

"What's wrong with your face, Jim?" Faye asked, when he shuffled into their awning the next morning.

"It lacks sleep. How does his snoring not keep you awake at night?"

"I'm just used to it. It's when he stops snoring I wake up –"

"To check he's still breathing," Jim remembered.

"But what happened to your face?"

"Why, what's wrong with it?"

Faye reached into her bag and pulled out a small mirror. Jim peered into it. His face was red and blotchy, like a bad rash. "What's wrong with my face?" he cried.

"I don't know. Allergies?"

"I don't have any allergies?"

"Is there … something in the caravan, you know, bed bugs or an insect infestation or anything like that?"

They both shivered. Jim lifted up his t-shirt and checked his skin, then lifted each leg of his jeans and checked there. Nothing, no rash, no bites. He'd slept in his clothes. It was just his face. "Was there something on that cushion you gave me?"

"No, it's brand new, but interesting that you slept in a festering pit of mould and then blame my lovely Dunelm cushion. Cup of tea? Antihistamine?"

"Love one," he said, falling into a chair in the awning, which was mostly taken up with Flo's bedroom tent.

"Don't wake her up," Brian warned, standing in the caravan doorway with a mug of tea. "This is the quietest it'll be all day, so keep your voice down. What's the matter with your face?"

Jim rubbed at it. "Just woke up like this."

"Allergies?"

"I don't have any allergies."

"Well, tomato head, you're in my seat, so shift yourself."

Jim moved to another chair and Brian sat down. Faye came out with a mug of tea and some toast. "Marmalade? Marmite?"

"We're not running a bed and breakfast," Brian huffed quietly.

"I can't see anyone go hungry," she huffed back.

"He won't go hungry; he can always eat his own head." Brian put a giant hand across his face to stop himself laughing.

Inside the bedroom tent came movement and the sound of deep breath being taken. "It's the only time she inhales," Brian whispered, putting a finger to his lips.

"Tea, Flo?" Faye bawled, and Brian slumped in despair.

"Thanks, Faye, that would be fan*tas*tic. Do you know what I fancy? Some croissants. You know when you just have a craving for something? I could just eat a couple of fresh croissants. Is there anywhere round here that does croissants, Bri? It's so strange, isn't it, I don't normally have a hankering for ...."

Mark came ambling over with his hands in his pockets. "You look well chill," Brian said, as Flo chattered away in the background.

"I'm always chill. I'm happy." He gave an exaggerated smile, which diminished into a normal one. "What's wrong with your face, Jim?"

"We think it might be allergies," Faye said, handing a cup of tea into the bedroom tent and then rushing back into the caravan.

"I don't have any allergies."

"Work? Monogamy? Fidelity?"

"Shut up."

"It's probably the rat dust."

"There you go with that phrase again," Faye called from inside the caravan as Brian rolled his eyes, "It's very horrible, I wish you wouldn't use it."

"Yes, mom. You want to put some cream on that, Jim."

"Before your head swells and explodes," Brian laughed.

"Why, does it look swollen? I can't lose my boyish good looks. Where's that mirror?"

"It's not swollen," said Faye, handing Mark a cup of tea as he sat down and giving Jim a tube of Savlon, "Put some of this on."

"Will it work?"

"Try it and see."

"Morning," came Olivia's sing-song voice as she strode across the grass towards them, her phone vibrating silently in her hand, "Did you all sleep well?"

There were some mutterings but no definitive answer.

"Oh Jim!" she cried, "What's happened to your face?"

"Does it look swollen to you, Liv? Tell me the truth, have I lost my boyish good looks?"

"No, it just looks …" She leaned in closer. "… sore."

Jim quickly squirted cream from the tube and rubbed it in.

"Morning, Liv, cup of tea?"

"Lovely."

"Any bacon sarnies?" Jim asked.

Brian growled.

"Sorry, Jim," Faye cried, "Forgot to bring the bacon, it's still in the fridge at home."

Jim tapped on his phone for a bit and scratched his head. "I feel a bit riffy."

"Ugh." Mark moved his chair out from under the awning and onto the grass, where Olivia sat, looking as pretty as a picture in her flowery summer dress, her phone vibrating gently next to her. "Do you want my chair?" he asked her.

She beamed up at him with her slight overbite, "Thank you, I'm alright."

"I might have a shower," said Jim.

"Good lad. Pop in at the reception shop on your way, they might sell lice powder."

"Have you got any shower gel I could use, Bri?"

Brian rolled his eyes again. "Have you not brought *anything* with you?"

"Just some clothes really."

With a huff, Brian stood up and lumbered into the caravan. He came out with a bottle of something purple and handed it over.

"It's not some fancy smelling stuff, is it?"

"Can you afford to be picky, rash face? Besides, what would be the point of me having fancy smelling stuff with Faye?"

"Oh, that's not very nice," Mark said. "Can't you two just make up instead of – "

"I meant because she has *no sense of smell.*"

"Oh yeah, I forgot."

Jim eyed the bottle suspiciously. "Doesn't actually say 'shower gel', Bri, it just says 'wash'."

"Yes, it's good as a bath wash, shower wash, window wash, car cleaner, floor cleaner, carpet cleaner, stain remover, silver polish, all sorts. There's rumours you can even use it in your petrol mower."

Jim looked up at Brian. Brian grinned down at Jim. Then Jim said, "Can I borrow a towel?"

"For crying out loud!"

"Here," Faye said, tossing a bath towel at him as she brought a mug of tea over for Olivia, "You can keep it, we don't want it back. Same goes for my cushion, consider it a gift."

Jim lumbered off towards the showers, scratching his head and his neck. Brian threw himself back into his chair and supped his tea.

"Faye!" cried Flo, "Can you give me a hand getting off the bed?"

Brian and Mark glanced at each other. Faye hurried into the bedroom tent, from which came the sound of much squeakiness, a bit of huffing, a short cry of alarm, followed by Flo stumbling into the awning in her nightdress, clutching at her heart and gripping a shaking tea mug. "I'm going to need a smaller bed." She pronounced 'going' as 'goo-win', just like Faye. "Oh, morning, Bill!"

"Morning." He waved over the hedge with a huge smile. "How are you this fine day?"

"All the better for seeing you. Do you have any plans for today?"

"Well, I thought I'd go and see Blenheim Palace again, it's been years since I last went, and since it's so close I thought I'd take a picnic and make a day of it. Would you like to come?"

Brian's eyes went as wide as dinner plates. He glanced across at Mark and crossed his fingers in front of his face.

"That would be fan*tas*tic," Flo said, and Brian turned his

crossed fingers into giant hands of shaking joy.

"Blenheim?" Faye said, standing in the caravan doorway. "Did someone say they were going to Blenheim?"

"We're not going," said Brian.

"Why not?"

"Can't afford it."

"I think the free return ticket we got last year is still valid."

"It's the gift shops I can't afford after the rampant spend-fest last time. I had to sell my spleen on eBay to pay off the credit cards. I miss it." I miss you, he thought, but didn't say.

"I'd like to go."

"I don't want to."

"Would you like to join us?" Bill asked. "It would be my pleasure to escort two such lovely ladies around the grounds of a stately palace."

Faye opened her mouth to answer, but then Brian lifted a hand to take hold of hers. She looked down at him, surprised. "I thought," he said quietly, "We might spend some time together, you know, some alone time?"

Faye's face softened. "Thanks, Bill, but you two go off and enjoy yourselves."

"No problem. Shall we say an hour, Flo?"

"Fan*tas*tic."

Flo dashed back into the bedroom tent to get ready, giving a running commentary as she did so, which nobody paid any attention to. Brian and Faye glanced at each other. He was still holding her hand. Mark smiled.

"Oh!" Olivia suddenly cried, "You know what we forgot to do yesterday?"

"Leave Jim's Caravan of Doom on the pub car park?" Mark said.

"No, fill out the first impressions survey. I have some here. Maybe we could all walk around and have a proper look?"

"It's the least we can do for a free holiday," Brian said.

"I'll just have some toast first."

"Toast?" Faye said. "You never asked for toast?"

"You do me toast every morning."

"Not when we've fallen out, I don't."

"You feed everyone else except your husband?"

"Everyone else appreciates it!"

"I've got to make my own toast?"

"No," she huffed, "I'll do it."

"My eternal gratitude."

"Yeah, whatever."

Brian glanced over and saw Jim coming out of the showers wearing nothing but a towel around his waist and a bundle of clothes under his arm, just as a car pulled through the entrance gates and stopped in front of him. The driver handed him a brown paper bag through the window, chatted for a moment, then reversed and drove off. Jim came hurrying over to their caravan and tossed out the contents of the bag to everyone. "My mate works in McDonald's," he said, "Double bacon and egg McMuffins all round. Two for you, Bri."

"You've actually paid for something?" Brian gasped, catching them both, "I thought I'd never see the day."

"You can just leave the money on the table when you've finished," Jim said. Then, noticing Brian's glare and the twitching of his beard, added, "Kidding! Breakfast's on me."

"I don't know whether to eat it," said Mark, staring at his in awe, "Or frame it with the caption, 'Jim Paid for This'."

"Where's mine?" Flo asked, coming out of the bedroom tent.

"Ah," said Jim, "I forgot about Flo."

"Thanks very much! Out of sight, out of mind –"

"If only," Brian breathed.

" – and I was just saying how much I fancied a croissant, didn't I, Faye, but a McDonald's would have been a fan*tastic* alternative. Oh, they do smell nice." She leaned over Brian's shoulder, sniffing. "My mouth's watering now, such a shame you didn't get me one, but never mind, sometimes life throws you a curve ball and you just have to accept disappointment – "

With a heavy sigh, Brian handed over his second McMuffin.

* * *

Mark was pointing at the cut-back brambles around the edges of the field. "Pay particular attention to the landscaping," he said, "All done by my own fair hands."

"Good job," Faye said, scribbling it down on her piece of paper, "Makes the field look so much bigger, tidier."

"And notice the wire fencing all around the perimeter to prevent small children wandering off and getting lost in the woods. I've put a few child-lock gates in too, and cleared the trails up to the main path into the village. It's a popular walk."

"I doubt Tel would agree," Faye laughed, remembering his shredded feet after his hike in boots too small. "You have been busy!"

"It's a nice place," said Flo, "Everyone looks happy. Did you know that in France people take their cats on camping holidays with them and walk them around in harnesses? Isn't that fan*tas*tic? I always thought, if I ever went abroad, I'd take Kat …"

"There's just one pole in the middle of the field with six hook-up points and a water tap," Mark said. "They want to keep it as open as possible so children and dogs have plenty of space to run around, but they'll use it when it gets really busy. There's a shepherd's hut over there." They all looked at what was clearly a small, artistically painted shed, on a wooden platform, on top of a chassis with four black carriage wheels. A small set of steps came down from the door at the front. "It's only just come onto site, I think Chelsea got it more for decorative purposes. You can hire games and barbecue equipment in the reception shop. Oh, and those picnic tables in the middle are for anyone to use. Hefty buggers though, takes two men to lift them, stops them from being nicked."

"They've thought of everything," Faye said, impressed. "They obviously know what they're doing."

"So, you've met the new owner then?" Brian asked.

"No, they just leave instructions with the pub manager, Chelsea, who used to be Ant's girlfriend, you remember, the old landlord?"

"Oh yeah, lethargic chap."

"She practically ran the pub herself when she was here, Ant was so lazy, and the new owner offered her a job. She's really good, keeps everything running smoothly. Feisty, though," he laughed, "She doesn't stand much nonsense."

"I like that," Faye said, pointing with her pen, "There's a children's play area at the bottom."

"Far enough away not to bother other campers," Flo said "I mean, I don't mind the sound of children, it's just when they get to that certain pitch, you know, that constant shrieking noise that bores into your brain and sends you a bit bonkers ..."

"Know it well," Brian breathed.

"Showers are good," said Jim, "Same as last time but a lot cleaner."

"Chelsea runs a tight ship, the whole block is cleaned twice a day."

They wandered out of the field towards the wash area and had a quick look. There were containers of flowers and hanging baskets everywhere. "I had free rein over the plantage," Mark said proudly. Next to the shower block stood an enormous wooden cabin with windows all down one side. Inside was a fridge, chest freezer, cooker, long countertops, cupboards full of kitchen equipment, a washing machine, dryer, a large TV screen mounted on the wall with a DVD player, a bookcase full of DVDs and books and board games, and several tables and chairs. "Campers can come in here in bad weather," Mark said. "I suggested it to Chelsea after the deluge last year, do you remember? She mentioned it to the owner, and voila, an all-weather emergency station!"

"That's fantastic, such a good idea, isn't it, Faye."

"Books!" said Faye, wide-eyed.

"It's not you, is it?" Brian asked Mark. "You're not the new owner, are you?"

He laughed. "No, no, it's not me."

"Chelsea?"

"No, I've heard her talking on the phone to the owner, and she couldn't afford to buy a pub anyway."

"Intriguing."

Olivia's phone vibrated again. She glanced at it, then cried, "Oh, it's Sophie! Hello! Oh lovely! Yes, the others are here. Okay, see you in a bit. She's almost here," she said to them, "I can't *wait* to see her!"

"Me neither. I hope she hasn't fallen out with Tel."

"We'll soon find out."

They walked back to the caravans with their surveys and sat around the awning again. "Are there any amenities missing?" Olivia read from the sheet. They looked at each other and shook their heads. "Is there anything else we can do to improve the site?" Again, they all shook their heads. "Excellent, that's that done then."

"Oh, that's taken the pressure off," Mark laughed.

"I'll get the kettle on," Faye said.

Bill peered over the hedge. "Ready, Flo?"

"I'll just get my bag, I don't go anywhere without my bag, it has my whole life in it and I'm not even joking. Have you seen my bag, Faye? I'm sure I put it in the flour bag of a bedroom. Where is it? Just a sec, Bill. Where is it?"

Faye handed her her bag from inside the caravan and then, suddenly, Flo and her constant flow of verbiage squeezed through the hedge, making Mark wince, and was gone. For a long moment they all sat still and quiet, savouring the silence, and then Brian sighed, "Good luck, that man."

"He seems a bit of a yakker himself," Mark said, "It could be a match made in heaven."

"Romance?" Olivia giggled.

"Oh no," Faye said, handing out mugs of tea, "Flo's not

into that sort of thing, isn't interested in men at all."

"And yet she galloped off into the car of another man with some incredible speed," said Brian.

Faye peered over the hedge at the sight of her sister's head giggling and disappearing into a bright red BMW. "I hope he's not a murderer or a gigg-leo," she breathed.

"A what?"

"Gigg-leo. Why, how do you say it?"

"Properly, but I'm saying it like that in future."

"I think they're both just lonely," Olivia said. "They're a bit of company for each other."

"Bit of silence for us," said Brian. Faye pierced him with a look and he thought he'd best keep his opinions to himself for a bit if he wanted a heart-to-heart chat during their precious alone time.

"Are you lonely, Liv?" Mark finally dared to ask, wondering if he was overstepping the boundaries they'd laid out so long ago.

She looked at him and gave her cute, slight overbite smile. "Sometimes," she said, "But it's still preferable to being with Dick."

"Maybe someone new?"

"Maybe."

And then Sophie arrived.

* * *

The women squealed as a huge car pulled up on the driveway next to them, their smiles splitting their faces. The men admired the sleek and grace of the Bentley Flying Spur, anticipating the sleek and grace of the woman inside.

"It's the bloody queen!" Jim cried. "Who knew she was a camping enthusiast!"

"I'm so sorry about the car!" Sophie gasped, as the driver held open the door for her. "I don't have a car in London, and dad was using his, and mum spends more time at the stables than she does at home, so I had to use the firm's Bentley, complete with hatted chauffeur, would you believe? Ridiculously pretentious!" She gave Faye and Olivia a huge hug and they all squealed together. "I'm *so* pleased to see you, you all look so well. Well, apart from you, Jim, what happened to your face?"

"Don't get too close," Mark said, "It could be contagious."

She hugged Jim, keeping her face at a distance, then Brian and Mark. Behind them, the hatted chauffeur unloaded the boot of suitcases and bags and placed them carefully on the grass. "Don't hold it against me," she said. Then, to the driver, she said, "Thank you, Barry, that will be all."

"Yes, madam."

"Madam!" mouthed Faye.

"I know, I know, I'm totally embarrassed."

The Bentley started reversing off down the driveway when Jim suddenly cried, "Oh, I could do with a lift to the shop, do you think the driver would mind dropping me off?"

"Help yourself."

"Me too," Mark cried, chasing after him.

"I'll come," said Brian, pushing Mark inside and clambering onto the back seat next to Jim.

The Bentley slowly and smoothly drove to the entrance gates and stopped. They all clambered out.

Sophie laughed. "Men, what are they like!"

"Talking of men," Faye began, but Sophie held up a hand, "Let me at least unpack first before the barrage of questions begins. Still okay to shack up with you, Liv?"

"Of course!"

"Let's help with the bags," Faye said, snatching up a suitcase and running to the motorhome with it.

* * *

"Come on then, spit it out. What's happening with Tel?"

They were in Olivia's motorhome, helping to hang and

fold Sophie's expensive but casual clothes into the bedroom furniture.

"There's nothing to tell," she said casually. "Tel got seconded to the Leeds office two months ago and we try and see each other as much as we can, which admittedly isn't often, but everything's fine."

"Fine," Faye repeated. "Not the best way to describe a relationship."

"Those are the cards we were given."

"You're being coy."

"Am I?"

"Hello," Olivia said, waving at her, "We're your best friends, you can tell us anything."

"Well, *we* don't get to see each other much and we're 'fine'."

"She has a point," Olivia said to Faye, who frowned.

"Why isn't he here?"

"Work."

"Too busy to come and see us?"

"Too busy to come and see me," Sophie said, slamming a dresser drawer shut.

"So, there is a problem. Tell us, maybe we can help. I'd be happy to be chauffeur-driven up to Leeds and bundle him into the car for you. Oh," Faye gasped, thinking about it in more detail, "More than happy, actually."

"Stop imagining my boyfriend naked."

"Not *naked*!"

"Oh," Sophie sighed, staring off into the distance, "Just me then. It's difficult keeping up a long-distance relationship. He's busy, I'm busy, all of that heady 'new love' excitement has gone."

"Oh, don't say that!" Olivia cried, "You and Tel are so good together."

"Not everything is meant to last, Liv, and if Tel was still interested in us as a couple he'd be here, but he isn't, so I'm guessing he has better things to do."

"Call him!" Faye said, "Beg him!"

"It's the men who usually do the begging," Sophie laughed, but her eyes looked sad.

"I'm WhatsApping him," Faye said, pulling out her phone.

"Don't you dare!"

"No!" cried Olivia.

Faye video-called Tel. It rang twice, then Tel's horrified yet still incredibly handsome face appeared on screen. Before Faye could utter a word, he gasped, prodded frantically at his phone, and was gone again.

"Told you," Sophie said, "He's a very busy man."

"Looked like he was driving."

"Busy, busy man. Anyway, enough about me, tell me about you two, what you've been up to since we last met. Liv, all that travelling you've done! Faye, all that …"

Faye let the pause linger. "It's okay," she sniffed, "I know I live a very boring life."

"Boring?" Sophie laughed. "With Brian?"

"They're having a spat," Olivia said, "They're hardly speaking, and when they do it's only to bicker at one another. It's horrible."

Sophie pulled a face. "The golden couple, *fighting*? Something must be done! This can't be allowed to happen!"

"Okay, you take Brian into the woods for a damn good thrashing," Faye laughed, "And I'll just nip up to Leeds in the Bentley."

"AHOY THERE, WOMEN FOLK!" Brian bellowed from outside.

"Ah, the dulcet foghorn of my giant husband."

"Oh God," Sophie gasped, "I've just remembered, does he still snore like a jet engine on take-off?"

Faye reached into her jeans pocket and pulled out a couple of small plastic bags.

"Drugs?" gasped Olivia, "Sleeping pills?"

"If only my life was that interesting," she sighed. "No,

they're earplugs. Take a pack, take two, you're going to need them."

"YO! WOMEN!"

"I think we're being summoned," Sophie said, raising her immaculate eyebrows.

Outside the men stood in a line on the gravel pitch in front of the motorhome, licking at ice-creams and grinning like children, each with a hand behind their backs like sailors.

"Where's ours?" Sophie asked, sticking out her bottom lip.

The men brought ice-creams out from behind their backs, and they sat on the grass eating them and chatting about ice-creams and campsites and Olivia's travels, all the while ignoring her constantly vibrating phone lying face-down next to her.

* * *

Olivia's phone started vibrating again as she was in the middle of describing her trip to New York. She glanced nonchalantly at the screen and then jumped to her feet, saying, "Sorry, I have to take this." She walked over to the far corner of the caravan area with the phone at her ear.

"Looks like Liv might have a secret admirer," Jim grinned.

"Shut up, Jim."

"Why? Oh, has Mark got a crush?" He burst out laughing. Brian reached out and gave him a hefty shove, and Jim catapulted sideways onto the grass, still laughing. He shuffled back towards the women, crying, "Make the brute stop, I'm being bullied."

Brian turned to Mark, who was watching Olivia talking on the phone. "You okay?"

"Yeah."

"What happened with you and Liv?" Sophie asked. "Last time we were here it looked like something might be starting."

"We talked about it, spent a nice week together. Nothing happened, nothing like that anyway, we just enjoyed each other's company. She's so lovely," he sighed, staring, "But in the end we decided to ... well, leave it for a bit. We both agreed it was too soon after our relationships had ended, and we should take time out before rushing into anything else."

"Sounds sensible."

"A year," Mark sighed. "We agreed to give it a year and then see if we still felt the same about each other. I haven't stopped thinking about her every day since. I've been counting off the hours to come here, like a kid waiting for Christmas to arrive."

"What about Liv, how does she feel?" Faye asked.

"I don't know." He picked at the grass. "We haven't had a chance to talk yet, but ... I don't know, she hasn't given me any signs or hints or anything. She's been around the world, met so many people. I mean, look at her, Bri, it's ridiculous to think she hasn't been snapped up by now. She deserves better than me."

Brian nudged him with a giant shoulder and Mark toppled over. "Bloody hell, Bri!"

"Distraction technique," Brian said, "Works well with dogs, apparently."

"You nearly broke my arm!"

"Don't know my own strength sometimes. Worked, though, didn't it."

"Leave him alone," Faye snapped. What on earth's the matter with you?"

"Yeah, Brian the bully," Jim added.

"What's the matter with me?" Brian suddenly boomed, shocking them all. "I'll tell you what's the matter with me, shall I? I can't get a word in edgeways in my own home, I'm being driven completely round the bloody bend by a woman who *never stops talking*, and I miss spending time with my wife!"

There was silence.

Faye got to her feet and very quietly said, "I think it's time we had a talk, Bri."

"Yes, I think it probably is."

He got up and started walking with Faye to their caravan, when Olivia rushed over, still holding the phone to her ear, and said, "Bri, can I have a word?"

"I'm just about to have a long-overdue word with my wife, Liv."

"It's an emergency."

* * *

"Where are you going?" Faye asked, when Brian rushed into the caravan to grab his car keys.

"It won't take long."

"What won't take long?"

He looked at her and said, "I can't tell you."

"Why can't you tell me?"

"Faye, you're just going to have to trust me."

"Are you ...?" She gulped hard. "Are you leaving me, Bri?"

"Don't be daft, woman, of course I'm not leaving you!"

"Then where are you going?"

"I have to run an errand for ... Liv."

"What kind of errand?"

"I have to go."

"Go where?" She got up and followed him to the car. He seemed to be in a big hurry and she had to jog to keep up with his huge footsteps. "Where are you going, Bri? When are you coming back?"

"I won't be long."

"How long is not long?"

He was in his car now, putting the keys in and starting the engine. The group on the grass watched anxiously. Sophie shouted, "Everything alright, Faye?"

"I'll come with you," she said to Brian.

"No!" He said it so abruptly that she immediately stopped running round to the other side of the car and came back to the driver's window.

"What's going on?" she breathed, sensing the tension in him. "Tell me, Brian."

"I can't. It's … it's a man thing, pride and honour and all that."

"What's a man thing?"

"I'll be back as soon as I can." And he drove off.

"Liv?"

"I can't tell you," Liv said, "I've been sworn to secrecy."

"Sworn to secrecy by who?"

"I'm sorry, Faye, I really can't say. He shouldn't be long, he's just helping me with … something."

Faye growled in frustration and stormed off into the caravan. Sophie quickly followed her in.

"What's occurring?" Mark asked Olivia, as she sat back down on the grass next to him.

"A friend asked me to ask Brian for a favour."

"What friend?"

"Honestly, Mark, I can't tell you."

"A close friend?"

"Yes."

"It's another woman," Jim said, "Flo's driven him into the arms of another woman, possibly a mute."

"There you go, judging people by your own standards again. We're not all lecherous, unfaithful morons like you, you know. Brian certainly isn't."

"It's always the quiet ones."

"Brian's hardly quiet!"

"You mark my words, it's another woman, it always is."

"Fancy a walk?" Mark asked Olivia, "To get away from the blotchy gob monster?

Olivia bit her lip, but nodded. They got up together and wandered off towards the woods, disappearing through the child-lock gate in the chain-link fence.

"Marky's got a girlfriend," Jim chanted after them, "Marky's got a girlfriend."

Mark, not breaking his stride, held a couple of fingers high in the air.

"Nah, that's alright," Jim called after them. "I'm fine being left all alone with nothing to do."

"You could try cleaning that cesspit of a caravan," came Mark's voice through the trees.

CHAPTER 4

"How the hell did you manage that?"

"I lost count of the turnoffs at the traffic island," Tel said. "I took the wrong one and ended up … here."

'Here' was down a long, narrow lane with a farmhouse at the end. In the farmyard, a car and caravan were jack-knifed quite spectacularly between the farmhouse and a brick barn that smelled of cows. An irate farmer stood menacingly to one side with his arms crossed, his tractor still running in the field behind the caravan. Chickens ran around. A sheepdog lay low on the cobbles, growling up at them both.

"How long you been stuck here?"

"About three hours. I left Leeds at five o'clock this morning. I wanted to surprise Sophie."

"I don't know about Sophie, but I'm pretty surprised, and the farmer looks quite shocked too. Alright, mate." He raised a large, jovial hand. The farmer clamped his arms tighter across his chest and grunted, "You gonna move the damn thing, or what? I got cattle to feed."

"I can't get it out, Bri! I've tried!"

"I can see you've tried." Brian slowly shook his head. "Takes some incompetence to get a rig wedged like that."

"I must have done a thousand backwards and forwards. I think," he said quietly, "I think I might have squashed a couple of chickens under there."

Brian walked down one side of the caravan, squeezing between it and the stone farmhouse. He walked up the other side, noting the car hood was a hair's breadth from the barn wall. It looked good and wedged. He stepped back over the hitching.

"What can I do, Bri? The farmer's pretty pissed off."

"As well he might, with you barricading his entire farmyard. As far as I can see, there's only one thing for it. We're going to have to unhitch and manhandle."

"Unhitch and manhandle?"

"Yeah, that's the technical term for getting the hell out of here before the farmer fetches his shotgun."

"Shotgun?" Tel risked a glance back at the farmer, who glared back at him with slitted eyes beneath thick, bushy eyebrows. Tel thought he looked every inch the type of man who would shoot first and ask questions later.

"Are you going to give me a hand?" Brian snapped.

"Yeah, I was just weighing up our chances of survival."

"My chances are high, I can drive out of here any time. You, however – "

"Don't leave me, Bri."

"Come on, let's get this jockey wheel down. Put the brake on first, Tel."

They unhitched the caravan from the large car and, half inch by half inch, edged the back of the caravan away from the farmhouse. When it sat parallel, there was just enough room to manoeuvre the car into a seventy-nine-point turn away from the barn. The car was now in the middle of the farmyard, facing the exit. The caravan was not. Brian and Mark heaved from the back, across the cobbles, turning just enough not to bash the back end into the house or the front end into the barn. There was a slight incline and they strained to push, both of them gasping.

"Couldn't lend a hand, could you?" Brian asked the farmer.

"Ain't my caravan, ain't my problem."

When the front hitch of the caravan was almost touching the barn bricks, they let it gently roll back, carefully turning it, then pushed again, rolled again, just missing both the stone wall of the house and the brick wall of the barn by mere millimetres. Finally, they managed to turn it enough to get the caravan in the middle of the farmyard behind the car, both now facing the exit. They hitched them together again. Suddenly, unexpectedly, Tel threw his arms around Brian as far as he could and cried, "I thought I was going to die here!"

"Come on, lad, pull yourself together and let's get the hell out of Dodge."

Brian gave a cheery wave at the farmer, now walking across his empty farmyard to his tractor. "Pleasure doing business with you!" he yelled, "I'll recommend your dairy to all my friends. Cheers, now."

* * *

On the way to the campsite Tel flashed his lights and they pulled up at a layby. Brian ambled back to Tel. "You okay?"

"Not really, still a bit shaky. Just needed a breather. It's quite exhausting, facing and escaping death."

"He looked harmless enough, just a bit peeved to have you in his farmyard. Why are you here anyway? Sophie said you weren't coming."

"I told her I couldn't make it, I wanted it to be a surprise. Things have been a bit strained between us lately, with Sophie in London and me all the way up in Leeds. I was supposed to work all weekend on a case that's coming up before the judge on Wednesday, but then I thought, 'What the hell am I doing? This is just a job. Sophie is my life'." He screwed up his face. "Not sure I'll still have a job on Monday, though."

"I'm sure Sophie won't mind keeping you in the lap of luxury while you bum it for a bit."

"Bum it for a bit?"

"You posh folk," he tutted, "Not knowing yer common slang. Sophie turned up at the campsite in a Bentley!"

"She never did!"

"With a chauffeur in a peaked cap, no less. So yeah, she can afford to take care of you, she's a good egg."

Tel was about to open his mouth to question 'good egg', then thought better of it. "My heart's stopped racing now," he said.

"Let's go surprise your lass then. Can't wait to see her face."

"Me neither."

* * *

"It's been terrible," Faye was telling Sophie. "I feel torn between my husband and my sister. I know she talks a lot and I know it's driving him mad, but she's my *sister*, Soph, what am I supposed to do? He just seems so angry all the time, it's never been this bad for this long before."

Sophie patted her hand across the table in the caravan. "It'll be alright. Brian's a good man. You two will sort it out, I know you will."

"I'm not so sure. I think I've really – " She lowered her head and her voice. " – *screwed up* this time, and I don't know how to make it right again."

"You haven't, I'm sure you haven't. All relationships hit rocky patches, I read it in Cosmopolitan. You just have to grit your teeth and get through it."

"He's been going to the pub after work almost every night. When he comes home he glares at me, glares at Flo, grunts, and stomps off to bed. By the time I go up he's fast asleep, snoring. When I get up in the morning he's already gone. Sometimes he texts me and all they say is, 'Is she still there? When is she leaving? I can't take much more of this.'"

"Oh, you poor thing."

"I think he wants to leave me, Soph. I've driven him away."

"Don't be silly, he loves you to bits."

"I just don't know how to make it right again. I can feel him getting more and more distant, and I miss him, I really, really miss him. I know it's Flo, but she was so distraught when she lost her cat I was afraid to leave her on her own."

"Perfectly understandable, Faye. You did what you had

to do, what you thought was best."

"But I don't want to lose my husband."

"You'll work it out, just give it time. Sit down together and have a proper heart-to-heart."

"We were going to, then he just suddenly dashed off, wouldn't tell me where he was going or how long he was going to be."

"I'm sure there's a reasonable explanation, Faye. I don't know him as well as you do, but he seems like a perfectly decent man to me."

"He is, but I've pushed him too far, expected too much of him. It's all my fault."

* * *

Out on their walk through the woods, Mark said, "How have you been?"

"Good. You?"

"Yeah, fine. Garden centre keeps me busy, it's doing really well."

"Glad to hear it."

"You enjoyed your travels then?"

"I did, very much."

"I loved all the WhatsApp photos you sent, you did a lot."

"I did."

"Did you … meet anyone?"

"I met loads of people."

"Don't tease, Liv, you know what I'm asking." He stopped on the path and turned to her. "We agreed last year that it was too soon, we'd just ended our relationships and we were both keen not to jump into another one too quickly. We said we'd wait a year and see how we felt then. It's … it's been a year, Liv. Do I still have a chance or shall I *tear out my heart and stamp it into the cold, cruel ground.*"

She laughed at his hamming. "Very good."

"Thanks, I've been practising. I was aiming for Richard Burton in Who's Afraid of Virginia Woolfe."

"I got that."

"Did you? Good. I feel like I'm walking on thin ice here."

"Take my hand," she said, holding it out for him, "I'll stop you from falling through."

"Will you, Liv?"

"I will."

"But not in a Titanic kind of way, where Kate just lets Leonardo go even though there's clearly enough space on the board for two people?"

"No, I won't let go."

They held hands, swinging them like children. "I've not met anyone else," she said.

"Good. I mean, not good, I don't want you to be lonely or anything, but … good."

They walked on in silence for a while, holding hands, neither of them really knowing what to say but both enjoying just being together, touching. "I was so excited to see you again, Liv, I've been counting down the days. It felt like Christmas was coming."

"Me too." She gave a cute, awkward smile, staring down at the leaves on the ground.

He took a deep breath. "How do you feel now, a year later?"

She turned her head to look at him, and said, "I feel the same."

"You do?"

"Yes."

Mark wanted to jump up and down and holler at the top of his lungs. He wanted to cartwheel down the path and hug her and sing all at the same time. Then he thought to ask, "About me? You feel the same about me?"

"Yes," she laughed.

He raced back to her. They held hands at chest height, standing close, staring into each other's eyes.

"Just to be absolutely clear, you don't feel we should give it more time? I mean, it's been a long year of waiting, I'm not sure I could – "

"I'm ready," she said. "I'm sure."

The sound of a man screaming 'Whooooo-hoooooo' echoed through the woods. Mark clasped her in his arms and hugged her. "I've never been so happy," he said, squeezing her tightly.

Olivia muttered something he couldn't hear. He pulled back. She took a deep breath. "Hearty hug," she giggled, "Couldn't breathe."

"Oh, sorry, sorry." He beamed from ear to ear. "I'm just so happy!" He ran down the path a few steps, shaking his fists in the air. Olivia gave her high, tinkling laugh. He ran back.

"Shall we date? We'll date, I'll take you nice places, I'm not without means and I promise to spoil you. We'll see lots of things together, new things, exciting things, or not, it's totally up to you. I'll come to Oxford to see you, you can come and stay at … at my house."

"Can we take it slowly?" she breathed. "I've only ever dated Dick, and that wasn't really dating, more like organising my place in his universe. I'm not really sure how dating works or if I'm any good at it. I actually feel quite nervous."

"Don't be nervous." He hugged her again, gentler this time. "We'll take it as slow as you want, you set the pace. Oh Liv, I could literally burst. I'm so happy to see you, so happy to have you back, and really bloody happy you still want me, I was so afraid you'd meet someone else and forget all about me, I couldn't even contemplate – "

"Mark."

"Yes, Liv?"

"Could you stop talking now and kiss me."

* * *

Jim sat on the grass for a while, strumming his fingers

on his knees, sitting back and staring up at the sky, whistling. Faye and Sophie were still in the caravan, he could see them talking animatedly at the table. Mark and Olivia clearly weren't coming back any time soon, and Brian was still out in his car.

He was bored and lonely.

He rang Beth. "Are you popping in later? Oh good, what time? We'll probably be in the pub by then, we can have a meal together and I can introduce you to everyone. Okay then, see you later. Love you."

He picked at the grass for a bit, before glancing over at the water tap at the end of the caravan area. There was a hosepipe curled up next to it, one of those crinkly things that looked like shrivelled snakeskin. He got up and went over, screwed it on, turned it on, and dragged it down the driveway to his green, listing caravan.

He might as well clean it.

* * *

At some point they turned on the path and started walking slowly back towards the campsite, holding hands, glancing at each other and smiling like naughty children.

"Can I call you my girlfriend?"

"You can, and you can be my boyfriend."

Mark pulled a face. "Girlfriend and boyfriend sounds a bit … young, teenagery?"

"I'm not calling you my male friend, that's too boring for words."

"Other half then, you're my 'other half.'"

"I'm not half of anything," she giggled, "I'm a whole, complete person, never been wholer, never been more complete."

"Better half?"

She laughed.

"Beau?"

"Are we in the 18th century?

"Okay, how about 'partner'?"

"Too business-like."

"Bae? Significant other?"

"Old man?" she giggled, "'Hello, can I introduce you to my *old man*?'."

"'And here's my *old woman*'."

"Him indoors."

"My girl."

"My man. Yes, I like that. 'This is Mark, he's my man'."

He lifted her chin to kiss her again. "My lady."

"Shall we tell the others?"

"Let's wait until they're all together and then do a big announcement."

"It's a bit exciting."

"It is."

They walked on in silence, arms around each other. Olivia bit her lip, fighting the conflicting emotions whirling round and round in her head. Mostly she felt relief that she could tell someone at last, but there was also fear, fear of admitting her deception and fear that it might change things before they'd even had a chance to begin. "Mark," she said.

"Yes, my lady?"

"Now that we're officially a couple I think I have something to tell you."

"You gave birth to triplets in America?"

"No, silly."

"You bought Google and now you're the CEO of a huge conglomerate with evil plans to take over the world?"

"Not exactly."

She told him, and he stopped dead in his tracks. "You're kidding!"

* * *

Jim dashed across to the reception shop and bought

caravan wash, spot remover, four cans of fabric spray cleaner, disinfectant, a wash brush with a long pole, wash cloths, a bucket, bin bags, paper masks, and air freshener. It cost him a fortune and his eye twitched as he handed over his money, but it would be worth it, and his mate would appreciate the effort. Also, he wouldn't be able to persuade Beth to take up caravanning with a van that looked like it had spent years in a swamp.

He filled the bucket with hot water from one of the washing-up sinks, and hauled it heavily and sloshily back to the caravan. Putting on a mask, he entered the dank interior of the caravan and began dragging the sofa cushions outside, where he left them on the grass to 'air'. He emptied out the cupboards, the contents all black and damp to the touch. There were more dead rats in the bottom cupboards, some more dried up than others. He scooped them out, retching at the smell, and piled them into a bin bag.

He squirted a good slug of disinfectant into the bucket and quickly started wiping everything down. The door under the sink and a drawer front fell off, but he thought Brian might have some tools to screw them back on again. Leaving every surface dripping wet to 'sterilise', he started on the outside, turning on the hosepipe and spraying it down. He directed it at a particularly mouldy bit on one side and a window fell out. He wouldn't be able to clean the rest of the caravan with a big hole in the side, so, sighing, he dashed across to the reception shop and bought a large bottle of Gorilla Glue, quickly glancing at the instructions as he walked back. He squirted a generous dollop all around the inside of the rectangular hole, using quite a lot on the rotted wood, and around the window itself, then he pushed it back in. The instructions said it reacted to water, so he sprayed the whole thing with the hosepipe and watched as the glue oozed like foam from around the window and started to expand. And expand. And expand some more.

"What the -?"

The window was pushed out by the ever-expanding

foam and splatted onto the gravel pitch, still oozing. Foam poured down the side of the caravan. He tried to spray it off but it just kept growing. Panicking, he raced back to the reception shop and brought masking tape. Racing back, he taped a couple of bin bags over the window, hoping that would stop the oozing avalanche, but it just made the bin bags bulge and fall off.

He decided to ignore it, Brian would tell him how to fix it later. He continued to hose down the rest of the caravan, before using the brush on the long pole to slosh on hot, soapy water from the bucket. He was disappointed to see that the green moss and mould didn't just slide off the surface, and started scrubbing with the brush, before hosing the whole thing down again. It wasn't a vast improvement. The roof of the caravan was still filthy, there were actual plants growing in the sills.

He rested for a bit, splayed out like Da Vinci's Vitruvian Man on the grass, before moving his small van closer to the caravan. He climbed up between the van and the caravan, clambering first onto the van roof and then on top of the caravan, feeling quite proud of himself, until he saw the bucket and brush on the gravel pitch below. He climbed down again, put the cleaning equipment on the roof of his van, and then ascended once more.

* * *

Brian pulled in through the entrance gates. Tel was about five minutes behind, he wanted to make a grand entrance and had pulled over into a layby on the main road.

He noticed it straight away, his eyes drawn to it like two magnets to metal. It stood out like a sore thumb against the blue sky. It was a man, standing on the roof of his caravan, apparently mopping it.

"What's the idiot doing?!"

As he pulled up level with the now drenched caravan, Jim raised an arm. "Hi, Bri," he shouted, "I might need to borrow your drill and a couple of – "

Jim disappeared when the roof collapsed under his weight. One whole side of the caravan fell outwards like a collapsing deck of cards, landing on the hedge and narrowly missing Brian's car. He jumped out. Several people on the campsite rushed over to stand and gawp. Faye and Sophie ran across the grass, their mouths forming perfect Os.

"I'm okay!" cried a little voice from inside.

"WHAT THE HELL ARE YOU DOING?" Brian boomed, horrified.

"Well," said the tiny voice, "I *was* cleaning the caravan, but now I'm just sprawled across a sofa and a broken table, and it still bloody stinks in here!"

Mark and Olivia raced up. "What happened?"

"Jim cleaned the caravan, and broke it!"

"The muck and the mould were the only things holding it together."

"Do you think it can be fixed, Bri?" asked the voice, to the accompaniment of things creaking and cracking ominously inside.

"FIX IT?" Brian cried, "*FIX IT?!*"

"Yeah, I've got some Gorilla Glue and some tape."

"ARE YOU COMPLETELY OUT OF YOUR TINY MIND?"

Jim appeared in the space where a caravan side used to be, covered in dust and bits of wood. As he tramped across the debris, rocking the caravan, the other side fell down. Faye and Sophie had to jump out of the way.

"YOU NEARLY KILLED MY WIFE, YOU IMBECILE!!"

"I'm okay," Faye whimpered, "Calm down."

Brian took some deep breaths and let the shock of two near-deaths wash over him.

"So, what do you think, Bri? Is it fixable?"

Mark started laughing, so hard he had to bend forward with his hands resting on his knees. Olivia sniggered guiltily behind her hand. Then Brian started laughing, shaking his head as he got back into his car – Tel would be here soon and he needed to get out of the way of his 'grand entrance'. He parked the Kia in front of his caravan and got out, looking back at the crumpled green mess.

"Bri?" cried Jim, climbing out of the debris on their side, "What should I do, Bri?"

"Search Google for a local scrap man and get them to pick it up."

Mark was still bent double, struggling to catch his breath. Faye and Sophie couldn't stop sniggering.

"Are you saying it can't be fixed, Bri?"

Brian shook his head some more. Mark was now laughing so hard he could hardly breathe, and a concerned-looking Olivia was gently rubbing his back.

Faye came over to Brian and said, "Were you worried about me?"

"Of course!"

"You don't hate me then, you know, because of the sister stuff?"

"Oh Faye, can't we just go back to the way it – "

A car and caravan crunched slowly through the entrance gates and into the caravan area.

"Brian?"

"Shush, watch this, you'll like it."

Sophie was busy helping Jim clamber out of his wreck. The car and caravan stopped level with them. She glanced briefly at it, then turned back to Jim. Car seems familiar, she vaguely thought, looks just like the Range Rover Tel uses in Leeds. She suddenly straightened up, let go of Jim's arm, and glanced at it again. Jim gambolled onto the grass.

"Tel?" she breathed.

Tel got out of the car and grinned at her across the bonnet.

"TEL?"

He came round the front of the car and strode towards her. She stepped towards him, hardly able to believe her eyes. "What ... what are you -?"

He pulled her into his arms and kissed her like Rhett Butler kissing Scarlet O'Hara. The others cheered and clapped. "Sophie Forbes," Tel said with feeling, "I've really bloody missed you."

"What are you doing here? I thought you were working this weekend?"

"I was, then I came to my senses and realised this is where I needed to be." He gave her another quick kiss and turned to the others. "Whatcha, plebs!"

"Whatcha, posh git!"

"Whose caravan is this?" Sophie asked.

He wrapped an arm around her shoulders and led her towards it. "It's ours, I bought it on Monday from a dealer. It's for us, to go travelling."

"Oh Tel!"

"Get a room!" Brian cried, as they embraced with some considerable passion, "Nobody needs to see that before lunch."

Tel finally pulled away and shouted, "I've got a room, I just need to park it."

With Brian guiding him, Tel reversed onto the pitch and parked on his first attempt.

"See!" Mark called back to Jim, who was trying to tape a caravan side to the still upright back panel, "That's how a competent driver does it."

"Nice that you're all helping Tel when I clearly have a crisis on my hands!"

"That's not a crisis, that's an eyesore of your own making."

They helped Tel unload his camping equipment and pull out the sun canopy, while Faye and Olivia made tea. Faye couldn't resist saying something.

"I saw you and Mark together earlier," she said.

"Yes, we went for a walk."

"Nice walk, was it?"

"It was lovely."

"Is there anything you might want to tell me?"

"Not yet," Olivia said, blushing a little, "Maybe later."

"I already know." Faye gave her a wink. "I'm very happy for you both, and don't worry, I won't breathe a word."

They hugged and poured out the tea. When they took it out chairs and tables, still with labels and price tags on them, were being hauled out of the caravan. Jim was standing on the roof of his white Transit, trying to tape the sides of the caravan together without much success. The smell coming out of it wafted across the campsite.

"Any chance of a bacon sarnie, Faye?" he said, taking his tea and wiping the sweat off his blotchy face.

"Caravan demolition hungry work, is it?" Mark shouted across.

"It is, actually."

"Sorry, Jim, still no bacon."

"How fortuitous," Tel said, grabbing hold of Sophie's hand and pulling her into their caravan with a squeal of surprise, "You'll all have to go to the pub for lunch." He slammed the door shut behind them and Sophie started giggling from within.

"Pub it is!" Brian cried. "Do you two in there want anything bringing back?"

"No, thanks," Tel yelled, "Got everything I need right here."

"They do sandwiches?"

"No, thanks."

"There's a well-stocked shop if you -?"

"Bugger off, the lot of you!"

* * *

Tel and Sophie's new caravan had a fixed bed at the back which someone, probably Faye, had already made up with the new duvet and bed linen he'd bought.

"Purple and orange bedding?" Sophie snorted.

"I was in a hurry," he said, sidling up to her. "Besides,

you won't notice the colour soon."

They lay down on the bed. It was very comfortable, and the new pillows were soft and lush. They cuddled up together.

"It seems such a long time since we've done this," Sophie said.

"The universe is conspiring to keep us apart, but I won't let it."

They kissed. Sophie snuggled up to him. He felt happy to have her in his arms again.

They were warm and comfortable and together.

And tired. So tired.

They promptly fell asleep.

CHAPTER 5

They lingered over a ploughman's lunch outside the pub in the sunshine. Lots of others lingered with them, eating and drinking and laughing. It was a good atmosphere.

"Did we put 'good atmosphere' on the surveys?" Brian asked.

"I think we did."

When they'd finished, Tel and Sophie still hadn't appeared.

"They can't still be at it!" Jim said, just as the barmaid walked past and gave him a wink.

"The stamina of youth," Faye sighed.

"My memory doesn't go back that far," Brian said. "Couple of quid each towards the tip, since we're not actually paying for anything?"

"I'm all out of funds," Jim whined. "All that cleaning equipment cost me a fortune."

"And all for nothing," Faye said.

"Changed man indeed," Mark said. "You're still the same old stingy git."

Jim raised his arms, "I'm skint! Plus, I'm saving to take Beth on a surprise holiday."

"Butlins at Bognor Regis?"

"Ten day cruise in Egypt."

"Is this for your 20th wedding anniversary, if you make it that far?"

"No," Jim drawled, "This year, that's why I'm saving so hard."

"And by 'saving' you mean scrounging off other people."

In a high voice, Jim said, "I have always depended on the

kindness of strangers."

"I wish we were strangers," Mark said, throwing down a few pound coins, "That way we wouldn't have to keep paying for you."

"First and last time this week, I promise."

"Yeah, yeah, heard it all before."

"It's just a couple of quid each, Mark," said Brian.

"Yeah, that's for me and Liv."

"That's very kind of you, Mark," she said with wide eyes.

Faye laughed. Brian said, "Come on, you two, we're old, not stupid."

"What do you mean?" Mark's face was overly innocent. Olivia's was expressionless.

Brian gave a grin behind his beard. "What do we do now, risk going back to the caravans to listen to an X-rated soundtrack, or something else?"

"I'm actually a bit tired," Olivia said, "All that driving from Oxford and … everything. I might take an afternoon nap."

"Yeah," Mark gave a yawn that could have easily earned him an Oscar. "Me too, it's been a busy day, and that lunch was quite heavy."

"Lunch was a hefty cheese teacake and salad," Brian laughed.

"Teacake?"

"Oh, don't start him off," said Faye, "It's a weird Yorkshire thing. Do you know, I think I'd quite like an afternoon – "

"No, you wouldn't," snapped Brian.

"Er, I would, actually."

"You can't."

"I can and I will!"

"Well, you'll be doing it on your own."

"Why?"

"Because we haven't resolved our differences yet and we don't know when The Sister is coming back, that's why."

Faye pulled a sulky face.

"I'd quite like a doze myself," Jim whined, "All that cleaning's done me in, except I don't actually have anywhere to sleep."

"Déjà vu, anyone?" Mark laughed, walking off with Olivia.

"Mark, could I -?"

"No!"

"Bri, could I -?"

"No!"

"Well, what am I supposed to do then?"

"Reception shop sells airbeds and sleeping bags," Brian said, "You could sleep in your van again."

"But I'm skint!"

"Not my problem," Brian said, walking off.

"Where are we going?" Faye asked excitedly, "Are we having an afternoon nap after all?"

"And risk Flo barging in on us in flagrante?" He glanced down at his wife's confused face. "Naked and *at it*."

"I know what it means," she lied. "So where are we going then?"

"To get the car and go for a drive. Do you still have those earplugs in your pocket?"

"I'd rather stay here and wear them," she grumbled.

He stopped and touched her arm. "Let's go for a drive and find somewhere quiet."

"I'm not doing it in the car, Bri!"

"No, we need to sort this out once and for all, Faye, without interruption and without Flo dragging your attention away."

They walked through into the camping field, pushing their earplugs in, just in time to see Olivia inviting Mark into her motorhome. "They're a bit rubbish at deceit and subterfuge, aren't they!"

"What?"

"I said … oh never mind." He noticed Faye walking on

the grass and tip-toeing exaggeratedly over the gravel pitches. "What are you doing?

"What?"

Brian pulled his earplugs out. Faye did the same.

"What are you doing?"

"Being quiet."

"And you don't think the engine starting and a heavy car crunching over the gravel might raise suspicion? They might come out thinking our car's being stolen, and nobody wants to see four naked bodies on a campsite." He paused.

"Stop thinking of naked women, Brian."

"I'm not, I was having a flashback to Jim and Julie bending naked at the water tap last year." He shuddered. "Come on, let's go talk."

* * *

"Hi, Steve. Yeah, I got the caravan okay." Jim paced up and down the pub car park with the phone at his ear. "I was just wondering, how much did you say you paid for it? And that was how long ago? So it would be, what, worth half that price now or even less than that, maybe nothing at all? Oh really? Sounds a lot for a really old caravan, I don't think you'd get that much for it. No, no, just asking.

"To be honest, Steve, it's a bit bloody knackered, mate. The inside is full of mould and dead rats. Yeah, dead rats under the sofa, all dried up, been there ages. Stinks, too. Listen, Steve, I'm going to have to be straight with you, the caravan's a wreck, unsuitable for human habitation, and I think the best thing to do is … Bring it back? I was thinking about having it towed away, purely as a favour to you so you don't have to bother with it yourself. I've a friend who knows a scrap man and … You want it back? You sure you want that green thing parked on your driveway for another couple of years? I think the best thing to do is just scrap it, tyres are knackered and the only thing holding it together is …

"Okay, Steve. No, that's fine, everything's fine. I'll bring it back at the end of next week, no problem. Okay, Steve, catch ya later."

He hung up and hissed, "Bugger!"

He went into the pub for a pint and a think. He vaguely considered going home, but then he really didn't want to miss out on any fun with his camping buddies. Also, the idea of just abandoning ship, or caravan, and making a run for it was somewhat mooted when Chelsea, the pub manager, put his pint down in front of him and said, "What you doing about that wrecked caravan? It's an eyesore and I've had complaints."

"I'm dealing with it," he said.

"*When* are you dealing with it?"

"As soon as I can."

"Today?"

"I'm working on it."

"Today," she said, giving him a firm eye as she walked away.

Melissa, the barmaid who used to work in the pub down the road from him, sidled up. "How have you been?" she asked, twirling her hair in her fingers and smiling at him.

"Okay," he said, smiling back, "How've you been?"

"Alright. Broke up with my boyfriend."

"Have you? That big chap with the skinhead?"

"Yeah, weren't my sort after all."

"What's your sort, then?"

"You," she said.

"I'm married."

"You were married last time."

"Yeah, but I'm a changed man now."

"Are you?" She gave him a cheeky look and wandered off.

Jim thought he might stay after all, a bit of harmless flirting would do him the world of good.

* * *

"OH BRIAN!"

They'd been cruising down a country lane, looking for somewhere to pull over, preferably with a view, when there was a sudden noise and the car lurched violently to the right. Brian had to slam the brakes on pretty fast to stop from going right across the road and into a ditch.

They both sat there for a full second, shocked to the core.

"What –?"

"Tyre blew out." He put the car into first gear and drove back to the left-hand side of the road.

"Oh my God, Bri, if a car had been coming the other way –"

"I know."

He drove the car very slowly up the lane

"You'll ruin the wheel driving with a flat, Bri."

"I'll park up on this blind bend then, shall I, and we can just wait for something to hit us."

"Okay, no need to be sarky."

Away from the sharp corner he pulled onto the grass verge and got out. A car flew past, blasting its horn. Brian muttered furiously under his breath.

"What are you going to do, Bri?"

"Change the wheel." It *would* be the front driver's side, he was going to be exposed to traffic while he changed it, risking life and limb.

"Have we got a spare?"

"In the boot." Except, when he went to the boot, narrowly avoiding an Astra that was going much too fast, the spare wheel also had a flat – he'd meant to have it fixed months ago and forgot. He muttered a few choice words.

"What was that, Bri?"

"Nothing, just muttering a few choice words."

She came and stood beside him, just as a blue car sped by blasting reggae music from its open windows. "Are you going to change it, Bri?"

"Can't, it's flat."

"Why is it flat?"

"Because I meant to get it fixed and forgot."

"Oh Brian!"

"Yes, I know, don't nag."

"You should have got it fixed."

"I know!"

"What are we going to do now?"

"I'll have to call the AA."

"How long will that take?"

"I don't know."

She huffed. He glared at her. She went and sat back in the car again. Brian called the AA, then got in with her to wait.

"Well, it's not a scenic view," he said, "But I guess we could chat here."

"I don't feel like talking now, I still feel a bit shaky, and – " A car roared past, rocking the car. " – it's not very quiet. Oh Bri, if a car had been coming the other way! You shouldn't have taken that corner so fast."

"I wasn't going fast!"

"It felt fast."

"Are you blaming me for getting a flat?"

"No, I'm just saying, if you hadn't been going so fast round that bend – "

"Your sister's driving me round the bend," he suddenly blurted.

"I know, you've told me, *several* times."

"And yet nothing changes. It's like talking into a void, you listen, you nod, you do nothing."

"What am I supposed to do, Brian, she's my sister!"

"Send her home!"

"She's upset and alone and lonely."

"It was just a *cat*, Faye!"

"It was her *baby*, Bri."

"Then why doesn't she get another cat?"

"Oh, so when I die you'll dash straight out and get another wife?"

"It's not the same!"

"It is for Flo."

"She has to go!"

"Don't shout at me, you know I don't like it when you shout."

"I'm not shouting, I'm just loud!"

Faye sighed. "This is a waste of time, we're just saying the same things over and over again."

"Then say something different, say something like, 'I completely understand where you're coming from, Bri, and I'll ask Flo if she's ready to go home.'"

"Or *you* could say, 'I totally understand your sister needs us at this difficult time and of course she can stay for as long as she wants,' instead of complaining all the time."

"I have cause for complaint! I can't get a word in in my own home! You completely ignore me and lavish all your attention on a woman who will simply *not stop talking*!"

"Oh, so you're feeling neglected, are you? Is this what this is all about, I'm paying too much attention to Flo?"

"No!" he growled, "It's about getting our life back, our happy life, our quiet life that doesn't have someone yakking at us and around us from morning till night. Faye, I'm losing my mind!"

Faye stared out of the window, torn, angry, frustrated. She was about to say something, when the police arrived.

* * *

The police officer, who looked like he was still in school, made Brian drive two feet further away from the blind bend for safety reasons, and then parked directly behind them, which shortened the gap between the bend and the cars, which was shortened even more when he put a yellow triangle further down the lane, narrowly avoiding death by truck. The officer was clearly having a slow day and lingered awhile, standing next to the driver's door and asking questions about the blowout, if he was going too fast (Faye wisely kept quiet), meticulously checking his driving licence and insurance details. Every car that skimmed past blew its horn at the policeman, who was literally standing in the middle of the road, some yelling expletives out the window, but he seemed oblivious to it all. He was, Brian thought, a Heartbeat wannabe with Poirot aspirations.

"I could fine you for not having a working spare tyre," he said.

"You couldn't," Brian countered, "Having a spare isn't a legal requirement."

Another car flew past, sitting on its horn. The officer was blown against the driver's door.

"I might ask you to drive to the nearest garage, sir."

"You can't, the Highway Code requires tyres to be inflated t'correct pressure, so my flat-wheeled car is deemed unroadworthy and you can't ask me to drive it anywhere."

"Don't antagonise him, Brian."

"I'm not, but he should know the Highway Code better than me and he obviously doesn't. New on the job, are you, lad?"

"No."

Brian was tempted to ask him if his mother knew he was out playing policemen, but decided against it. "Tow truck should be here soon anyway."

"Fine, I'll leave you to it then, sir."

The officer collected his yellow triangle, narrowly avoiding death by screeching Land Rover, and drove off.

Brian and Faye sat there in silence for a while, until Faye said, "I'm too upset about our near-death experience to talk now, and you're obviously too angry."

"I'm not angry, I'm frustrated."

"You think I'm not?"

"I don't know how you feel, we never get the chance to talk anymore, but you seem pretty happy to have your sister living with us, despite my protestations. I'm telling you, Faye, I can't take much more."

"Are you asking me to choose between you and my sister."

"I assumed it wouldn't be a choice, but maybe I'm wrong."

There was silence. They both glared out of the window.

"I'm going back to the caravan," Faye said. "I think I need to be on my own for a bit."

"It's a good few miles."

"I'll call a taxi."

She got out, made a call on her mobile, and stood solemnly by the side of the road.

Brian stayed in the car.

* * *

Faye got back to the caravan. There was no sign of the others, so she slumped in a chair under the awning, ostensibly reading a book but mostly sobbing silently behind the screen of Flo's hanging bedroom.

It was another two hours before Brian got back.

"Did the tow truck come?" she asked.

"Yes."

"Did you get both tyres fixed?"

"Yes.

"Was it expensive?"

"Yes."

They didn't speak again after that, or even look at each other. Faye moved her chair out onto the grass, in the sunshine. Brian snatched a can from his coolbox and moved his chair onto the grass about two feet away, dragging a plastic side table with him.

They both felt very unhappy.

* * *

"Tel!" Sophie gasped.

"Hmm?"

"We fell asleep!"

"Towing a caravan is exhausting work."

"It's been hours!" she said, glancing in horror at her watch. "They'll think we've been at it all this time."

"Let them." He pulled her back into his arms and they kissed in the warm aftermath of sleep. "Best snooze I've had in ages."

"Me too." She lay blinking against his chest. "Why are you here, Tel?"

"I told you, I missed you."

"There were ... rumours in the office."

"Oh? Do tell Tel." It was a familiar joke, but it did nothing to lighten Sophie's mood.

"Apparently the big boss in Leeds has a very beautiful daughter."

"He has. Elle, who is what's known in legal terms as 'drop-dead gorgeous.'"

"Don't tease, Tel."

"I'm not teasing, I'm just stating facts."

"Were you ...?" She couldn't believe she was saying this but couldn't stop herself. "Were you *close* to her?"

He rolled her onto her back and peered down at her beautiful but anxious face. "Is that what the office rumours are about?"

"Yes."

"There's some pretty malicious people in that office."

"I know, but I still have to ask, for my own peace of mind. Were you close?"

"We were. She was fun. I liked her a lot."

Sophie felt a pain in her chest, which increased when he added, "I'm sorry, Sophie." He was sorry? Why was he sorry? The hurt was just starting to rise to anger when he said, "I shouldn't tease you. Yes, me and Elle were close, like brother and sister." She said nothing. All perfectly innocent? Isn't that what they all said? She should scratch out his eyes. She felt like slapping him, and crying.

"Sophie," he said, stroking her face and kissing her nose, "Elle's gay, she makes no secret of the fact she's got a girlfriend. Bet the rumours didn't mention that, did they?"

"No."

He kissed her again, and she said, "Why didn't you say you were coming?"

"I haven't, yet," he laughed.

She slapped him on his chest. "You know what I mean."

"I wanted to surprise you."

"Why?"

"Because I missed you." He sighed and fell onto his back. She leaned over him, stroking his hairy chest. "I had a revelation," he said. "I came out of the office last Sunday night, well, early hours of Monday morning really. The streets were empty. I'd just done an eighteen-hour stint on a case and there was this ... heaviness inside me. I thought it was hunger, or just exhaustion, but when I prodded it, this heaviness in the pit of my stomach, it had your name all over it. I stood looking up at the office block and something just ... clicked. I thought, 'What the hell am I doing here, so far away from the woman I love?' Was I willing to risk losing you? I was not." She lay her head against him. "If it was a choice between me making partner or being with you, I choose you. I went home, went to bed, and slept like a log. The heaviness was gone. I knew what I had to do. I got up early on Monday morning and rang the office, said I'd be in late. Then I went shopping."

"Shopping!" she laughed.

"For a caravan. Found one, bought it, went into the office and said I wanted to be transferred back to the London office and that I was taking the following week off. Boss wasn't best pleased, to put it mildly, but I didn't care, it didn't matter, all that mattered was you."

"Oh Tel."

"I cleared my workload like a man gone mad, I had something more important to aim for. You. And here I am."

"I'm glad you came."

He laughed.

"I thought we were finished. I thought it was over."

"Not over," he said, "Just starting."

They lay still and comfortable for a while, then Sophie said, "We'd better get up."

He groaned. "Five more minutes. In fact," he said, pulling her close again, "Maybe ten."

* * *

Sophie stepped out of the caravan, her curly black hair wild around her face. Tel followed, looking smug and bleary-eyed.

"The creatures emerge from the pit and blink blindly in the sunlight," Brian shouted across.

"Brian!" Faye admonished.

"Stop saying my name," he growled. "I'm not a child that needs reprimanding, I'm a *grown man* and I can *do what I want!*"

Faye slammed her book down.

Sophie and Tel came over with fold-up chairs and beaming smiles, which faded a bit halfway across. "Blimey," Sophie said, fanning a hand in front of her face, "Jim's caravan *stinks*. Oh sorry, Faye, forgot you can't smell."

"I can smell barbecue," Brian said, sniffing the air.

Sophie sat down. "We fell asleep," she laughed.

"A likely story."

"So, what have you two been up to?"

"Arguing, mostly."

"Oh no! Please make up."

"I won't ask about your afternoon," Brian laughed.

"No, best not," Tel smirked, and Sophie looked at him. He shrugged. He quite liked the idea of being seen as an energetic sex symbol rather than someone who couldn't follow a satnav and got stuck in farmyards.

"Where's Mark and Olivia?" Sophie asked.

Brian nodded towards the motorhome and she raised a perfect eyebrow. "Really?"

"Yeah, but it's not official yet so don't say anything."

Sophie pinched a finger and thumb across her lips.

"Cup of tea?" Faye asked.

"Something stronger."

"I'll get the champagne," Tel said, running back to their caravan.

"Ooh, champagne."

"Tel's brought a crate. Won't last the week, of course, but we can replenish."

He raced back with a bottle in one hand and a tinkling box of flute glasses in the other. "Let the champagne flow!" he cried, popping a cork.

"Here's to caravans and champagne," Sophie said, raising her glass, "And to good friends."

They tapped glasses

"Brian," came Mark's distant voice.

"Yes, Mark?"

"Would you lot mind standing up and looking at the camping field for a sec?"

"Any particular reason, or do you just want to make us look stupid?"

"There's a reason."

"What is it?"

A pause, and then, "I can't tell you."

"If you want us to stand up and move onto the driveway so that we can stare like zombies at the camping field, just so you can sneak out of Liv's motorhome and into your own caravan, then we're all wasting our time. I mean, you're talking to us *from* Liv's motorhome."

A pause, and then, "We fell asleep."

"What happens in the caravan stays in the caravan."

"Unless you like outdoor pursuits," Tel laughed. Then, catching Sophie's inquisitive look, he raised his eyebrows and

Sophie notched up her smile.

"Come join us," Brian yelled, "We have champagne!"

The motorhome door swung open and Mark sheepishly stepped out, turning to help Olivia down the steps. She was carrying two bottles of her own. "Let's get sloshed," she giggled.

Sophie stood up to hug Olivia and asked, "Are you two together now?"

"Oh," said Mark, grabbing a glass as another bottle popped, "You know already? I was going to make a big announcement and everything."

"Speech! Speech!" they all cried.

"Go on, darling," Olivia urged, and Mark grinned; he would never tire of her calling him darling.

He raised his glass. "Unaccustomed as I am to making speeches, in fact, apart from staff meetings I haven't done much – "

"Get on with it, lad."

"Right, okay. I'm very proud to announce that – "

Faye gasped out loud and squealed, "You're getting married?"

"Give us a chance, Faye, we've only just got together."

"Ignore the hysterical woman and continue," Brian said.

"I'm not hysterical!"

"Shush, woman."

"Don't shush me."

"Can you two stop bickering for one minute and let me do my thing?"

"Continue."

"I'm beyond happy to announce that the very lovely Liv has agreed to be my ... lady? Doesn't sound right, does it."

"Just say girlfriend," Olivia said.

"Has kindly taken pity on a poor, lovesick man and allowed him to proudly call her his girlfriend."

They all cheered and raised their glasses. "To Mark and Olivia!"

"Long may they love," Sophie cried.

"Long may they take afternoon naps," Brian laughed.

"Oh," Olivia cried, "We really did fall asleep."

"We believe you."

"No, honestly, we – "

"It's okay, Liv, we're just winding you up."

"It's been a long, hard year," Mark continued, "We wanted to do it right, not rush into anything on the rebound, and so we waited until – "

"Bored!" Brian boomed.

"Brian!"

"*Faye!*"

"I give up," said Mark.

Tel refilled everyone's glasses. "It's a huge responsibility, being role models," he said to Faye and Brian. "I think you should take it more seriously and make up, for all our sakes."

Brian remained silent. Faye held out her glass and pretended she hadn't heard.

"Kiss and make up," Olivia urged softly.

"Oh, we're way beyond the kissing stage," Brian replied, "We're at the duel at forty paces at dawn stage, soon to be followed by – " He caught Faye's eye. She looked so unhappy. He hated this. He leaned sideways in his chair and puckered up beneath his beard. The others cheered. Faye was just about to lean forward and kiss him, when Flo arrived.

"Oh, champagne!" she cried, bursting through the hedge next to them. "Fan*tas*tic. I won't say no to a glass of champers, thank you very much. Love the stuff, all those bubbles, and it never gives me a hangover the next day, unlike some other drinks, especially whisky, whisky gives me a massive headache so I tend not to touch the stuff, but champagne, fan*tas*tic. Who are you?"

Slightly shocked by the sudden onslaught, he said, "I'm Tel, I'm with Soph-"

"Good looking man," Flo said. "I can say that

because I'm old and no one takes offence at an old woman complimenting a young man. Youth is so attractive, isn't it? Not that I've lost my looks or anything, our mother has fan*tas*tic bone structure, hasn't she, Faye, it's why Faye and I have aged so well, our entire body hangs off our cheekbones. Our mother was beautiful right into her seventies, still is." She laughed heartily, while they all sat wide-eyed, stunned by the sudden explosion of words, their mouths hanging open, ready to speak at a millisecond's notice but not holding out much hope. "Had a fan*tas*tic time with Bill, Blenheim is just fan*tas*tic, what it must be like to live somewhere like that! We sat and had prosecco by the lake, oh it was brilliant, and all those antiques and old things, especially the library room, I bet you liked the library room when you went, didn't you, Faye, all those books."

"I – "

"As much as I'd like to stay and 'chew the cud' with you fan*tas*tic people, I can't hang around here, Bill's taking me out to dinner – "

"Oh, thank the Lord!" Brian cried.

" – and I've got to change and get ready." She swigged back her champagne, hurried into the awning and unzipped the bedroom tent. "Can't keep the man waiting, can I." Another peal of laughter and the sound of zips being undone, bags being moved. Outside, they looked from one to the other, each having lost the will to speak. "Faye," Flo shrieked, "Do you think I should wear the blue dress or the green?"

"I – "

"I think the green suits my colouring more, but I've only got black elastic sandals, do you think they'd be okay in a restaurant? I'm not sure how posh it is but they look okay, they can hardly throw me out for wearing elastic sandals, can they, or can they? I'll risk it. Can I borrow some of your lipstick, Faye, it's a fan*tas*tic colour? Does my hair look okay?"

Flo came out of the tent and gave a twirl in a large summer dress and elastic sandals. "What do you think? Not bad for an old bird, eh?"

"Are you ready, Flo?" Bill called over, "I booked the table for six o'clock, but we can have a drink in the bar first."

"Oh, that sounds fan*tas*tic, Bill. He really knows how to treat a woman, doesn't he? Yeah, I'm ready. Lipstick, Faye?"

Faye jumped up and dashed into the caravan as Flo regaled them all with the finer details of her summer dress, where she'd bought it, how much she'd paid for it, and how shops didn't really cater for normal sized women. Faye returned with the lipstick, which Flo put on blind before pushing her way through the hedge again to the other caravan area. Mark winced as branches snapped.

"Right, I'm off now, people. Have fun while I'm gone, don't do anything I wouldn't do, although that's not saying much and certainly won't keep you on the straight and narrow. Try not to miss me too much, tara a bit." A screech of laughter, and then she was gone. They heard a car door slam shut and an engine start, and then the crunching of gravel as it pulled away.

No one spoke for several seconds, and then Mark croaked, "I feel like I've just been verbally assaulted."

"How does she breathe?" Tel asked, "She doesn't pause for breath at all, it's quite remarkable."

"Don't you mean 'fan*tas*tic'?"

"I take it that's your sister, Faye?"

"Yes. Flo."

"Flo in full flow," said Brian. "Now you know what it's like. Imagine listening to that day in, day out."

"Brian!"

"*Woman!*"

"Don't speak to me like that!"

"*Then stop saying 'Brian'!*"

"Come on, you two," Mark said, "Kiss and make up."

Brian stood up. "The smell of barbecue is making me hungry. I'm going t'pub for some grub. Anyone else?"

The others finished off their champagne and stood up.

"Faye?"

"I think I'll stay here," she said, "I don't think I'm much wanted."

Brian bent down and planted a gentle kiss on her cheek. "Come on, y'dopey cow, let's go eat."

* * *

The Woodsman pub now sported a banner hanging from its upper windows reading, 'SATURDAY NIGHT IS BARBECUE NIGHT!" Brian rubbed his hands together in glee and entered the surprisingly empty bar.

"Where is everyone?" he asked the barmaid, who was wearing a SUE nametag.

"Out back, where the barbecue is."

"And out back is where?"

"Out back," she said, nodding her head to the right.

"Any hint as to how we can get 'out back'?" Brian persisted. When she looked at him blankly he said, "Cryptic clues, a spot of charades, finger pointing or – "

Faye jabbed him in the side and he shut up.

"You can either go back out the way you came and go down the side of the pub, or you can go to the end of the bar and turn left, then head towards the sunlight. I could scribble a map on the back of a coaster, if you'd like?"

"A barmaid with a caustic sense of humour, this could be an interesting week. Mine's a pint, love."

Sue started pouring, saying, "Just pay the barbecue man – "

"*Don't pay the ferryman,*" Tel sang.

" – and help yourself to food."

"We're not paying," Sophie said.

"Then you don't get food," Sue laughed.

"No, I mean, we're here to give our first impressions, everything's paid for."

"Oh, you're the survey people? Just use your password

when you order anything, but try to be discrete about it so the other campers don't get jealous of you being given free stuff."

"We don't have a password. We weren't given one, were we?" Faye looked at the others, who all shook their heads.

Sue pulled her phone from the back pocket of her jeans and pressed a button. "Hi, Chelsea, just a quickie." Faye scoured Brian's face. Brian determinedly kept his expression blank and unmoving. "What's the password for the survey people? Okay, thanks. No, everything's fine." She hung up and said, "'Cute campers.'"

"Thanks, love," Brian said, flicking back invisible hair, "I try my best."

Sue burst out laughing. "You're going to be trouble, you are, I can tell. Your password for food and drinks is 'cute campers'."

Olivia giggled.

"We have to say that every time we order something?" Sophie asked. "Sounds a bit … egotistical."

"Chelsea thought you'd like it. She's been on her hands and knees for most of the afternoon."

Brian sensed Faye's eyes upon him again and set his expression to stone.

"Hands and knees?" Mark asked.

"Burst water pipe in one of the bedrooms. They're trying to dry the carpets out with hair dryers and electric radiators, whole bedroom is like a sauna and we've got guests arriving at six. Now, just to let you know, there's no waiter service so you'll have to come in here for your drinks. Is that all clear enough for you, darlin'?" She winked at Brian.

"As crystal."

Faye was jabbing him in the side again. "Are you flirting?" she hissed.

"I wasn't aware."

"Yes, you bloody were."

He turned and winked at Sue, "And a Zinfandel."

"For *his wife*," Faye snapped.

They called out their orders one by one and carried them to the end of the bar.

"LEFT!" shouted Sue.

Brian turned with a wry smile beneath his beard. Sue grinned back and said, "You might want to leave breadcrumbs for your return journey, wouldn't want you getting lost now, would we."

"Yes, a very interesting week," he muttered, following the others.

Double patio doors were open and, beyond them, a large, grassed garden full of round benches under bright yellow umbrellas. Pots of summer plants were everywhere.

"Brand new patio doors," Mark said. "A shutter comes down at night for security. Clearing the garden was a nightmare, but it was worth it, it's a good outdoor space."

"Excellent job, that man," Tel said, admiring it all.

"It's fabulous," Faye said.

They walked out onto the patio and saw a giant barbecue smoking away to the left, laden with meat and tended to by a man in pub t-shirt serving a queue. Even as they looked, a girl in kitchen whites came out with a tray of meat and placed it on the table next to him. On the right was a giant table full of plates and buns, salads and sauces and paper napkins.

"Landscaping and pots all done by moi," Mark said proudly. "It was all overgrown before."

"Oh, it's *gorgeous!*" Faye gasped.

"Beautiful," said Sophie.

"Fan*tas*tic," Tel said, making Brian give him the evil eye.

"All the tables are full though," Faye added, looking around.

"Look," Sophie said, "There's Jim."

They walked en masse through the bustling tables to Jim, sitting at an empty table with a young girl next to him, rubbing knees.

"Oh God," said Mark, sitting down. "Leopard never

changes its spots, does it."

"Give up," Jim snapped, "We were just having a chat."

"He's married, you know," he said to the girl wearing a MELISSA badge.

"I do know," she cooed. "Anyway, I'd better get back before the boss notices. Shout if you need anything, or," she said, winking at Jim, "Call me."

"You two looked very cosy," Mark said, when she'd gone.

"I told you, she used to work at the pub down the road from me, known her years."

"Does Beth know?"

"Does Beth know what?"

"That the girl you've known for years is working at the campsite you just happen to be staying at for a week?"

"I can talk to other women, you know."

"Talk?"

Jim sighed. "I'm getting pretty fed up of your sarcastic remarks, Mark, I wish you'd bloody well pack it in."

"Come on, lads," said Brian, "Settle down now."

"You *were* flirting with her," Faye hissed at him.

Brian exhaled loudly. "If I was, it was subconscious, urged on by my desperate need to have a woman *talk* to me instead of *hissing* for a change, and she didn't keep saying, '*Brian! Brian! Brian!*'"

Faye pulled a face and slumped into a sulk.

"Behave yourselves, fallen role models," said Tel.

"I do wish you'd kiss and make up," Olivia said, her phone vibrating on the table, "I don't like seeing you like this."

"Me neither," Brian said, and reached out to squeeze Faye's hand. "Come on, lass, let's get some grub before I fade completely away." He stood up and looked down at himself. "If I turn sideways you can hardly see me! Liv, can you see me now? Soph, do I vanish when I do this?"

Everyone was laughing, and Brian bellowed, "Right, food!" He reached down for Faye's hand and helped her up. She dropped her bag and spent a minute or two picking up the scattered contents, with Brian standing over her, whining like a starving dog and glancing frequently at the barbecue.

Mark put his hand on top of Olivia's on the wooden table and said, "Shall I get you a plate?"

"No, I'll come up."

"Aye up," Jim grinned, "What did I miss?"

"Quite a lot, actually," Sophie said.

"Lots of people – " Brian did air quotes with his huge hands. " – 'taking afternoon naps.'"

"Nice," Jim said. "Does that mean I can sleep in your caravan, Mark, if it's going free?"

Mark huffed loudly and walked with Olivia to the barbecue queue, holding hands. Brian rushed after them, past them and in front of them, pulling Faye alongside him. Tel and Sophie followed.

"Queue's a bit slow," Brian eventually said, staring at the people nearest the barbecue. "CAN YOU HURRY IT UP A BIT?" he bellowed, "STARVING MAN ABOUT TO EXPIRE BACK HERE!"

The man in front of them snapped, "We're all bloody hungry, mate!" He turned, looked up at Brian, and quickly added, "No offence, mate."

"None taken, but you should know that if I pass out from famishment you'll be first in the topple zone."

"HURRY UP AT THE FRONT!" the man yelled.

They all waited and waited, taking one step forward. "It'll be all gone by the time we get there," Brian fretted. "HEY, LASS WHO CAN'T DECIDE BETWEEN A LAMB CHOP OR A BURGER, GO WILD AND HAVE BOTH!"

"He gets grumpy when he's hungry," Faye said, as faces turned to see where all the shouting was coming from.

Brian felt a tug on the back of his t-shirt. At first he thought it was Faye, getting a bit frisky, but when he turned he saw a small child standing next to him. Without looking down he cried, "Who's tugging on my shirt?"

"It's me," a tiny voice giggled.

"Who said that?"

Another giggle. Brian lowered his head and saw the cutest little boy staring up at him. "You're very small," he said.

"You're big," said the boy, "Are you a giant?"

"Sorry," the boy's mother said, standing a few people back in the queue, "Is he annoying you?"

"No, I like children." He looked down at the boy and added, "I couldn't eat a whole one though."

"Brian!"

The boy's eyes widened. "You eat children?"

"Only the naughty ones."

The boy considered this for a moment, then he laughed and jiggled like an amused toddler. Brian smiled at the parents. "Cute kid," he said, and turned round again.

Finally, they reached the front of the queue. The barbecue was full and sizzling.

"Ten pounds, please," said the barbecue man.

Brian leaned forward and breathed, "Cute campers."

"Excuse me?"

"Cute campers."

"I've been too busy to notice, but if you say so."

Brian whispered, "We're the survey people, we get our food and drink for free."

"Ah, right. What will you have then, sir?"

"Everything!"

* * *

"Funny, isn't it," said Sophie, taking another delicate bite of a chicken leg, "We had a barbecue on our second night last year, too."

"Oh yeah."

"Most people have barbecues on Saturday, Soph."

"Yes, I suppose. Smart of you to reserve a table for us, Jim."

"'Smart' and 'Jim' don't naturally go together in a sentence, do they," Mark snorted.

"Shut up. Reserved sign was already there when I got here."

"Maybe it's somebody else's reserved table," Faye gasped.

Jim turned the plastic sign round. It had 'Brian' written on it. Faye smiled, relieved.

"We're the survey people," Mark said, "They want good reviews from us, not, 'I was wandering around the garden waiting ages for a table'."

"How's your steak?" Olivia asked Brian.

Brian made a noise and vigorously nodded his head. He hadn't spoken since he'd sat down with his heaving plate of meat.

"Teacakes okay, are they?" Mark laughed.

"Teacakes?" Sophie asked.

"They call cobs 'teacakes' up north, apparently."

"You mean, bread rolls?"

"Crusty cobs?"

"Teacakes," Brian said, slapping a beefburger into one.

Jim turned to Mark. "So, if you're not using it your caravan – "

"I *am* using it!"

"I thought you and Liv were a couple now?"

"We are, but, unlike you, we don't jump into … we don't participate in … we haven't – "

"Why not?"

"I don't have to explain our relationship to you!"

"Why not?" Jim was grinning now, enjoying himself.

"Are you deliberately winding me up?"

"Not deliberately, no, it's a gift."

"A curse, more like."

"Can I divert and avert a fight by asking you to pass me the salt, please, Mark?" Faye asked.

Mark passed the salt and Jim said, "So, you two aren't sleeping together yet?"

"It's none of your business!"

"Just askin'."

"We got together *yesterday!*"

"So that's a night wasted already."

"Jim," Brian boomed, "You're making poor Liv blush."

He laughed. Mark huffed. Sue, the barmaid, came over with a sheaf of papers. "Chelsea asks if you can fill out these questionnaires about the food before you leave tonight."

"Extra points for the personality of the staff," Brian grinned.

"Why, thank you, kind sir."

"You're welcome, lass."

"Stop it," Faye hissed, as Sue walked off.

"I'm not doing anything!"

"You are, and I don't like it."

"Wow," said Sophie, using a knife and fork on her burger bun, "The bickering around the table tonight is off the scale."

"No, it's not," Tel snapped, laughing.

"Oh my God!" Olivia suddenly gasped, staring across the table towards the back of the pub.

Mark followed her gaze. "You have *got* to be kidding me!"

They all turned to look.

Richard was walking across the garden towards them.

CHAPTER 6

Richard stood next to the table, glaring at them with the annoyed and angry expression they all remembered.

"Dick!" Olivia gasped. "What are you doing here?"

"It's *Richard*, and I need to speak to you. I've been trying to call you *all day*!"

"I've blocked you." She couldn't bring herself to do the same with her father, hence the permanently vibrating phone on the table in front of her.

"That's why I'm here, you *forced* my hand."

"How did you even know I was here?"

"I know you've been here for a week."

"Go away," she snapped.

"I don't know *why* you're here," he said, looking around, "The place is a dump, and it's where this whole breakdown of yours started, thanks to you lot!" he spat at the table.

"Go away, Richard."

"I think she wants you to leave, pal."

"I need to speak to you, Olivia, about a *very urgent matter* and it *can't wait*!"

"She doesn't want to speak to you."

"I'm not talking to *you*, am I?" Richard spat at Mark, "This is a private matter between me and my *wife*, so kindly mind your own business!"

Mark made to stand up, but Olivia put a hand on his arm. "I have an injunction against you, Richard, you're not allowed to harass me like this."

"It's a criminal offence if you continue to bother her," Sophie said.

"You can be arrested and sent to prison," Tel added.

"*You* made me come here, Olivia! This is all your fault.

Now do me the courtesy of explaining this letter your father and I have received."

"It's Liv," she said, "My name is Liv, and I don't have to explain anything to you, that's my solicitor's job."

Richard glanced around at the others. "She's put me through hell," he snarled, "It's been a complete nightmare and she's *ruined my life*!"

"Richard!"

"You won't find any sympathy here, pal."

"No, you're all on *her* side, aren't you, waiting for your little hand-outs like blood-sucking leeches."

"You're the only blood-sucking leech around here," Mark said.

"I think you'd better leave, Dicky-boy," Brian growled, "You're not welcome here."

"Oliva, you can't ignore this and bury your head in the sand, you have to deal with it! I need answers! All I'm asking for is two minutes of your time, you owe me that much at least!"

Olivia glanced at her watch and said, "Say what you've got to say and then go."

"Not *here*, in front of everybody, in front of *them*!"

"It's here or nowhere."

"Over there." He motioned towards the side of the pub.

"Here," she said, "And you have ninety seconds left."

Richard's thin lips pursed tightly, angrily, and Brian said, "There's the Dick we're familiar with. Better make it quick, lad, we're busy digesting and you're giving me heartburn."

A couple stood up from the small bench at the back of the garden, and Richard snapped, "There."

Olivia hesitated, biting her lower lip, then made to stand up. Mark said, "You don't have to if you don't want to."

"No," she said, "Let me get rid of him, I won't be a minute."

"We'll be here." He looked up at Richard. "Watching."

Olivia gave her cute, overbite smile and stood up, walked to the empty table with Richard following her. They sat down.

They all watched.

* * *

"I don't know how you can do this to me," he began, "And to your father, your *own father!*"

"Get to the point, Richard."

"We've had letters from your solicitors, outlining the financial settlement."

"I know."

"It's *absurd!*"

"Get your solicitors to contact my solicitors if you want to negotiate, that's what we pay them for."

"*I can't afford solicitors!*" he hissed, glancing back at the table of faces watching them. "They won't *do* anything until I've paid them and I *can't afford it.* You've *got* to help me out!"

"I don't have to do anything."

"The settlement is nothing short of ridiculous. Your father's fuming, have you spoken to him? He rang me this morning, absolutely beside himself with rage."

"Yes, I guess he must be." She was glad her mother was out of the country, away from all this.

"I'm broke, financially and mentally." He dropped his head into his hands, breathing heavily. "You've destroyed me. I have *nothing.*"

"Nothing?" She gave a dry laugh. "You have the car and the little flat in London that you insisted on buying, a share of the house, and the settlement's very reasonable, both mummy and I tried to be as fair as possible."

"*FAIR!*" From the corner of his eye he saw one of *them* standing up, and lowered his voice. "It leaves me with nothing, *nothing!*"

"That's not true, it's just less than you expected. You're

hardly destitute, Richard."

"I looked after you! I took care of you!"

"You stifled me, controlled me, you don't get rewarded for that."

"How can I possibly compete against your expensive lawyers and fight for my rights *as your husband* if I don't have the money to pay for decent legal support?"

"I don't know, it's not my problem." She felt empowered by her year of freedom and safe with her friends close by, but Richard's anger still alarmed her, she'd forgotten how aggressive and overbearing he could be.

"I need money," he said. "I need to pay for better legal representation to get what I *deserve*."

Olivia looked at him across the table, at his beady little eyes and his excessive sense of entitlement. "You want *me* to give you money to fight *me*? Do you know how ridiculous that sounds?"

"Olivia, if you feel anything for me at all – "

"I don't."

"I'm still your husband!"

"Only until the decree nisi is finalised. The gravy train's over, Richard, you're on your own now. Good luck."

She stood up.

"Olivia, *sit down!*" He suddenly snatched at her wrist, gripping it tightly, making her turn and gasp out in surprise.

Mark was on his feet in an instant, as Sophie yelled, "That's assault!" Everyone in the garden turned to look. "You can be arrested for that!"

Olivia lifted her gripped wrist in front of her face and put her other hand underneath Richard's, squeezing it and pulling it away. When she was free, Mark was at her side, snarling, "Don't you ever lay a finger on her again! She's with me now."

"With *you*?" Richard burst out laughing. "My God, Olivia, how the mighty have fallen. With him? Really? Isn't he a *farmer* or something?"

Olivia saw Mark's hands clench into fists, saw Brian standing up at the other table. "You should leave now," she said, "Go away or I shall call the police."

Richard stood up. "You're going to regret this, you'll rue the day you turned me away when I needed you."

"Goodbye, Richard."

With a final lip curl at Mark, he stomped off. Everyone in the garden watched. "What are you all looking at?" he yelled, throwing his arms out, "Have you never seen a man being kicked when he's down by his *own wife* before?" He spun round and leered at Olivia, fury flashing in his eyes, before storming off down the side of the pub.

Brian followed to make sure he left.

"Are you okay?" Sophie asked, her face full of concern as they came back to the table.

"Yes, it's just Richard, I'm used to it, or I *was* used to it, kind of caught me off guard for a second there. However did I put up with it before? He just sucks the life right out of me, like an emotional, manipulative vampire."

"Good moves though," Tel said.

"Self-defence classes," she grinned. "Feel a bit shaky now."

"Here, take a sip of this."

"What is it?"

"Whisky."

She took his glass and gulped it straight back. Tel laughed, "That was a double!"

"Was it? Sorry, I'll get you another one."

"Drinks all round, I think," Brian boomed, almost back at the table and doing an immediate about-turn, "I'll get them in."

"Brian!" Faye shouted, "Why does it have to be you that fetches the drinks?"

"Because I'm already up and halfway there."

"Wait, I'll come with you."

"If he ever tries to bother you again, call the police,"

Mark said, as Faye chased after Brian.

"Don't even hesitate," Sophie said. "He's not allowed to harass you in any way. That's what I advise my pro bono clients at the women's shelter to do."

"How did he even know you were here?" Jim asked.

They all looked at her iPhone on the bench in front of her, which, even as they looked at it, started vibrating. 'Daddy' came up on the screen.

Mark said, "You don't think …?"

"I do," said Tel.

"What?" Olivia asked.

"Have you changed your phone since you left Richard?"

"No, I've had this for a couple of years. It's a good phone and I know how to work it. Why?"

"We think he's been tracking you, Liv."

"What does that mean?"

Tel pointed at her now silent phone. "Can I have a look?"

"Of course, just don't bring up all the photos of naked men," she giggled. "Ooh, I think the whisky's kicked in."

Tel tapped on her phone. "He has."

"He has what? Not that anything Richard does surprises me anymore."

"He can see where you are anywhere in the world using an app on his phone."

"Oh. I did wonder how he always seemed to know when I was back in the country."

"Do you want me to disable it?"

"Yes, please."

He did.

She looked at Mark. "Another tie broken, yay."

He nodded and smiled, but she saw something in his eyes.

Brian and Faye came back carrying two trays of drinks. "Are you doing it deliberately?" Faye was saying to him.

"No."

"You are, you're doing it on purpose to make me

jealous." They put the trays on the table. "Well, it won't work, I'm not the jealous type." Brian handed the drinks out. "Not a jealous bone in my body."

He sat down and looked up at her, standing with her hands on her hips. "What's up with you, woman?"

"You know what's up with me. Flirting with that barmaid again, right in front of me!"

"I merely asked her for the drinks."

"You *looked* at her."

"Quite hard not to look at someone who's serving you, but I'll pluck out my own eyeballs as soon as possible."

Faye threw herself down. "You know what I mean, there was a *look*. She saw it too, and now she thinks you fancy her. Do you fancy her?"

"She's not an unattractive woman."

Mark sucked in air.

"Who, Sue?" Jim asked.

"See! She clearly has a reputation, even Jim knows who she is."

"Jim knows all the barmaids within a 20-mile radius," Mark laughed.

"Do not!" He grinned. "Maybe ten."

"Do you, Bri?" She looked at him, waiting for an answer. "Do you fancy her? Are you ... going off me?"

"Faye, I don't 'look', I don't have to, I already have the best, I'm not interested in anyone else."

A smile slowly grew on her face.

"Can I borrow that Little Book of Men's Answers later?" Mark asked, and they all laughed.

"I thought your wife was coming, Jim?"

"Yeah, she's running late, been shopping with her mother, but she's popping in later."

"Is she staying overnight in your luxury abode?" Faye asked.

"I'm sure she'd loved the smell of decomposing wood and the husks of long-dead rats," Mark laughed.

"Rats?" said Sophie.

"What rats?" Faye asked.

"Blabbermouth," said Brian.

"It's just a joke."

"There's no rats in my caravan."

"Not now there isn't."

"Tel," said Brian, "You're the closest, whack Mark round the back of the head to shut him up, would you?"

Mark snatched up a squirty sauce bottle and aimed it at Tel. "Back, back, you scoundrel!"

Jim sipped at his beer and spied Melissa coming through the double patio doors. She looked across at him and sat at the nearest table, ostensibly searching through her bag whilst luring him with her eyes.

"Just be a sec," he said, jumping up.

* * *

"You alright?" Jim asked, joining her at the table.

"Yeah, you?"

"Good, good. Finished your shift?"

"Yes."

"And what wild plans do you have for a Saturday night?"

"Nothing," she said, pulling a sad face, "I'll be alone and lonely all night long."

"A disgrace."

"Isn't it?"

"You still living in that flat by the pub?"

"Yeah, why? Do you fancy nipping over later for a nightcap?"

"Very tempting," he grinned, lowering his eyes to the temptation. "Sadly, I don't do nightcaps anymore."

"Who's to know?" She was twirling her hair in her fingers and smiling at him.

"Him upstairs?" Jim chuckled, raising his eyes to the sky.

"Who, Pete on the floor above? Nothing to do with him who I have visiting my flat."

Jim laughed and leaned closer across the table, whispering, "Hypothetically speaking, what kind of nightcap would you be offering?"

"I have a vast variety of nightcaps," she breathed. "What kind of nightcap were you thinking?"

"I was hoping you'd tell me."

"Do you remember the nightcaps we used to have?"

"I do, but why don't you remind me?"

She straightened up, her smile vanishing. "Are you just talking the talk here, Jim?"

"There's no harm in talking."

"There is if you're just wasting my time."

"I thought we'd reminisce a little."

"I don't want to look back, Jim, I want something to look forward to."

"Don't we all."

She tutted. "Do you want a nightcap or not?"

"Yeah, Jim," said a woman standing by the barbecue, casually eating a hotdog, "Do ya?"

"Beth!" He quickly dragged a smile across his face. "I didn't know you were here!"

"Clearly not." She looked at Melissa. "If you'd remove yer claws from my 'usband I'd be grateful."

"I wasn't – "

"Save your breath, love. You do know that if he comes for a nightcap you'll have to keep him, don't ya?"

"I don't know what – "

"If he strays again the unfortunate woman gets lumbered with him for good. I should mention, he snores, he's pretty crap at housework, and you'll never be able to fully trust him. Now sling your 'ook, love, and if I catch you with me 'usband again I'll slap ya."

Melissa snatched up her bag and stormed off.

"We were just talking, Beth."

"They have telephone chat lines for what you were doing, babes." She popped the last of the hotdog into her mouth and chewed languidly. "What's up with your face? It's very ... rashy."

"Allergy to caravan material I think."

Beth took a couple of steps towards him and put a hand on his cheek. "Poor," she said, slapping him lightly, "Baby," and she slapped him again. "Now, introduce me to your friends."

* * *

"Wow," Tel gasped, watching Jim and a very striking-looking woman walking towards them, "Jim's scored *big* time! There's no denying he's got talent if he can pull someone like that."

Sophie turned, looked, turned back again and said, "Shove your eyeballs back in your head, Tel."

"A man can look!"

"Apparently not," said Brian, "No looking, no talking, and definitely no indication of admiration."

"Yes, *Tel*!"

He carried on staring regardless and said, "She reminds me of someone. I'm sure I've seen her before somewhere. Bit of a stunner."

"That's his wife," Mark said.

"*That's* Jim's *wife*? How did he manage that?"

"I've heard he can be very charming when he wants to be."

"This is Beth," Jim grinned, standing next to the table and looking quite proud of himself, despite the handprint smarting on the side of his face. "The old ball and chain."

"Alrigh'," she cried in a thick, cockney accent, "Really pleased to meet you all."

"It's Adele!" Tel cried.

"Nah," she said, laughing and throwing her hands forward, "But I get mistaken for 'er all the time, dunno why, I'm much better looking." Another burst of laughter. "I look completely different without me makeup though, don't I, Jim."

"You look beautiful with or without," he said, and Brian gave him a thumbs up.

The others greeted her with huge smiles and scooted round the bench to make room for her.

"Nice to meet a fellow southerner," Tel said.

"East End born and bred, darlin', not a part of London I'm guessing you're familiar with." She laughed as she sat down next to Mark, planting a kiss on his cheek. "How ya doing, babes?"

"Good, and yourself?"

"Not bad, still with this one."

"So I've heard. Is he being a good boy?"

"So far, so good."

"I am here, you know," Jim huffed.

"But you shouldn't be, should ya." He looked blank. She rolled her eyes and tutted. "You should be at the bar, gettin' me a drink. I quite fancy a cocktail, you choose for me, babes."

"I'll give you a hand," Brian said, starting to get up.

"No, you won't," Faye snapped. "I'll come with you, Jim, I quite fancy a cocktail myself."

"Now you're talking!" Sophie cried, jumping up. "Sit down, Jim, we'll get these. Want to come and choose a cocktail, Liv? Beth?"

"Anyfink'll do me," Beth said, "S'long as it's got alcohol in it."

Olivia nodded and the three of them excitedly wandered off. The table chatted and laughed, Beth louder than all the rest.

Jim felt very proud.

* * *

They returned carrying a tray of glasses and three glass jugs. "They do cocktail pitchers!" Olivia exclaimed, handing a glass to Beth. "We played safe and got a mojito, but I might try a Manhattan next."

"Get you with your alcoholic beverages!" Tel laughed. "Last year we couldn't get you to sip a glass of wine, now look at you, necking whisky and mojitos like there's no tomorrow, you *lush*."

"I survived a Dick visitation," she giggled, "That deserves to be celebrated, and of course, it's all free!"

"The barman was gorgeous," Faye said.

"Wasn't he!" Sophie sighed, "Just my type, tall, dark and handsome." She winked at Tel, who grinned and ran a finger over his eyebrow.

"Absolutely drop-dead gorgeous." Faye sat down next to Brian, pouring herself a cocktail from the pitcher and adding, "Totally my type."

"Except for possibly being half your age," Brian grinned.

"He wasn't half my age!"

"He was at least twenty-five," Olivia giggled.

"More than half then, lass."

"Shut up, Brian, a lady never divulges her age."

"Lady?" Brian gasped, looking around, "Where?"

"Besides," she said, "Lust knows no boundaries."

"Are you somehow trying to make me jealous?" Brian laughed.

"Is it working?"

"No."

"Oh. Well, drink up, Bri, get your beer goggles on so you can look at me like you looked at Sue the Barmaid."

"I don't need to drink to ..." He trailed off, suddenly looking away, and Faye stared at him in horror.

"You can't say it, can you," she gasped. "You can't say it because you won't mean it. You've gone off me, haven't you!"

The table was suddenly enveloped with a heavy silence. Brian looked pained. Faye looked on the verge of tears.

"Oh Brian," she breathed, "We really are in trouble, aren't we."

Brian didn't answer and the moment dragged on, until Sophie quickly jumped up with the pitcher, crying, "More cocktail, Faye?" Then, seeing her glass was already full, added, "You know what, Liv, I think I might join you for a Manhattan next. How about you, Faye, Manhattan, or something else?"

Faye tore her eyes away from Brian and stared at her glass.

"Oi!" Beth shouted, and they all looked at her, as did half the people in the garden. "'Eard a lot about you two. Don't waste what you've got, it's a rare commodity and you should look after it. Get yourselves sorted out pronto, or else I'll do my party piece in protest."

"Oh God," Jim sighed, throwing his head in his hands, "Not the party piece."

"Beth's party piece!" Mark laughed, strumming on an air guitar.

"What's your party piece?" Sophie asked.

Beth grinned and said, "I take me knickers off and dance Flamenco on the table, waving 'em above me 'ead."

There was some gasping and snorting, and the heavy moment, thankfully, was gone.

But Brian and Faye were unusually quiet for the rest of the night.

* * *

"So, where's this palace on wheels then?" Beth asked, as they all staggered merrily into the pub car park, a couple of them steadying themselves against the pub wall as they went.

"Ah," said Jim, "About that?"

"What about it? You said there'd be candles and music and a warm bed, which bit ain't you got?"

"All of it," Mark laughed.

"The caravan's currently in dispose."

"That's one way of putting it," Mark snorted.

"In dispose? What the 'ell does that mean?"

"He meant 'disposal'."

"Shut up, Mark!"

"Snog?" Mark asked, turning to Olivia, who obliged.

"So, where's the caravan then, Jim?"

"It's broke."

"Broke?" Mark cried, pulling away from Olivia, "It's in pieces! It's like a great big, 3D jigsaw puzzle."

"What's he mean, it's in pieces?"

"It's not up to your standard of cleanliness, Beth."

Mark screamed with laughter. "Cleanliness? There were rats in it!"

"Rats?" Sophie burped.

"Not live ones," Mark continued, "Dead ones, loads of them, all dry and crusty under the sofas."

"Make him stop, Tel."

"Pack it in, Mark, Sophie has a rat phobia."

"What's she doing with you then?"

"Oh, very droll and *very* unfunny."

"Hey, big man," Beth said, turning to Brian, "What's 'appened to Jim's caravan?"

"It arrived in one piece," Brian said, gently swaying on the spot, "And quickly deteriorated from there."

"He tried washing it!" Mark snorted, losing grip on Olivia again, who threw out her arms like she was freefalling. "He stood on the roof with a mop and a hosepipe, and it caved in!"

Beth looked at Jim. Jim glared at Mark, who was trying to catch one of Olivia's windmilling arms as she staggered backwards. "I think I'm a bit drunk," she giggled.

"Take my hand, I'll keep you steady," he said, promptly side-stepping like crab and dragging her with him.

"Will someone tell me what's going on?" Beth cried.

"There'll be no caravan capers tonight, lass."

"Not unless you like fresh air and open sky," Mark cried, falling over and taking Olivia down on top of him, where she stayed, kissing him and giggling hysterically.

Faye, who seemed remarkably undrunk, walked past Beth and said, "It's broke, love, you'll have to stay at the pub or go home."

"JIM!"

"Oh, you can't stay at the pub," cried Sophie, "I heard the sexy barman telling someone they were fully booked tonight."

"You can't even organize one night away?" Beth tutted and took out her phone. "Yes, I'd like to order a taxi please."

Faye was now by the entrance to the camping field. Tel shouted, "Wait for us! Mark, Liv, get up, I'm sure that would be more comfortable on a sofa bed."

"I've lost my wife," Brian suddenly blurted.

"Sorry to hear that, chap," said a man coming out of the pub, patting Brian on the shoulder as he passed.

"She's over there, Bri."

"Where?"

"By the gate. Oh, she's gone."

"WIFE!" Brian howled.

"Come on, Tel, let's catch her up, she can't be wandering around on her own. Brian, come with us." Sophie tried to tug his arm into motion, but he was like a man-shaped mountain and didn't budge. "Brian, come on! Lovely to meet you, Beth."

"Likewise, 'ope we can do it again soon."

They disappeared through the gate, a staggering, clashing mob, and Beth turned to Jim. "'Ow bad is the caravan?"

Jim decided that honesty would probably be the best policy since he was too drunk to do otherwise. "It's got no roof. Or sides."

"Bloody 'ell. What you gonna tell Steve?"

"I don't know."

"Well, you'd better think of something, Ellie's planning to go away in it next week."

A taxi pulled up onto the car park. "You were quick," she said to the driver.

"I was just round the corner."

"You coming home or staying, Jim?"

"I don't know, I'm too drunk to decide."

"Nightcap?" she grinned, and Jim dived into the back of the taxi.

"What would I do without you?" he sighed.

"You know exactly what you'd do, fall to pieces, like last time."

"I love you," he burped, resting his head back on the seat and closing his eyes.

"Love you too, babes, for my sins."

CHAPTER 7

Day 3: Sunday

Brian couldn't sleep, he had too much on his mind. Faye didn't even look at him when he got back to the caravan, and now she lay stiffly in bed with her back to him. They hadn't even kissed goodnight, and 'Never go to sleep angry' was their mantra; "Stay up and fight!" he'd say, and they'd laugh and the bad feelings would evaporate. This time it was serious. It felt like the world, his world, had tilted on its axis and everything was squiffy.

He couldn't sleep, couldn't stop thinking. He felt an enormous sense of doom bearing down on him, but what could he do, just put up with Flo, say nothing, do nothing, and slowly lose his mind? God knows he'd tried. He liked Flo, he really did, she was a nice woman, very similar to Faye, but he preferred her in small doses, more than a month would send anyone screaming into insanity.

Brian shifted in bed. He couldn't find a comfortable position. "Can't you just block her out?" Mark had said to him earlier, "You know, like parents do with their kids?". He'd tried, but it was the pitch of her voice that did him in, that endless shrieking in his head, grating on his nerve endings like fingernails down a blackboard. Her voice had that urgent edge to it, like someone who was about to fall off a cliff or be mown down by a truck, you couldn't ignore it, it demanded your attention. No, he couldn't just 'tune her out', and he couldn't insist she go home, Faye would never forgive him.

Brian turned over.

"Stop moving!" Faye hissed, "You're rocking the whole caravan!"

Brian rolled onto his back and stared up at the blackness. They'd been married twenty-four years, had raised two kids, and their relationship had never hit this kind of impasse before. Sure, they'd had arguments, but one of them always backed down, they always talked things through and reached a compromise somehow, and humour had always been an important part of the relationship, but not this time, this was beyond a quick joke and a hug.

He wanted to roll over onto his side but didn't dare. Maybe it was their age, maybe this was what happened as you got older, you just drifted away from each other, but his and Faye's parents hadn't, they'd always seemed happy. He'd never cheated on her, never felt the need, and he was pretty certain she'd hadn't either. She had seemed unusually jealous about the barmaid tonight though, that wasn't like Faye at all. She must be feeling insecure, he'd made her feel insecure. He didn't think he'd ever given her cause to be insecure before.

He rolled towards her, put an arm gently on her waist. She didn't snap and she didn't wriggle away. He breathed, "Faye, I'm sorry. I miss you. Can we fix this, please?"

Faye was just turning to face him when, from outside, came that intolerable pitch, getting nearer and nearer. It wasn't loud, it was just constant, the distant murmuring turning into endless words that flowed like a tidal wave into the awning.

"Oh, Bill, that was such a fantastic night! Wasn't it a fantastic night?" The awning zip was quickly pulled up and Brian sensed bodies entering. "The food was just divine, and you're *such* good company, very funny man. Oh, I can't remember the last time I laughed like that, certainly not since Kat passed away. You're a tonic, Bill, the universe sent you to me just when I needed – "

"Can you keep the noise down?" Brian whispered hoarsely.

"Yes, sorry, Bri." The bedroom zip was pulled open. "Come and have a look where I sleep, Bill. S'like a flour sack, innit! But that bed! Oh my God, it's *so* uncomfortable! Here, sit on it, give it a try. It's one of those double blow-up beds but it's just so high, for me anyway, I'm just a little short thing."

"Have you got a man in my awning, Flo?"

"Leave her alone," Faye grumbled, "She's old enough to have a man in her room if she wants to."

"It's not her room, it's my awning, and I certainly don't want to hear her with a man."

"Don't be ridiculous, she's not into that sort of thing."

"Really? And yet here she is, with a man in my awning."

"Oh, don't start!"

"You're going to have to help me up, Bill." There was the low whisper of a man's voice, followed by a screech of laughter and the squeaking of plastic, which just kept on squeaking as the cackling continued.

Brian huffed loudly. "Do you see what happened there, Faye? We were just about to make up and get things back on track, and then Flo turns up and we're shitty with each other again."

"That's not Flo's fault, it's yours!"

"My fault, of course it's my fault. Why wouldn't it be my fault? It usually is. God forbid I should express an opinion or vent an emotion, what *was* I thinking?"

"Stop being such a drama queen, Brian."

"Oh Bill," Flo hooted, "You're so strong! Can you push me into the middle a bit more? That's it, I don't feel like I'm clinging to the edges now, about to fall off ..."

"I can't listen to this!" Brian snarled.

"Flo," said Faye, "Can you keep it down a bit?"

"Of course, Faye. Sorry, Faye. Sorry, Brian. Didn't mean to wake you up. I mean, it's actually only 11.30, you people have no stamina if you're in bed at this time. Talking of bed, I've just realised, I've found the one comfy spot on this one but I'm fully dressed!" She shrieked with hilarity. "Oh, what am I like? Can you pull me off again, Bill? Yeah, just pull my arm and I'll wriggle my way towards you."

Squeaking. Laughing. Bill whispering. Flo talking. Talking. *Talking!*

"Is that you, Flo?" Tel shouted across.

"YES, LOVE, IT'S ONLY ME."

Brian growled, low and deep.

"Can you keep it down a bit, only we're trying to sleep."

"SORRY, SORRY!"

"SHUSH!" yelled someone else.

"YES, I'M SORRY. I MEAN, IT'S NOT EVEN MIDNIGHT YET, YOU'RE ALL SUCH LIGHTWEIGHTS ABOUT – "

"*JUST SHUT UP!*" Brian hollered, and everything fell silent, except for Mark's distant voice, shouting across from his caravan, "Deep breaths, Bri!"

"Now you've woken *everyone* up," Faye whispered.

Brian scuttled heavily and quickly off the bed.

"What are you doing, Bri? Don't make a scene."

Brian threw open the caravan door, glad that he'd decided to keep his underpants on as there didn't seem any reason to remove them with Faye being so huffy. "Will! You! *Please*! Be! *Quiet!*"

Flo came up to him, looked up at him, and said, "I'm a bit thirsty, Bri, could you pass me a bottle of water out of the fridge, the one with the blue label, I don't like the other one, tastes a bit salty. Oh wait, don't bother, there's one in the coolbox, forgot all about that one, and it's a blue label too, that's very ..."

Brian stared off through the plastic windows into the distance, wondering if madness would offer him any sense of peace and quiet. Maybe that wouldn't be a bad thing after all. He could just let the voice wash over him, accept his fate, and relent to the inevitable. He vaguely wondered if Amazon did straitjackets, he thought they might. And there it was, a click in his head. It had happened, he'd finally lost it. It had all become too much and his brain had cracked under the pressure.

But it was just Flo, opening her bottle of water.

* * *

It's very difficult to ignore someone in a caravan, Brian thought the following morning, there simply isn't the room. They got wedged passing in the middle bit, and had to negotiate not touching in doorways, at the cooker and at the sink. Every time they tried to open a cupboard the other one would be standing in the way. So Brian and Faye huffed a lot and avoided eye contact.

Even the awning space had been halved by the bedroom tent, so there was just the top bit to stand in and huff. Brian unzipped an awning doorway as quietly as he could, praying to Odin and Zeus and any other deity that might be listening *not to wake her up*, not yet, he wasn't ready.

Faye stomped out of the caravan with a mug of tea, and plonked it heavily on the table next to him. He winced at the noise and waited for movement from the flour sack. There was none, so he snatched it up, spilling it down himself. He grunted. Faye tutted.

This was not, he decided, going to be a good day. Good days were a thing of the past.

He moved his chair onto the grass and sat with his wet t-shirt drying in the sun, sipping at his tea. She hadn't put enough sugar in, probably on purpose, her way of telling him *he was in the wrong*.

Another day, another chip in what was left of his brain.

Mark came over with his own mug of tea, dragging a chair with him. "Y'alright?"

"I've hit rock bottom and it's not as bad as I imagined." He forced a smile behind his beard. "I've decided that insanity isn't such a bad thing after all and to just give in to it. It's quite peaceful actually, letting go. Well, apart from the dribbling and the night terrors that turn out to be not nightmares after all but your actual life."

"You losing it, Brian?"

"I didn't lose it, it was torn from me."

Mark laughed, then stopped, then laughed nervously. "I'd suggest you need a holiday, but – "

"Padded room and a long-armed jacket are what I need."

"Seriously though, Bri, you okay?"

Brian sighed, sipping at his tea before saying, "It starts to get a bit like Groundhog Day after a while. It starts off quiet and peaceful and you think, 'This isn't so bad'." He nodded towards the bedroom tent. "You think you'll be able to cope, and then it begins and doesn't stop, and then the screaming starts inside your head."

"You're worrying me, Bri."

Brian looked at him and laughed. "Pay no attention, I'm just tired. Oh!" he wailed, "So tired!"

Olivia shuffled over in her dressing gown, listlessly dragging her chair. "Just got up," she muttered, "Don't speak to me yet, I'm not human. How much did we have to drink last night?"

"Lots," Mark grinned, kissing her cheek.

"Morning, darling. I forgot to buy tea. And coffee. I would literally *kill* for caffeine."

"Tea, Liv?"

"Oh, yes please."

As Faye rushed back into the van Brian mimicked, "Would you like another cup, Bri? Oh, that would be lovely, thank you so much."

"You've just got yours!" Faye snapped, "You can't have finished it already."

Brian glanced down at his crisping t-shirt, then at the bedroom tent, listening, waiting. Nothing. He breathed out.

Sophie and Tel came over with their chairs. "Oh my God," Sophie groaned, "Cocktails give killer hangovers."

"It was the *gorgeous* barman," Faye said from inside the caravan, tinkling a teaspoon against mugs, "He didn't use a measure, he just poured them by rack of eye."

"The left eye that looked off in the opposite direction,"

Sophie laughed.

"Yep, and for extended periods of time as the night progressed."

Tel seemed fine, he didn't drink cocktails, only spirits. "Plans for today?" he asked, flopping into his chair.

"Just keeping a tenuous grip of my sanity," Brian said, "Not sure it's worth it."

"Then don't bother," Sophie said, "Just set yourself free."

"If only."

"You two want tea?" Faye asked.

"Please, Faye."

Brian quickly emptied his mug. When Faye appeared with two steaming mugs, he pulled a face and said, "My tea's all gone."

"You know where the kettle is, don't you?"

"You two are not *still* bickering, are you?" Sophie groaned. "You're giving me flashbacks to my childhood. My parents were evil to each other until they got divorced, now they're like best friends."

"Maybe we should get divorced?" Brian casually asked.

"Don't bloody tempt me."

Brian's eyes widened in horror. What had he done! They were on the edge of a precipice and he thought it was *funny* to mention the D-word? He wanted to slap himself.

"Cup of tea, Flo?" Faye yelled at the bedroom as she passed it, and Brian sucked in air, held it, listening, waiting. Nothing. He exhaled and looked at his watch. "That's thirty minutes so far. If I can make forty it'll be a new record."

"So, what are we all doing today, does anyone know?"

"Too early to think," Olivia croaked, sipping at her tea. "I might just nurse my hangover and feed it loads of junk food, that always seems to help."

"Suffer a lot of hangovers, do you?" Tel laughed, "You *lush*."

"Meanie."

"We thought we might drive out to Stow-on-the-Wold,"

Sophie said, "Take a look around, have an indulgent pub lunch, then maybe the Cotswolds Wildlife Park. Anyone fancy it?"

Mark considered it, nodding his head. Olivia definitely didn't look like she was up for it. Brian said, "Sounds good."

"Faye!" Sophie yelled, and Brian winced, "Fancy a village, lunch, and some animals?"

There was a plastic squeak and an inhalation of breath from the inner tent. "Brace yourselves," Brian said, "It's coming." He ignored Faye's pinched expression as she handed mugs of tea to Tel and Sophie. The squeaking turned into a hollow bouncy sound. A slight cough. "Clearing the pipes ready for rev up," Brian said, poised in anticipation and giving his watch another glance. "If she can just not speak for two more minutes I'm ahead of the game."

"Faye," cried Flo, and Brian groaned with disappointment, "Cup of tea would be nice."

"Coming."

"I could do with a top-up," Brian said.

"Kettle's in the kitchen."

"But if you're making one anyway."

"I'm making one for Flo."

"But not your husband?"

"My husband is perfectly capable of making his own."

"So is Flo."

"I don't *mind* making Flo one."

"Nice, and – "

"Oh my goodness!" Flo cried, "That bed is so uncomfortable, I can't begin to tell you how uncomfortable it is." She came out of the tent in her dressing gown and peered at them all in a crooked, hand on the back way. "I've been floating around like flotsam and jetsam all night, it's like sleeping in a dingy, hardly got a wink of sleep. Morning, everyone." They all muttered in reply. "I'm so seasick, it's the worst bed I've ever slept in."

Brian had the urge to say, 'Go back to your own bed then', but he wasn't quick enough.

"Oh dear, I feel quite ill. Oh, thank you, Faye." She wandered towards them, mug in hand. "Couldn't offer your seat to a suffering person, could you?" she asked Tel, and he stood up and sat on the grass next to Sophie. "Oh, that's so kind of you, thank you. My back is killing me, absolutely killing me, that blow-up bed offers no support at all, I'll be bent double all day. I can't sleep in it anymore," Flo said, and Brian felt something like hope spring up inside him. "I just can't." In his mind he could almost hear her saying, 'I'm going to have to go home, Faye, I can't spend another night,' and he was fully prepared to drive her there. "It's just so uncomfortable, it really is."

"You staying here then, Liv?" Sophie asked, as Flo continued her barrage of complaints, "And you too, Mark?" She winked at them. "Spend some alone time together."

"Alone time," Brian said dreamily, as Flo talked, and talked, and talked.

"Yeah," Mark said, "I think we're going to stay here and eat junk food all day." He wanted to ask Olivia something that had been on his mind anyway. She gave him her cute, overbite smile, and he wondered if he should maybe just forget it.

"Brian, want to come?"

"Why not?"

Faye was still concentrating on Flo's aches and pains. They waited for a moment to jump in and ask her, but it didn't come.

"... I was clinging on for dear life, and I'm sure it's deflated. It was a bit easier to get off it than it was getting on, but of course that makes it less supportive on your back, doesn't it, if it's sagging. I really can't sleep in it another night."

What happened next Brian witnessed as if in horrific slow motion. Faye, turning her head to look at him. Her mouth opening. Words coming out. Words that exploded in his head. "What?" he said quietly.

"I said, you can sleep on the airbed tonight and Flo can sleep with me in the caravan."

One of Brian's eyes started twitching at the corner. Flo was still talking but he wasn't listening, he was trying to comprehend the enormity of what Faye had just said.

"Bri?" said Mark, "Are you okay?"

The others were quiet, just staring at him. His face went red, his eye twitched. His giant hands gripped onto the plastic chair handles and tightened. Faye seemed oblivious. "You don't mind, do you, Brian, swapping beds with Flo so she can get some –?"

"WHAT?"

"It'll only be for a few nights. I mean, what is it today, Sunday?" She counted off the days on her fingers. "Five nights."

"Brian?" Sophie glanced at Mark, who was staring at Brian, who was crinking his neck and breathing quite heavily.

Faye, still oblivious, said, "Yeah, it's only five nights, and then Flo can get some – "

"YOU WANT ME," he boomed, so loud that several campers went quiet and peered over the hedge, including Bill, who looked quite concerned, "TO LEAVE *MY* BED IN *MY OWN* CARAVAN AND SLEEP ON AN AIRBED *IN THE AWNING*?"

"Retreat!" Mark cried to the others, "He's gonna blow!" He grabbed his chair and hurried off. The others did the same. Mark flung himself into the chair outside his caravan and picked a book up off the table, hiding behind it. Olivia shuffled into her motorhome and closed the door behind her, immediately turning on a radio. Tel and Sophie sat on the plastic bench outside their caravan, covering one side of their faces and pretending to talk, to not notice, to not hear.

"You don't have to make such a big deal of it," Faye said, "Flo's been sleeping on it and it wouldn't hurt for you to – "

"YOU'RE KICKING ME OUT OF MY OWN BED IN FAVOUR OF YOUR SISTER?"

"Calm down, Bri, you're causing a scene."

"A SCENE!" he hollered. "HAVE YOU TOTALLY LOST YOUR SENSES, WOMAN?"

"Don't talk to me like that, Brian."

"Calm down," Flo said to him, "You want to be careful of your blood pressure, you've gone a bit of a funny colour. For a man of your age you should be – "

"STOP! TALKING!" Flo immediately snapped her mouth shut, her eyes wide as Brian hollered, "I WISH TO SPEAK TO MY WIFE *WITHOUT INTERRUPTION* AND I WISH TO DO IT *NOW*!"

"Brian, don't speak to Flo like that!"

Bill was beckoning from the other side of the hedge, and Flo scurried through it, into his embracing arms. Brian stood up and lumbered like a furious steam engine passed Faye and into the caravan. "FAYE!" he cried, "WE NEED TO TALK!"

Faye got up slowly and followed him in. The door was slammed shut and the shouting started.

"What time is it?" Tel said, glancing at his watch from behind his shielding hand. "Right, it's late enough." He dashed to his car, unlocked it, threw open the door and turned the key. Switching on the radio, he tapped through the stations until Whitney Houston wailed *I Will Always Love You*, and turned up the volume. He cracked open all the windows so that Whitney and her warbling dampened the yelling coming from the slightly shabby, slightly rocking caravan, and locked the car.

"Breakfast at the pub?" he shouted across to Mark, who nodded. Olivia came out of her motorhome, hurriedly adjusting the clothes she'd thrown on in a hurry, and went with them.

Leaving Brian and Faye to fight it out.

* * *

Jim was just walking into the pub car park as they were going in. "Whatcha?" he grinned.

"Join us for breakfast?" Sophie asked.

"Love to."

Jim had barely reached the bar when Chelsea, diminutive in size but fierce in nature, dashed up to him and said, "I want that caravan moved *today*."

"I'm still working on it."

"Work faster, get it gone. I want it off the campsite *this morning* or I'll have it towed away."

"Alright, keep your titian hair on."

With a final glare, Chelsea stormed off.

"Nice start to a Sunday morning," he said to Melissa, who raised an eyebrow. "Buffet breakfast is out the back," she said curtly.

He followed the others towards the smell of cooking, muttering, "Probably for the best."

They sat out in the garden. "So, did I miss anything interesting last night?" Jim asked, tucking into his bacon and sausage with the men, while the women delicately sipped on fresh orange juice.

"You missed a lot," Sophie breathed.

"Like what?"

"Like Flo coming home drunk and waking us all up, and then, this morning, Brian just lost it, *big* time."

"Lost it?"

"Faye asked him to sleep in the awning so that Flo could sleep in the caravan."

Jim sucked in air.

"He went ballistic," Tel said.

"I'm not surprised."

"Do you think Faye will be okay?" Olivia asked softly, "Brian looked *really* angry."

"It's Brian we're talking about here," Mark laughed, "The gentle giant with the big gob."

"But good that you're staying and having a junk food day," Sophie said, "You'll be around if Faye needs a shoulder to cry on."

Olivia nodded. "I hope they sort it out, I hate seeing them like this."

"Me too. Fingers crossed, eh?"

They all crossed fingers, and then Jim went back to the

breakfast buffet for seconds.

* * *

They shouted at each other for a long time. A *long* time. Brian released all his pent-up emotions and they exploded into the caravan like booming fireworks. Faye screamed out her frustrations and threw a few things she knew wouldn't break. He bellowed his argument and she countered with her own. He bawled and pounded the table, and she yelled and threw a few more things.

"And I asked you three weeks ago to fix that door downstairs!" Faye shrieked.

"I tried! God knows I tried! Every time I got my toolbox out Flo was there, asking what I was doing, if she could help, if there was anything I needed, screeching down my ear the whole time! *That's* why it never got fixed! And while we're raking over old stuff, what's with the meals?"

"What do you mean, what's with the meals?"

"Suddenly we're eating everything Flo likes!"

"You don't like what I'm cooking?"

"I didn't say that, but what about some of *my* favourites for a change?"

"I'm just trying to cheer her up, Bri!"

"I know, but to the detriment of *me*? You're ignoring me, Faye, not listening to me. 'Oh, it's only Brian, he'll put up with anything'. Well, I'm sorry, I can't put up with it anymore in my own home, my own *caravan*." He threw up his arms up, hitting the ceiling. "There is no escape!"

"She's my sister! She's hurting! What do you want me to do, throw her out?"

"Let her go back home! She wants to go home!"

"No, she doesn't!"

"She does, Faye!" He took a deep, calming breath. "Remember when we had that big row the other week and Flo came running up to you afterwards, said she didn't want to cause any problems between us and wanted to go home? You told her to stay, I heard you. You said, 'No, it's just Brian being Brian, he doesn't mean anything by it, don't take any notice of him.' Take no notice! How do you think that made me feel, Faye?" She lowered her eyes. "That's when I realised we weren't working as a team anymore, and it's been downhill from there."

Faye, caught off guard, suddenly snapped, "It's all about *you*, isn't it! You're so *selfish*!"

"Selfish?"

They stood still in the middle of the caravan, staring at each other, Brian surprised, Faye regretful. Brian was the least selfish person she'd ever met.

"I'm your soulmate," he said softly, "Your best friend. Don't I even count anymore?"

"I ... I just want to take her sadness away."

"What about my sadness, Faye? What about my pain? I'm tough enough and ugly enough to withstand anything, but not this." He seemed to slump on his feet then, his enormous shoulders sagging. "I can't take anymore. I don't want to give you an ultimatum, but something *has* to change, I ... I can't do this anymore, I really can't."

Worn out and shocked by their mutual rage, they slowly sat down on opposite sofas, the table between them.

"We've never argued like this before," Faye gasped.

"We've never been in this situation before."

"I'm ... I'm frightened, Bri."

"So am I."

"I don't want to lose you."

Brian reached across the table for her hands, and then dropped his head. She couldn't see his face. His shoulders shook.

"Brian?"

He didn't answer. His breathing was stilted.

"Brian!"

She spun onto the sofa next to him and wrapped her

arms around him as far as she could, resting her cheek against one huge shoulder. "Brian, don't cry, please don't cry."

"I'm sorry, Faye, I can't do it. I want to, I really do, but it's the incessant talking, the pitch of her voice, all the time talking, talking, talking." He looked up and out of the front window. Tears crawled from his eyes into his beard and Faye thought her heart would break. "I know she's your sister, I know you want to help her, I know you're a lovely, caring person." He turned to look at her and squeezed her hand on his shoulder. "I'm on edge *all the time*, and even when I'm not in the house I can still hear her in my head. It's like a form of torture."

"Oh Brian." She tightened her arms around him, letting her own tears fall.

"I like her, I really do," he said, "But there's no let up, and no matter what I say or do it's always wrong."

"I'm sorry, Bri, I really am."

"It's so overwhelming and – "

"I'm not here!" Flo cried, running through the awning and into her hanging bedroom. "Just grabbing my clothes and leaving you in peace. Bill's taking me out to get me out of your hair. Call me if you need anything, we won't be far." There was a sudden silence and for a moment they both thought she'd gone, but then she said, "I'm sorry, Brian, I can't help it. I just … felt so alone after Kat died, I had nobody to talk to, and … I do like to talk."

"I know, Flo, I know."

"I don't want to cause any problems, not between you two, you've been so good to me and I love you both." There was a flurry of movement, and then there was silence. Flo had gone.

"Cup of tea?" Faye asked softly.

"Love one." He turned his head to look out of the front window again, and noticed Tel's car with all the windows open. Barry White was blasting *You're the First, the Last, My Everything* across the campsite.

"Faye," he said.

"Yes, Brian?"

"You're my first, my last, my everything."

"You're mine, Bri."

They hugged for a long time. A *long* time. And then, over their mugs of tea, they began to talk, just as The Righteous Brothers started singing *Unchained Melody* out of Tel's car and somebody outside yelled, "Will ya turn the bleeding music down!"

* * *

Tel quickly answered his phone. A familiar voice said, "Tel."

"Yes, Bri? Is everything okay?"

The others stopped talking around the table, listening intently. Olivia chewed on a nail.

"People are complaining about the noise," Brian said.

"Ignore them, a bit of shouting never killed anybody."

"No, about the noise of the music pounding from your car."

"Oh, right. Shall I come and turn it off?"

"You could, or a man in a caravan next door is offering to shut it off for you with some box cutters."

"I'll be right there ... if that's okay? I don't want to intrude."

"The man with the box cutters is coming, Tel."

Tel jumped up and started running.

* * *

"We wondered where you'd dashed off to," Sophie said, when Tel came back to the table.

"Had to turn the car radio off."

"You could have said before bolting off like that, you gave me quite a turn."

Tel bent to kiss her on her neck. "A turn?"

"Yes, the speed you were going I thought it must surely

be a case of life or death. I was quite impressed, actually, you were like a blur of panic."

"We didn't know whether to follow you or not," Olivia said. "How are they?"

"I don't know, everything was quiet once I turned off the radio."

"Do you mean like the calm after a storm quiet, or an ominous, sinister silence?"

Tel shrugged. "It was just … quiet."

"You didn't see them at all?"

"No. I mean, I didn't look over, didn't want to interfere, I just assumed they were in there."

"Maybe they're not," Jim said, still eating his second plate of breakfast, "Maybe he's dragged her into the woods to bury her!

"Jim!"

"What? It's just a joke."

"Car was still there," Tel added. "I suppose they might have gone for a walk."

"Into the woods, with a hatchet and a spade."

"Stop it, Jim!"

"I just hope they can sort themselves out."

"It would be awful if they can't, for them, I mean. Well, for us too."

"We'll just have to wait and see."

"Meanwhile," Tel said, getting up, "We have a drive, a pub and a wildlife park waiting for us. You sure you don't want to come?" He was looking at Mark and Olivia, but Jim, finally putting down his knife and fork, said, "Yeah, I'll come."

"Don't you have a scrap caravan to sort out?" Sophie asked.

"Oh yeah. Oh!" he gasped, spotting Chelsea stomping through the patio doors towards them and jumping up. "I'm on it, Chels!" he yelled, giving her a wide berth and sprinting down the side of the pub.

"You'd better be!" she called after him, "You've got two

hours before I call the scrap man."

"Do you two fancy it?" Tel asked.

Mark looked at Olivia and said, "Thanks, but Olivia and I have some catching up to do." He gave her a sideways hug and kissed the top of her head. "If Brian and Faye are still at it, we'll go out for a drive."

"Lovely," Olivia grinned.

* * *

They saw the handsome couple hurrying down the gravel driveway to their car. Sophie glanced very briefly over at their caravan and saw them through the big window.

"Everything okay?" she mouthed.

They both raised a thumb, and Sophie smiled, got into the car, and zoomed off with Tel.

"*Is* everything okay?" Faye asked.

Brian held her hand in his across the table. "I think so. I hope so."

"So, we're agreed?"

"We are."

"I'll tell her."

They kissed and hugged, and then Brian got up and lumbered out of the caravan for some much-needed fresh air. He dragged a chair over to the grass area and threw himself into it, feeling like a great weight had been lifted off his huge shoulders. He felt they had narrowly avoided a relationship death knell by the skin of their teeth. He let out a long sigh and lifted his hairy face to the sun. He heard the crunching of feet on gravel and opened his eyes. Mark and Olivia were quickly walking past.

"Sorry to disturb," Mark said, "We'll just get in the car and – "

"No, no need to rush off on our account, it's all good."

"Is it?" Olivia asked nervously.

Faye came out of the caravan, smiling, and stood with her hand on Brian's shoulder. He said, "Sorry about all the shouty stuff, it was long overdue, but we've sorted it now." He squeezed Faye's hand.

"Oh, I'm *so* glad," Olivia sighed.

"All back to normal then, is it?" said Mark.

Brian was about to answer, when Olivia stared off into the distance and said, "Oh, it might not be."

They all turned to follow her gaze, and saw a white Bentley coming through the entrance gates.

"Bit posh for a campsite," Brian said. "Is it Sophie's driver? Maybe she left something in the car."

Olivia's smile had completely gone. "No," she said, "It's daddy."

CHAPTER 8

The Bentley crawled along the driveway. As it turned into their caravan area they could see Olivia's father, Harry, behind the wheel, his face clamped in fury. Next to him sat Richard, looking equally angry. They came to a stop next to the group on the grass and Harry jumped out, waving a piece of paper in his hands. His first words were, "Why aren't you answering my calls, and what the hell is the meaning of *this*, Olivia?"

Mark automatically moved in front of her as Harry stormed towards them. Brian stood up. Olivia looked anxious and, in a high, nervous voice, said, "Hello, daddy."

Brian stepped up next to Mark. Faye rushed to Olivia's side and put a protective arm around her.

"Explain yourself!" Harry cried, "Explain the meaning of this right this bloody minute!"

Mark took a step forward to stop him reaching Olivia. Harry glared at him, then pushed him sideways, snarling, "Get out of my way, farmer boy!" He went to push Brian away, but Brian didn't yield, didn't budge at all, just bent his head and said, "Maybe you should come back when you're a little calmer."

"Olivia, call these goons off, I want to *speak* to you."

"Goons?" Mark said, turning to Brian.

"Goons," said Brian, shrugging. "I've had worse."

"Daddy, you didn't have to come all the way up here to – "

"Explain this!" he said, furiously shaking the paper in front of him as he stepped around Brian, who took a step back, closer to Olivia. "What is the meaning of *this*?"

As he thrust the paper into her face, Brian thrust an arm between them and gently but firmly pushed Harry back with his forearm. Harry was spluttering, his eyes wide, his nostrils flared. Fight face, Brian thought, sensing the anger pulsing off him.

"Daddy, I – "

"Explain it! I'm your father! How dare you treat me like something to be disposed of and *paid off so cheaply*!"

Olivia looked like she was about to burst into tears. Faye stood next to her.

"That's enough," Mark said, "You're upsetting Liv."

Brian said, "Go and have a drink in the pub to calm down."

Harry took a deep breath and stared up at Brian. "I remember you," he hissed, "You're the man mountain who stood in my way last time. *Move!*"

Brian remained motionless.

"Daddy, our solicitors agreed, it's the final settlement."

"There's nothing *final* about this, and I certainly didn't agree to anything so outrageous. It's an *insult*!"

"Mummy's been very generous – "

"*Generous!*"

"You get to keep the car, the villa in Spain, the flat you didn't think mummy knew about in Bristol, stocks, shares, a portion of the house valuation, and a very substantial lump sum. It's more than fair, daddy."

"Fair?" he spat, "And how long do you think that's going to last me?"

"It's a comfortable sum, daddy, it should last a long time, if you're careful."

"Careful?"

"Yes. Perhaps if you stopped splashing out on your mistresses?" She felt strong now, surrounded by her friends. She felt the frightened little child inside her stand up, ready to fight back. She took a step away from Faye and said, "Have you thought about getting a job?"

"A *job*? Are you out of your mind?"

"Aldi are always hiring," Faye said.

Harry was red in the face now, the goatee beard quivering with rage. "Where's your mother?" he snarled. "I want to speak to her!"

"She's not here, and you're not to bother her."

"I think you should go," Brian said, "Ranting and raving isn't going to solve anything."

"I'm not going anywhere until I've had it out with *my daughter*. Now get out of my bloody way!"

The passenger door of the Bentley sprung open and Richard started to get out. "I suggest you stay exactly where you are," Brian boomed, and Richard crawled back in again, slamming the door shut. Several campers were staring at them, even the kids were quiet.

"If you don't get out of my way right this minute – "

"You'll what?"

"I'll have you arrested!"

"For?"

"Unlawfully preventing me from seeing my own daughter! What's this got to do with you anyway?"

"Liv is our friend, and I hate bullies."

"I'm her father! You can't stop me talking to her!"

"Do you want to talk to him, Liv?"

"I … I don't think I do, not while he's like this."

"There you go," said Brian, "You heard her, now leave."

"Don't you tell me what to do! How dare you try and tell me what to do! Olivia, get in the car so we can – "

"No, daddy."

"Olivia!"

Brian sucked in air and expanded his chest like a balloon. He'd done this with the chaps in the steelworks when they got too obstreperous, the surprise usually de-escalated things. He bounced his bloated frame against Harry, who staggered backwards with a look of shock. "Oh sorry," Brian said, "Didn't see you there." He took a step forward and bounced against him again. Harry struggled to remain upright this time. "Well, it was nice to see you – "

"Not," said Mark.

" – but I think you should be going now. Cheerio." And he pounded his belly so hard against Harry that he fell against the bonnet of his car. Inside the car Richard's eyes bulged and his mouth fell open.

"Bye now," said Mark, waving.

Harry stood up and tugged furiously at his clothes. "You haven't heard the last of this," he snarled, glaring at Olivia, who, with her chin high and her face set as hard as stone, said, "Bye, daddy."

Harry snorted, spun around, and threw himself into the car. The Bentley fired up and skidded backwards down the driveway, showering them with gravel. They roared off.

"Are there any more bust-ups planned for today?" asked a man peering over the hedge, "Only I came away to get some peace and quiet and there doesn't seem to be much of either around here."

"Sorry, sorry," said Mark, raising a hand and walking towards Olivia.

"We'll try and keep it down," said Brian.

"Cheers, appreciate it."

"Drink, anyone?" Faye asked brightly.

"Double expresso," Olivia said, "A large one."

* * *

Jim had every intention of sorting the caravan out, but then it had seemed too difficult and involved a lot of effort, like finding and calling a caravan repair service, so he just ignored it. He couldn't risk hanging around at the campsite in case he bumped into Chelsea, who he knew could get a bit aggressive, so he'd jumped into his van and gone off to play pool with a mate at another pub. He stayed longer than he intended.

When he drove onto the campsite late that afternoon he

saw a breakdown truck idling in the caravan area. He noticed his caravan wasn't where he'd left it, was, in fact, being hauled onto the back of the flatbed. There were two thick straps wrapped around it, keeping it all together. The side walls curled in over a roof that was no longer there.

"OI!" he yelled, getting out of his van, "WHAT YOU DOING WITH MY CARAVAN?"

The man turned off the noisy winch and leaned against the edge of the truck. "What?"

Jim ran over, staring up at the broken, green-tinged wreck. "What are you doing with my caravan?"

"Got told to take it away."

"But it's *my* caravan."

"Don't look much like a caravan to me, unless it's one of those new-fangled kit things you haven't put together yet."

Jim looked back at the two couples scattered in chairs on the grass, holding steaming mugs and glasses of pop. Behind them, several people peered over the hedge, including the man who had pleaded for peace and quiet earlier. The man caught Brian's eye and Brian said, "It's not shouting though, is it."

"Didn't you try to stop him?" Jim shouted.

"Why?" shouted Mark, "It's knackered."

"But it's not my caravan, is it," Jim hissed.

"Oh?" said the man, "I thought you said it was."

"Well, *technically* it belongs to a mate."

"Did it look like this when he gave it to you?"

"No, it was a lot dirtier, I cleaned it."

"It was just the muck holding it together," Mark laughed.

"Listen," Jim said, "You couldn't just put it back, could you?"

"Woman who called insisted it had to be taken away today. I've had to leave my Sunday dinner for this."

Jim huffed. "Okay, how much will you give me for it?"

"Pardon?"

"How much for the scrap?"

The man looked amused. Behind them, Brian started laughing.

"How much were you thinking?" the man asked with a grin.

"It's worth about a grand."

"A grand." The man was now clearly struggling to control his facial features. "Maybe a decade or so ago."

"No, that's now much my mate paid for it about three years ago."

"And that's how much you expect to get off me for it?"

"Well, yes, but I'm open to offers."

Brian's boom of laughter was joined by several others.

"Is this just entertainment to you?" Jim shouted.

"Yes," Mark laughed.

Jim turned back to the man. "Sensible offers, mind."

The man shook his head.

"How much, then?" Jim asked.

"Fifty quid."

"Fifty quid! You're only offering fifty quid?"

"No, mate, I'm asking for fifty quid to tow it away, in cash."

"You want *me* to pay *you*?"

"That's usually how it works."

"Too funny!" Brian howled.

Jim looked up at the caravan again. "It's got salvageable parts on it."

"Then take them off and sell them."

"Me? Isn't that what you do?"

"No, it ain't."

"The wheel thing must be worth a few bob, at least."

The man glanced at the dry, cracked tyres and the rusty chassis, and shook his head.

"It's got to be worth *something*," Jim pleaded.

"Not to me, it's not. *You* pay *me* fifty quid to tow it away."

"But ... I don't have any money."

"Then we have a problem."

Jim turned to the others, watching on the grass, and they all shouted, "No!" He turned back to the man, who now had his hand outstretched in front of him. He stared at it a while, wondering what to do, when a wad of money was suddenly placed into the outstretched palm by a small hand. Jim turned and found himself looking down at a rather furious Chelsea. The man thanked her and set about securing his load.

Chelsea gave Jim an almighty push backwards and said, "You owe me fifty quid, and don't you dare forget or I'll call Beth and tell her. Now, clear this lot up." She indicated all the bits that hadn't made it onto the back of the truck. "You're making a mess of my lovely campsite. Come on," she said, swiping him round the back of the head, "Get on with it."

"Ow! What am I supposed to do with it all?"

"I dunno, stick it in the back of your van, stick it up your bum. I don't care, just get rid of it." She turned to give a big, beaming smile at the others and said, "So sorry about this, don't hold it against us," and tottered off back to the pub.

Jim picked up the foam-framed window, pulling a sad face at the others and saying, "Isn't anyone going to help?"

"Clear up your own mess, Jim."

"Well, that's not very nice, is it. Are you going to just sit there and watch?"

They all stood up, and Jim smiled. His smile vanished as they each picked up their chairs and moved them over to the driveway for an unhindered view.

The truck revved its engine and started reversing onto his now empty pitch. Jim heaved the window into the open shell of his mate's caravan, quickly bending to pick up the larger remnants and tossing them in too, bobbing up and down like a wonky piston and wildly tossing debris. By the time the truck pulled away it carried most of the caravan pieces with it. Jim proudly brushed his hands together, thinking of a cold beer from Brian's coolbox. Up at the pub, an upstairs window opened and Chelsea, surprisingly loud given her diminutive size, yelled, "AND THE REST!"

It took about an hour for Jim to pick up each individual particle of his mate's caravan, to the sound of the others pointing and crying, "Missed a bit."

* * *

"So, where am I going to sleep?" Jim whined, picking at the grass they were sitting on outside Brian's awning.

"Dunno, lad, but I'm sure you'll work something out."

"There's always the van," Mark chuckled.

"Van's full of work stuff, mostly concrete after the mixer went mad last week."

"Oh dear, what a shame, never mind."

Jim huffed. "I thought we were like – " He counted their names off on his fingers. " – the seven musketeers, one for all and all for one."

"There were only three musketeers," Mark said, "Plus D'Artagnan."

"Oooh, get you with your knowledge of old films."

"It was a book!"

"I think we're more like the Magnificent Seven," Brian said.

"We are," said Faye, winking at him.

Mark pointed at Brian and said, "James Coburn with a beard!"

"Charles Bronson!" Brian said, pointing back, "Without the good looks."

"Tel is Yul Brynner," Faye sighed.

"You're drooling, wife."

"I know."

"Can I have a can, Bri?" Jim asked. "All that clearing up has given me a right thirst."

"Has it? There's water in the tap, lad."

"Water?"

"Or you can collect your own liquid refreshment from the conveniently situated campsite shop over yonder."

"I don't have enough body juice in me to get that far,

Bri. You wouldn't see me die of thirst, would you? Besides, I'm skint and actually owe money. This is the most expensive free holiday I've ever had."

Brian glanced at his watch, then at Faye. "S'not five o'clock yet," he said.

Jim grimaced, then smiled and said, "So, Magnificent Seven, who wants to put the cheeky-chappy up for the night?"

"Pass," said Mark.

Olivia pulled a face.

Brian said, "We've already got Flo bunking with us."

"Oh come on, somebody must have some room for a lost, lonely – "

"Yoo-hoo!" cried Flo, bursting through the hedge and making them all jump. "I'm back, did you miss me?"

Brian looked at Faye. "That's the second time today I've said her name and she's just appeared out of the blue. She's like a genie in a bottle who comes out every time you say her name."

"Have you had a nice time?" Faye asked.

"Oh, it was – "

"Fan*tas*tic!" they all shouted.

"What are you all like?" she laughed, flapping a hand at them. "We had a lovely time." She said nothing else while they all sat and waited for the onslaught to begin. She appeared to make a physical effort to keep her jaw clamped shut as she shifted from foot to foot in front of the hedge. Mark glanced at Olivia, who looked at Faye, who shrugged when there was still no flow from Flo.

"You okay?" Faye asked.

"Yes. Well … actually … no."

"No?" Faye jumped up and hugged her. "What's wrong?"

"Don't restrain yourself on my behalf," Brian said, wondering if he'd actually broken his sister-in-law. "We had a bit of a fight, but we've sorted it now."

"Can we have a quick chat, Faye?"

"Yes, of course."

They disappeared into the caravan. The others pulled faces at each other. Jim said, "So, about my sleeping arrangements."

Nobody said anything, just looked off in different directions. The women reappeared again, both smiling. Brian gave a sigh of relief when Flo came over and said, "Phew, that's all sorted then, I'm glad that's over and done with now, but don't think badly of me, it's just the practical thing to do, and of course there's no hanky-panky involved or anything like that, oh dear me, no. Bill's got a spare pull-out bed in his caravan, and anything's better than that plastic squeaky thing. And," she said quietly, "I don't want to come between you and Faye."

Brian was about to say something, when Bill appeared on the other side of the hedge holding a bottle up. "Hi everyone, isn't the weather gorgeous. Champers, Flo?"

"Oh, I won't say no to a glass of bubbly. Sorry to kick the table leg and rush off again, but Bill's under the vain illusion that he can beat me at poker, and of course he can't, so we've got a bet on it. I think he's trying to win the upper hand, excuse the pun, by plying me with alcohol, but the poor man doesn't know what he's up against, I'm Lady Gaga on the poker face front. See you later, bye."

And she was gone again.

"She's like a little tornado, isn't she," Olivia giggled.

"Everything okay?" Brian asked his wife.

Faye nodded. "It wasn't the conversation I intended to have with her, in fact, I could barely get a word in edgeways – " They all feigned surprise. " – but everything's fine. She's staying with Bill tonight, he's taking her to Cheltenham Race Course tomorrow and they're leaving early, so it makes sense."

"Ooh, do I sense a romance brewing?" Olivia whispered.

Faye shrugged. "Who knows? At least she's happy, happiest I've seen her in yonks actually."

"So, everybody's happy then – "

"I'm not," said Jim.

" – including Flo."

She burst through the hedge just then and Mark rolled his eyes, making a mental note to put up a fence or take out a few bushes. Brian looked at Faye and said, "See, like a genie!"

"You carry on, I just forgot my overnight things." She unzipped the bedroom tent with gusto, rushed inside, talking to herself about what she should take, then dashed out with two heavy bags.

"Overnight?" Faye gasped.

"You can't be too prepared."

"Harlot," Brian breathed, laughing, and she blushed and disappeared through the hedge again.

Jim said, "So you've got a spare bed going then?"

* * *

Delayed by Jim's entertaining escapade with the now removed caravan, they had a late but magnificent carvery lunch at the Woodsman. When they wandered, stuffed as eggs, back to their caravans, Tel and Sophie had returned and were already lounging on the communal grass area outside Brian and Faye's caravan.

"Good time?" Faye asked.

"Brilliant. Ate our own weight in Sunday lunch at the cutest little pub, then staggered round the wildlife centre, which was good, you should go."

"I see they've taken the caravan away," Tel said.

"Yes, it was quite a spectacle."

"Got nowhere to sleep now, though," Jim muttered. "I couldn't kip under your canopy or inside your car, could I, Tel? Soph?"

"No," they said together.

"Some bunch of friends you are! Mark, you won't be using your caravan tonight, will you?"

"Yes!" Mark snapped, "My days of leaping from one maiden's bed to another are far behind me."

"What period was that then?"

Mark lifted his chin and said, "August 2011 to September ... 2011."

Jim laughed, then sighed and put on a sad face . "I'm not feeling included in this group, it feels like I'm not welcome."

"Give over," Mark said.

"No, I know when I'm not wanted. I might as well go home."

Silence.

"No, don't try and stop me, I know when I'm not wanted, I'll just get in my van and – "

"What about that?" Brian said, staring at the top of the camping field.

They all craned their necks.

"The shepherd's hut?"

"It's literally a shed on wheels?" Jim said.

"Oh well, if it's not good enough for – "

"No, no, it's fine, good idea."

"I doubt Chelsea would agree."

"I'll just call her," said Olivia, pulling out her phone. She spoke into it for a minute, then said, "She said okay, as long as you don't destroy it."

Jim grinned. "Come on then," he said, enthusiastically walking off.

"Come on what?"

"Come and help me push it over."

"Why?"

"Well I can't sleep in it all the way over there, can I, I want to be with the group."

"We wanna be together," Mark laughed. "I'm not sure we do, actually. If he was all the way over there we wouldn't have to listen to his whining and complaining."

"Shut up. Are you going to help me or not?"

"Not," Olivia giggled, "I've just had my nails done."

"Oh, they're nice," Faye said.

"Had them done at a little shop in ..."

"You're just going to sit there and watch me do it all by myself then?"

Brian rolled his eyes. Tel heaved himself up. Mark tutted. They all followed Jim to the green painted shed on wheels at the top corner of the camping field. There was a tiny window on the right panel and three wooden steps leading down from the door at the front. There was no hitch.

Jim, eager and excited, said, "You take the helm, Bri, and we'll push from the back." He raced to the back, Tel and Mark a little slower and much less enthusiastic. "You know," Mark said, "We seem to be pushing a lot of things around this campsite for you."

"I know, and it's much appreciated. Now push."

They pushed. The shepherd's hut hadn't had time to sink into the ground and started moving straight away, just not fast. The wheels squeaked and there was definitely some resistance. They pushed harder. Brian nudged the front as it moved, aiming it towards the caravan area, and the steps unhooked from the wooden base and fell off. He picked them up and waited to nudge again.

"Push!" Jim cried.

"We are pushing!"

"Push harder, it'll take all night at this rate."

"It'll take even longer if we just walk off and leave you to it."

"You're doing a great job, lads. More to the right, Bri."

Brian pushed it and admired the scenery, the little pub, the field, the surrounding woods. It was a nice place, 'good vibes' Faye would say. He was glad they'd made up, he hated confrontation and bad-feeling. He felt like his life was whole again, back on an even keel.

"More right, Bri."

He was even getting a much-needed break from Flo, and they'd worked out a compromise that he hoped would suit them all. He felt happy. Until the hut hit the slight incline up to the driveway and suddenly lurched to one side.

"GRAB IT, BRI!"

Brian dropped the steps and jumped to the side, throwing up his hands to stop it toppling over. The others stopped pushing to peer at him and the tilt of the hut. "Don't just stand there gawping," Brian gasped, "Push the bloody thing!"

They went back and pushed. It started tipping further against the incline. Brian wasn't sure he could hold it for much longer.

"IF SOMEONE COULD LEND A HAND!" he bellowed, and his voice echoed across the campsite. A couple of men came running over, one went to the back to push, the other hovered next to Brian, his hands up but not actually touching anything. "Push, lad!" he snapped, and the man pressed his palms to the wood in a non-committed, half-hearted sort of way. Brian thought he was as useful as a chocolate teapot, but didn't say, any help was better than no help at all.

The hut rose up the incline as three men pushed, one man held it up, and one huffed and puffed a lot but made no actual physical effort. Another man came running over, and then another. They all shouted instructions to one another, each wanting to be in control as they manoeuvred the hut onto the gravel pitch next to Jim's white van.

"LEFT A BIT, LEFT A BIT!"

"BRING IT FORWARD AGAIN!"

"IT AIN'T STRAIGHT!"

"THAT'S TOO FAR! PUSH IT BACK!"

"WATCH THAT LEFT CORNER!"

"IT'S NOT STRAIGHT!"

Brian ran a hand down his beard, puffing, and turned away from the shepherd's hut as it was pushed into place. He was startled by a man standing very close to him, holding a book and wearing a hangdog expression. "I just wanted a bit of peace and quiet," he said, as the men around them screamed and hollered. "That's all I wanted, just a bit of peace and quiet to read my book."

"Sorry," Brian said, "We'll try and keep it down."

"First the big argument with you and your missus, then some bloke in a posh car shouting his mouth off, then the caravan getting towed, and now this."

"I understand, I do apologise."

"I live next to M5 motorway and it's quieter there than it is here."

"I'm very sorry, we've finished now."

The man turned, shoulders drooped, face like a bloodhound, and wandered back to his caravan.

"Thanks, lads," Brian said, "Much appreciated."

They wandered off. Tel wiped sweat off his brow. Mark fell backwards onto the grass and lay there like a starfish, breathing heavily. Jim went and got the steps, slotted them back in, then threw open the door and stepped inside the hut. "My shed at home is bigger than this," he said. "There's nothing in here."

"Whinge, whinge, whinge," said Mark. "What did you expect, kitchen, bathroom and bed?"

"Talk about ungrateful," Tel said.

"No, no, it's fine, it's lovely. I'm sure the bare wooden floorboards are more comfortable than they look."

The women came running over in a chattering gaggle, carrying piles of sheets and blankets and cushions. They pushed Jim out of the way and, crushed tightly together inside the wooden confines, started planning where to put things. Jim watched them, rubbing his hands together and grinning.

"Get the airbed, would you, Bri?" Faye said.

"FLO!" Brian hollered, then, seeing the bloodhound man hadn't even got back to his caravan yet, Brian hurried to the hedge between the back of his caravan and the back of Bill's caravan and poked his head over. Flo and Bill were happily playing poker on a plastic table. "Flo," he whispered, "Are you sure you won't be needing the airbed tonight?"

"I'll never need it again," she said, not looking up from her cards. "I will never launch my body at that blue, plastic bag of air ever again as long as I live. Burn it for all I care, it will haunt my dreams for ..."

He dragged the bed out of the bedroom tent inside the awning and over to the hut. Faye pulled it up the wooden steps and tried to set it down inside. "Ah," she said.

"Ah?" said Jim.

"It's a King-sized mattress for a double-sized space."

"Let it down a bit," said Brian, "It'll be fine." To Jim he said, "No bouncing on it or the walls might collapse. You know all about walls collapsing, don't you?"

Olivia and Sophie got out of the hut to give Faye more space to work. They passed in the soft furnishings as she called for them. An orange cushion was considered and removed since it was deemed to clash with the others. They brought over bottles of water, a carton of milk, a glass, a bowl, some cutlery and a box of Weetabix. Sophie brought over a 'housewarming gift' and handed it to Jim, who said, "What is it?"

"Fortnum and Mason rye bread, sea salted butter, a jar of dark navy orange marmalade, and," she announced, holding it up, "A knife."

"Cheers, Soph. I think."

Olivia's phone rang. After checking it wasn't her father, she answered it. "It's Chelsea," she said, then listened. "She said Jim had better not break this one, and if he damages it in any way she'll ... what? Oh, I can't say that. No, I can maybe run to 'bugger'? That won't hack it?"

"Go on," Mark urged, nudging her, "Go wild, hit him with a few choice expletives."

"I can't say what she's asking me to say, even you would flinch. Hang on, Chelsea, I'll put you on speakerphone." She did, and held it out as Chelsea's voice yelled, " – if that disaster on legs breaks my eBay bargain I'll smash his face in and make him pay for a new one!"

"Fair enough," said Jim.

"Oh, and Liv," Chelsea continued, "There's been a

problem with the meat delivery – "

Olivia snatched it off speakerphone, spun round and held it to her ear, muttering quietly, before hanging up and turning back to them with a roll of her eyes. "T-bone steaks are off the menu tomorrow."

"Ugh, food," Mark grumbled, rubbing his full stomach.

Faye placed the last of the cushions at a jaunty angle, and the women stood back to admire their handiwork.

"Looks pretty cool," Jim said.

"Bohemian," said Tel.

"Cosy," said Brian.

"Padded shed," Mark laughed.

"Shut up. Oh," Jim said, as they started to wander off, "You know what would look nice just in front, don't you?"

"A set of stocks and a barrel of overripe tomatoes?" Mark suggested.

"No, a bench."

They all looked at the hefty benches halfway down the field.

"I'm not," said Brian.

"Me neither," said Tel.

Mark rubbed his stomach again and said, "Far too much exertion after such a big meal."

"Oh come on, camping buddies," Jim whined, "Last finishing touch."

They all wandered back to their chairs.

"Well, would you look at that!" Brian exclaimed, glancing at his watch. "It's almost five o'clock! Phew," he gasped, wiping his forehead, "All this hut pushing is hard, thirsty work."

"And the award for the best dramatic actor goes to … Brian," Faye cried.

With a grin, he went to collect his coolbox, unhooking and squishing the bedroom tent to the back of the awning. He dragged the coolbox over to his chair, opened it and cracked open a can. "Help yourselves," he said, "Except for Jim, who contributes nothing?"

"Where is Jim?"

Tel leaned back in his chair, peering round the front of the caravan, down at the camping field. "He's only trying to drag a table up the field," he groaned.

"On his own?"

"Yep." Tel got to his feet. "He'll give himself an injury."

Brian stood up, upending the can into his mouth and gulping quickly, before setting it down on top of the coolbox.

Mark stayed resolutely on his back on the grass with his hands behind his head as Tel and Brian lumbered off. After a few seconds he huffed and hauled himself to his feet. "It'll take four people," he said, stomping after the others, "They're pretty heavy."

* * *

"Oh my God, they're heavy!" Tel cried from one corner of the picnic bench. "What are they made of, concrete encased in lead-lined oak?"

"It's to stop them getting pinched," Mark puffed. "Are you lifting your end, Jim?"

"Yes."

"It doesn't feel like it."

"I am!"

They minced their way up the field, gasping and stopping every now and again to put it down to rest. A young woman came rushing over. "Excuse me," she said, "But when you've done that, could you bring one over to my tent? There's only me, you see, and my two kids, and I can't lift it on my own."

"Of course," Tel said, and they all glared at him.

So, having heaved one table up the field and placed it outside Jim's hut, they went back for another. Fortunately, the woman's tent wasn't too far from the herd of tables, and she was so grateful she gave them each a packet of chocolate buttons. Other campers, maybe not noticing them before or having been motivated by their efforts, began to haul off picnic tables. One man tried to carry one himself, crawling underneath and lifting it onto his shoulders; he stepped heavily towards his tent, his shoulders getting lower and lower, his knees bending beneath the weight, until they, feeling his pain, rushed over to lend a hand. He said he didn't need their help, and didn't give them any chocolate, buttons or otherwise.

Heading back to their caravan area they could see Faye stretching up to wrap some sort of wire onto the front of the shepherd's hut. "Look what I found!" she cried, turning on the switch, "Fairy lights! Battery-powered!" The hut looked very twinkly. Brian made a mental note to scour their caravan at some point to see exactly what Faye had stashed in there, it was like Mary Poppin's magic carpet bag.

They resumed their previous positions, talked a bit more, drank a bit more. A small child appeared through the hedge and stared at them. His mother peered over the hedge, watching him. "Hello," said the boy who'd tugged on Brian's t-shirt the night before, "My name's Hayden and I'm five."

Everyone laughed and said, "Hello, Hayden."

"If only adults could introduce themselves so succinctly," Tel said to Mark, "It would cut out all the boring small talk. 'Hello, my name's Tel and I'm thirty-two, in a relationship but not married, and I have ten children'."

"Ten?" Sophie gasped. "I hope that's a random figure and not something you have planned for our future."

The little boy approached Brian and said, "Are you Father Christmas?"

"No," said Brian, gulping from his can, "I'm his brother, Merry."

Mark choked on his beer.

"Hayden," his mother cried, "Don't annoy the nice people."

"He's fine," Brian said, "We'll push him back through the

hedge if he gets aggressive or starts drinking our beer."

"Is your beard real?" the boy asked.

"No, I take it off at night and let it have a run around before putting it in its cage."

"Can I touch it?"

Brian leaned forward, jutting his chin out. Faye whispered, "Don't do it, Bri."

The boy tentatively reached out a hand towards his beard. Just as he was about to touch it, Brian barked like a dog. The boy jumped back, holding his hand and giggling hysterically.

"Come back now, Hayden," called his mother.

"Bye," he said, waving his pudgy hand.

"Bye, Hayden."

The boy disappeared through the hedge again.

Four hours of beer and wine and chatting later, Brian finished his can of beer, stood up, burped and said, "Wife."

"Yes, husband?"

"Would you care to join me in the caravan for a spot of make-up intimacy?"

The others laughed. Faye, embarrassed, cried, "Brian!"

"What?"

"Could you not be a bit more discrete?"

"Why? We're all grown-ups. And besides, I'm from Yorkshire, we don't do discrete, it's against our culture."

"Yes, but – "

"Stop acting all coy," he winked, "Just get yourself in that van."

Blushing and tutting and silently laughing all at the same time, Faye hurried off.

"Do you know," Tel said, "A bit of snogging sounds like a thoroughly good idea right now."

Sophie was racing back to their caravan before he'd even finished his sentence.

Mark looked at Olivia. Now, finally, was the time to ask her about what Richard had said in the pub garden. "We could watch a film?" she said.

"Oh yeah?"

"I've got The Greatest Showman on Blu-ray and two sets of Bluetooth headphones."

Mark's eyebrows stopped wiggling up and down and just stayed down. "The Greatest Showman?"

"Yes. It's very good. Have you seen it?"

"No, I'm not really into musicals."

"Oh," she said, standing up and taking his hand, "You'll be into this one."

Mark's eyebrows shot up again. Maybe it was a ruse to get him alone in her motorhome. They hurried off.

Jim sat there for a while, puffing a bit, humming a bit. Then, realising none of them were coming back any time soon, he wandered over to his shepherd's hut and sat at the picnic table. He drummed on the wooden surface, admired the scenery, drummed some more, then started singing about being lonely, oh so lonely.

* * *

Olivia had paused the film to get them both a glass of water. "Makes a change from alcohol," she said, handing it to him, "I was starting to worry I was becoming a lush, just like Tel keeps saying."

"He's only joking."

"Yes, well, just in case." She settled down next to him on the sofa again. Before she had a chance to put on the headphones and start the film again, he mustered up the courage to say, "Liv."

"Yes, darling?"

He thought he would never get used to her calling him darling, and hesitated. He decided to take the direct approach and just blurt it out, like quickly pulling off a plaster. "Richard said you've been here for a week."

"I have."

"And ... and you didn't contact me?"

"I was quite busy, I had a lot of things to organise, and ... I had a lot of thinking to do, about us."

"Us? You still weren't sure about us a week ago?"

She turned on the sofa to look at him. "No," she said, giving him a huge smile, "I was sure about us a year ago."

"Then why didn't you call me, come and see me?"

"Because," she said, sitting up, "I was ... "

"What?" he said quietly.

"I was ... Well, I was afraid. Terrified, actually."

"Terrified of what? Of being in a relationship again?"

"No." She stared down at the water in her hands. "That you wouldn't ... want me."

"Oh Liv!"

"I thought you might have changed your mind." He hugged her tightly. "You gave no indication when we all met up at Christmas and I thought you maybe you'd gone off the whole idea."

"I didn't want to pressure you. I really wanted to push you against the pub wall and snog your face off."

"Did you, darling? I wish I'd have known, I'd have leapt across the table at you."

"All that lost time."

"Yes." She sipped at her water. "But at least now we know how we feel and we haven't just rushed into anything."

"And all good things are worth waiting for."

"When I drove up last week I guess I was sort of bracing myself for the worst-case scenario. I was putting it off, seeing you, in case that look in your eyes wasn't there anymore."

"I felt exactly the same. It was like Christmas was coming in July, but there was this terrible sense of doom, too, in case you'd met someone, in case you'd changed your mind."

"I thought about you every day, *every* day."

"Me too. What the hell were we thinking, waiting a year? It's been the longest year of my life!"

She was laughing now and smothering his face in

kisses. "We were being sensible."

"I've waited a year to have you in my arms like this, Liv. I'm never letting you go again."

They kissed.

They didn't see the rest of the film.

CHAPTER 9

Day 4: Early hours of Monday morning

Brian prised his eyes open. He wondered if there was a storm coming. He could hear thunder in the distance. The thunder got louder. He sat up, opened the blind on the window next to him and peered out. Jim's fairy lights were still twinkling in the darkness. Then he noticed more lights moving around in the camping field. Headlights of late arrivals? Campers rushing to the loo by torchlight?

He reached for his watch on the TV stand. 2am. The thunder got louder, the lights on the field brighter and more erratic.

The noise increased. It wasn't thunder, it was engines. And then he saw a flash of light outside the caravan area, a shadow of something thin and fast screaming past, then another, and another.

Suddenly a motorbike skidded into their caravan area, spinning the back wheel round in a circle, pulling doughnuts and spraying the caravans with gravel. It went to Olivia's pitch and did the same there, splattering the motorhome. Faces appeared at the windows. The engines, several of them, revved up. Some went down the field and Brian, as he lurched off the bed, heard the sound of canvas being slapped. People were shouting out as the engines squealed. Women were screaming. Children were crying

"What is it?" Faye asked, sounding frightened.

"Stay here," he said firmly.

Brian pulled on his dressing gown and went outside. The others came out too, and saw what looked to be several motorbikes rampaging across the campsite. Even as they looked they saw, in the flashing beams of light, a tent cave in on itself as a bike went past and kicked at the guy ropes. Kids started wailing, women were shrieking, men were clambering out of the tents and hollering. It was bedlam.

Another bike came into their caravan area, circling on the driveway and spraying them with gravel. The rider wore a helmet, they couldn't see his face. Another joined him and they all stepped back to avoid being pelted with stones. The riders yelled at each other, laughing, and roared off down the field. Men came running out of tents, chasing them, but they were too quick. They took down another tent, kicked over tables and chairs. A group of angry men ran to and fro, trying to catch them. Camping equipment was scattered, the bikes screeched. And then one biker stopped and leaned down and pulled up a newly planted bush. Another skidded up to the huge shed with the glass windows all down one side and kicked over pots, pulled down hanging baskets.

Mark ran to his caravan and came back out with a baseball bat, smacking it against his palm. Tel reached under his caravan and pulled out the socket bar for the stabilisers. Brian dashed into his caravan for the car keys and opened up the boot, took out a wheel wrench. Jim burst of out his shepherd's hut, looked at the bikes, looked at them, and reached for his own weapon. Together, the four of them left the caravan area to join the men running around the field. Two bikes roared past right in front of them. One threw out a leg and kicked at Brian. Brian swung his wrench at a wheel and missed. The bikes roared one by one through the entrance gates, kicking at pots of plants as they left. They chased after them, into the pub car park.

The engines squealed off into the distance, leaving chaos behind.

Chelsea came running out of the pub, her dressing gown billowing out behind her. "Oh my God!" she cried, "I've called the police. Is everyone alright? Is anybody hurt?" She burst into tears.

Olivia came galloping over and swooped Chelsea into her arms. "Everyone's okay, I think, it's just minor damage. They've gone now, it's over."

"Oh my God, Liv! Who was it? Who were they?"

"Young hooligans out to scare everyone," Brian said.

"My plants," Mark groaned, surveying the breakages in the dark.

Tel came walking up from the group of men gathered at the gate. "Everyone's okay," he said, "Kids are upset, obviously, but nobody's injured."

"Oh, thank God!"

"Little bleeders," said Jim.

Brian looked at him, then down at his weapon of choice. "And what, exactly, were you intending to do with *that*?"

They all looked at what Jim was holding in his hands.

"It's the first thing I could grab," he said.

They all stared at the cushion.

"Were you planning to smother them one by one?" Mark asked.

"It was literally the only thing to hand!"

"Could have at least thrown it at them in the hope of knocking one off."

"Oh yeah, I didn't think of that."

Olivia was leading Chelsea into the pub. Faye quickly checked on Flo, who was fine, and then she and Sophie went down into the field to help mothers to calm hysterical children. The men at the gate dispersed, a few of them helping others to erect fallen tents.

The police came half an hour later, lighting up the campsite with their blue lights. They took statements and left.

* * *

It was light when Brian woke up again, and again he could hear a noise. Not motorbikes this time, it sounded like someone digging.

He peered out the window that still had its blind up from the night before. The campsite was quiet, sleeping in after a restless night. There was a van parked at the top of the camping field with its doors open.

Brian got up, went outside. The neat gravel driveway between the caravans was scattered everywhere. Deep circular gouges ripped up the grass. He followed the sound of digging and saw the carnage in the camping field; camping equipment had been scattered, and one enormous tent lay on the ground like discarded clothing.

He found Mark on his hands and knees at the edge of the caravan area, using a trowel to re-plant one of the bushes that had been pulled up.

"You're up early."

"Lots to do, don't want these to die."

Brian nodded and went back to his caravan to get dressed. He plugged the hosepipe into the water tap and dragged it over to where Mark was still on his hands and knees. "You plant, I'll water," he said.

A short while later, Tel wandered over to the van and, without a word, took out a leaf rake and began raking the gravel off the grass in the caravan area, tamping down clods of turf with his foot as he went. Another man did the same for the other caravan area. Faye took them mugs of tea and packets of biscuits. Olivia and another woman helped Chelsea, who was taping up broken pots around the glass-walled hut to stop the plants drying out. There were three people snuggled into sleeping bags inside, refugees from the fallen tent, Sophie thought, replanting the hanging baskets as best she could and hanging them up.

Other campers woke up, some helping to put the campsite back together again. There was the gentle murmur of people just getting on with it. Even the kids helped out, making a game out of jumping on churned-up grass in the field. The flattened tent was raised again.

Flo hurried over to Faye, who was brushing up compost from around the pots. "I'd love to stay and help, I really would, but Bill's quite keen to head off to the racecourse and get there early so we can find good seats. Looks like you've got it all covered anyway," she said, looking around. "Can we get together for a meal tonight or something?" Faye nodded. "I'd like you to meet Bill properly, he's a lovely man, you'll like him and I think Brian will too, they have the same sense of humour, you know, blunt and sarcastic." She burst out laughing, then turned and hurried back to the caravan area and Bill. "Don't work too hard," she cried, "No idea when we'll be back, just expect us when you see us. Bye-eee."

* * *

Sophie and Olivia were carrying the spades and a hoe back to Mark's van, when Sophie looked at her and said, "That's a very enormous smile you're wearing there, Liv."

"It is."

"Just happy to be alive?"

"Well yes, but ..." She stopped and turned to face Sophie, whispering, "I didn't know it could be like that."

"What like what? Oh, *that* like that!"

"Amazing! I mean, it literally blew my mind! It never even occurred to me that it could be more than three minutes missionary style on a Friday night. I did wonder what all the fuss was about. Now I know, and ... wow."

Sophie burst out laughing.

"He's amazing," Olivia said, staring dreamily at Mark, loading up the back of his van. "Just ... amazing."

"Enjoy," Sophie said.

* * *

Chelsea arranged a free breakfast for everyone afterwards and the pub, with its taped-up pots and wonky hanging baskets, was heaving with people, both inside and out.

"I'm so sorry about last night," Chelsea kept telling everyone. "I hope it doesn't spoil your holiday or affect your decision to stay here again."

"Wasn't your fault, lass," Brian said, when she approached their table. "Just hoodlums letting off steam. Everyone's fine, don't worry."

She sat down. "Scared the living daylights out of me," she gasped. "Police said there's nothing they can do without witnesses who actually saw their faces."

"Nobody was hurt, that's the main thing."

"Anyone get the reg numbers?" Tel asked.

"No, it was too dark, and one of the campers said they'd smeared them with mud or something. I just hope it doesn't happen again." She looked at Mark. "You did a good job putting everything back together again."

"Wasn't just me, everyone mucked in."

"The kindness of campers," Faye said, patting her hand, "We've seen it before."

"Yeah," said Jim, chomping on a sausage, "And people get bored on holiday, they like something to do. Maybe you should make it a regular thing, camp and plant."

"Not funny, Jim," Chelsea said, piercing him with a stare, which shut him up.

"I'll nip to the nursery later and pick up some new pots."

"Thanks, Mark." She stood up and, as small as she was, hollered in a mighty voice, "Thanks to everyone who helped out this morning, it was very much appreciated."

"As is the breakfast," someone shouted, and people laughed, and ate, and everything seemed normal.

Chelsea turned back to them and said, "There's no plans for you cute campers today, so feel free to go off and explore, but conserve some energy for tomorrow, you'll need it."

"Why, what's happening tomorrow?"

She tapped the side of her nose and said, "You'll see. Be outside at 10 o'clock in the morning. You don't need to bring anything, all will be provided."

"Sounds intriguing," Brian said.

"It'll be abseiling," said Tel, when Chelsea was gone.

"Wingsuit flying," Jim said.

"What's that?"

He told them and they all went slightly pale.

"Parachute jumping," Sophie laughed, and Brian saw a look pass between Tel and Olivia.

"You always wanted to try that, didn't you?" Tel said, overly casual.

"Yes, Tel, back when I thought I was indestructible and had no care for broken bones and ruptured internal organs."

"And now?"

"Why are you asking?"

"Just curious."

"Now? I don't know. Possibly. You *have* booked a spa day for today, haven't you, Tel? You've not made plans to push me out of an airplane or anything like that?"

Tel laughed, but Brian noticed a look pass between him and Olivia again.

* * *

It was a good day for everyone. Tel and Sophie did indeed pamper themselves at a hotel spa, which curiously had a 'fairy farm' attached to it. Brian and Faye, happy again, just drove around the beautiful countryside, talking calmly, talking properly. And then Faye spotted a craft fair in a village hall and started hyperventilating. Like a dog let off the lead, she bought candles and jewellery and Mediterranean glassware; "Christmas gifts," she told Brian's horrified face.

"It's July, Faye, at least make an attempt to restrain yourself." He said this whilst purchasing a vast amount of cheese at one stall.

"Restraint?" Faye sneered.

"Yes, I walked straight past the hand-made sausages."

"Ooh, sausages." And she was off again.

Mark and Olivia went to his garden centre for new pots, and snogged in the office. They came back to the campsite and started repotting the plants, but kept glancing at each other and eventually raced to the motorhome for a proper snog.

Jim spent the day in the pub, talking to Melissa, who seemed a bit stand-offish at first after her encounter with Beth, but he eventually charmed her round; casting frequent glances over his shoulder just in case Beth turned up again. There was nothing wrong with a bit of harmless flirting, he told himself, but he kept it low-key, just for his own amusement. He'd never risk losing Beth again.

He eventually got bored of swapping innuendos with Melissa, his heart just wasn't in it. He went outside, into the pub car park, and called Beth. "Come and have dinner with us tonight."

"I can't, babes, I've got plans."

"I might come home then. It's a bit boring here, they've all gone out and left me."

"Oh, poor you, but you can't come home 'cos, like I said, I got plans with the girls all week."

"Just girls?"

"Don't make me come round there and slap you, Jim."

He grinned. "I might like that."

"Maybe when you come home," she laughed, "On *Friday*."

He hung up and sighed, bored. He considered going back to Melissa at the bar, but decided against it. He smiled to himself, thinking, 'I think I've grown up, well how about – " Two young women in pretty summer dresses sashayed across the car park towards him and, as they sidled past him with lingering looks, Jim thought his luck might have just changed. "Hello, ladies!" he said, following them in.

* * *

"My whole body is like warm jelly," Sophie sighed.

"I've never felt more relaxed."

They were lying on the fixed bed in their new caravan, on their backs, arms and legs stretched out as far as the mattress allowed.

"Good massage," he sighed.

"Mine was more of an angry pummelling, I'm sure my masseuse was working through a few emotional issues, but the hot tub was bliss."

They both sighed, neither willing to move.

"I like the caravan, Tel."

"I'm glad. I chose it especially for you."

"I think we're going to have a lot of fun with it."

"I'd indulge in some fun right now, except I'm just *so* relaxed."

"Me too," she sighed, and they both fell asleep.

o O o

"Brian."

"Yes, Faye?"

"I love you."

"I love you more."

"Not possible."

"Is too."

"Brian."

"Yes, Faye?"

"I'm glad we're back together again."

"Me too, Faye, me too."

o O o

"Are you going to tell them?"

"Yes, but not yet."

"Do you think you'll manage to last the whole week without saying anything?"

"I doubt it, but I'm going to try. I just hope they won't

think badly of me."

"Nobody could think badly of you."

"I hope not."

"I know not."

* * *

Over dinner at the pub, which was Steak Night without T-bone but with all the sides, Faye mustered up the courage to say, "Liv."

"Yes?"

"We have something to tell you."

"Oh?" Olivia immediately thought, 'They know, they know and now they hate me for deceiving them.' Underneath the table, Mark held her hand.

"We … well, this afternoon, when we were out driving, we …" Faye looked at Brian, who said, "We drove through the village and saw Richard and your father coming out of the pub."

"Oh." She felt both relieved and alarmed.

"Looks like they're hanging around awhile."

"We thought you should know," Faye said.

"Yes."

"You should have called the police," Sophie said, "They would have arrested Richard and made him think twice about doing it again."

"I know. I will if he does it again."

"Wonder why they're sticking around?" Tel asked.

"They'd better not hassle Liv again," Mark snapped, "I'd quite happily knock that snotty smirk off – "

"It's okay, darling, I'll take care of it."

Afterwards, full and happy, they wandered back to their caravans to relax and enjoy the sun, and each other. All around them were the sounds of children, someone playing music somewhere, and the ever-present smell of barbecues. Dogs chased each other on the field, and friendships were being made outside tents.

"Been bored out of my brain all day," Jim said, sitting on the grass. He expected at least one of them to say, 'You should have come with us then', but they didn't. "I was thinking of going home, actually, I don't feel as if I'm wanted here."

"Don't be silly, Jim!" said Faye, "We kitted out the shepherd's hut for you."

"And chased your caravan down the field and pushed the bloody thing back again," said Brian, rolling his eyes, "*And* we pushed the shepherd's hut over for you. Wouldn't do that for just anyone, you know, lad, I have a creaky back and aging bones to consider."

"Of course you're wanted," Sophie said, leaning forwards in her chair to hug him round the neck, "You're part of the group."

"We won't let you go," Olivia giggled.

"I just feel a bit left out and … lonely."

"Don't fall for it," said Mark, reaching out a foot and pushing him over onto the grass. "He's just looking for sympathy and free stuff."

Jim straightened up again, pouting. "I don't even have my own chair. You all have chairs."

"Because we thought to bring our own," said Brian. "There's a couple of fold-ups in the back of my car, go help yourself."

Jim jumped up like an enthusiastic child to fetch one.

"Is there anything you *don't* have in the boot of your car?" Mark asked.

"I like to be prepared for any eventuality."

"How about a saw, in case a tree falls into the road?"

Brian nodded.

"How about emergency supplies in case you get trapped in a snowstorm?" Tel asked, and Brian nodded.

"Flares?" Sophie asked, laughing.

"Flares are more for seafaring, but I have a very cute orange triangle that flashes."

"Wellies?" Tel asked.

"Of course."

"A blow-up dingy," Olivia giggled.

"A blow-up anything?" Jim laughed.

"I think there's a blow-up alien and a hammer left over from a Halloween party we went to last year."

"Kidding!"

"Not."

"Impressed."

"Talking of preparedness," Brian said, turning to Faye, "I think I'd like a stocktake of everything we have stashed in the caravan, for weight purposes."

"Blimey," Faye said, "I'll need a couple of weeks."

"We could be carrying a vast amount of useless items."

"None of them are useless, Bri."

"What's the weirdest thing you've got in there?" Tel asked, and Faye thought for a moment.

"French boules," she said, and they all fell silent for a moment. "They're metal balls, you play them like lawn bowls. Picked them up in France."

"I didn't know that," Brian said.

"There's a lot you don't know about the contents of our caravan, Bri."

"That's what I'm afraid of."

"Says the man who has a blow-up alien in the back of his car."

Brian glanced at his watch. "Flo's late back."

"Yes," said Faye, "Hope she's alright."

"That bloke, what's his name, Bill? He could be anyone," Jim said casually, "A mass murderer, a psychopath, a white slave trader."

"He wouldn't get much for Flo," Brian laughed, stopping abruptly when he saw Faye's face.

"*Always look on the bright side of life,*" Tel sang.

They heard a car pull up on the other side of the hedge and Flo's head suddenly popped up.

"Genie," Brian mouthed to Faye, "Incredible!"

"Cooo-eee," Flo cried, "I'm back, did you miss me?" She slammed the car door shut and immediately pushed her way through the hedge. "Oh, we've had the most fan*tas*tic time, we really have, haven't we, Bill."

"Sure did," he called over.

"I won! Look at this!" She took a wad of money out of her handbag and shook it at them. "Bill says it was just beginners' luck, didn't you, Bill, but I've got a gift, my chakras told me which horse to bet on and the names just called out to me, Wizard of Hogwarts, Magic Mare, I mean, how could I not bet on those?" She gently pushed Jim on his shoulder and he vacated the seat for her. "Just an amazing time. Are you coming over, Bill?"

"Just a minute."

"The horses were so beautiful and the crowds were fan*tas*tic. Oh!" she suddenly cried, "You're not drinking?"

"No," said Tel, "On account of us not being alcoholics who drink every night."

Olivia pulled a face, thinking she quite fancied a Merlot, or maybe a crisp Chianti.

"I never knew watching horse racing could be so *exciting*! The size of them running past right in front of you, the thudding of their hooves on the ground ..."

Bill came through the hedge carrying two substantial camping chairs, which got caught on the branches, so he had to yank them free. Mark assessed the damage to the hedge and made a mental note to do something about invasive campers.

"Hello," Bill cried, opening up a chair and setting it down for Flo, who changed seats. Jim immediately bounced into the vacant chair.

Brian scoured Bill's face. He didn't look like a man who'd been verbally attacked all day, he looked quite calm and cheery. He immediately started to talk to Faye about the horses, managing to find gaps in Flo's endless, excited spiel. Brian was impressed by his tenacity and impeccable sense of timing.

"We're not stopping long, are we, Bill. I thought, as Lady Luck and my chakras were upon me, I'd thrash him at poker again, although we don't play for money, do we, Bill, well, not real money, we use pennies. Oh, Faye," she suddenly cried, "Before I forget, can we have a quick chat?"

They wandered off, walking towards the gate in the perimeter fence that led into the trees, but stopping before they got there. They all watched as Faye and Flo talked – well, Flo seemed to be doing most of the talking and Faye just nodded. Brian felt a bit nervous. Maybe Flo wanted her old airbed back in their awning. Jim was not going to be pleased. He wasn't going to be, either.

"Lovely woman," Bill was saying, "Very bubbly, very enthusiastic about everything." Brian felt a tinge of guilt. Maybe it was his fault after all, not being able to tolerate Flo like everyone else seemed able to do. "Talks a lot though," he added, and Brian felt vilified, "But that's not a bad thing. She's taken me out of myself a bit and I think I needed that. I've been quite down in the dumps since losing my partner."

They all murmured their condolences.

"But Flo's been like a breath of fresh air. Lovely woman," he said again.

"Drink?" Brian asked.

"No, no, I'm practically teetotal, except for the odd spot of Dom Pérignon. I used to have a problem with alcohol back in the day," he added, and Olivia frowned, wondering if she did, "But it's all under control now."

Faye and Flo came back and resumed their places. "I'm going home," Flo said, and Brian thought he was hearing things, hallucinating, or maybe he'd dropped off and this was all a dream. "My friend called me today, said poor old Tom from three doors down has died and his cat needs a new home, so of course I said I'd take it. It's a lovely pussy, white and fluffy, a bit like Kat, except Kat was tabby and short-haired."

"That's great," Mark said, "Not about poor Tom, obviously."

"Going home?" Brian repeated, as nonchalantly as he could manage.

"I feel I've overstayed my welcome," Flo said, putting her tiny hand on top of Brian's giant one. "I wanted to go home a couple of weeks ago, but Faye insisted I stay and I didn't want to seem ungrateful or anything, but now I have something to go home for and I won't be alone anymore."

"You won't be alone anyway," Bill chipped in.

"Oh yes!" she cried, "You'll never guess where Bill lives! He's just in Harborne, ten minutes away! We've already made plans to get together regularly, haven't we, Bill, it'll do us both good."

"It's very fortuitous that we met," he said.

"It was written in the cosmos, Bill, I could feel it coming in my chakras."

Faye wondered if she could get the contact details off Olivia for her private investigator. Jim was right, he could be anyone, they knew nothing about this man who had charmed her sister. "So, what do you do for a living, Bill?" she asked.

"I'm a curator at the Birmingham Museum and Art Gallery."

"Nice," Faye said, thinking maybe she didn't need the private investigator after all. "We were a bit worried that you were a kidnapper or a psychopath or ..."

Bill laughed when she trailed off. "No, not a kidnapper or anything like that, just a perfectly normal bloke."

"Except his name's not really Bill," Flo laughed.

"Bill's not your real name?" Faye asked, thinking again about the private investigator.

"No. Bill is what my partner called me." His eyes misted over. "He always said I looked like Bill Nighy, you know, the actor?"

"I see that," Sophie said.

"Oh yeah," said Faye.

"And when you say 'partner'?" Brian asked.

"My soulmate," he replied, and Faye glanced at Brian

and winked, "My best friend. We were together for seventeen years. I miss him so much."

"*Him?*" Jim blurted.

"Yes, Lawrence, my long-time partner."

"You're gay?"

"Subtle," Mark tutted.

"Yes, I'm gay, very much so."

Jim burst out laughing. "Didn't sense that in your chakras, did you, Flo."

"I did actually," she said, "First time I laid eyes on him I knew he was a special person with a great sadness inside him."

"We all thought there was a blossoming romance," Sophie said.

"No, not a romance, a friendship." Bill patted Flo's hand. "A blossoming friendship."

"What is your real name then?" Jim asked.

"It's Ralph. It's actually Ralph Fiennes, but everybody always asks me the same questions about Red Dragon, Harry Potter, or Budapest hotels."

"Why?" Jim asked.

Mark reached over to pat him on the head and said to Bill, "Our resident philistine, as you've probably gathered."

"Shut up." Jim looked over at Tel. "Philistine's an insult, right?"

Tel laughed and nodded, and Jim leaned over and gave Mark's wrist a furious Chinese burn. Mark raised his hands and flapped them at Jim's flapping hands, like fighting hares.

"So," Bill continued, "I just call myself Bill now, makes life much easier."

"Come on then, Bill," Flo said, standing up, "Let's see how many pennies I can take off you. I'm staying at Bill's again tonight, Faye, and he's taking me home tomorrow."

"Tomorrow?" Faye gasped, "So soon?"

Four weeks, six days and – he glanced at his watch – nineteen hours was hardly 'so soon', Brian thought, trying to control his mounting excitement. Then he felt a pang of guilt and hoped he hadn't been too horrible to his sister-in-law, now that she was going.

"I have a cat to look after," Flo said, "I'm needed, I have to go."

"Of course. I'll miss you."

Flo hugged Faye and said, "Thanks for everything, sis, you've been fan*tas*tic and I'm really grateful. You, too, Brian."

Brian stood up to hug her, and to shake Bill's hand. "S'been nice to meet you," he said, "Hope to meet you again soon."

"I'm sure we will."

"I knew you'd like each other," Flo cried, "I knew it." She seemed very happy.

Bill leaned down to shake everyone's hands.

"It's been fan*tas*tic to meet you all," Flo said, waving at each of them. They waved back. "Hope we can do this again sometime. Cheerio, be good, bye."

Flo and Bill dragged their chairs through the hedge and were gone, although they could hear Flo talking and cackling about her poker wins for the rest of the night.

The gang sat outside Brian and Faye's caravan, talking and laughing and having a good time in each other's company. It was nice. Relaxing. Comfortable.

Until later that night.

CHAPTER 10

Day 5: Early hours of Tuesday morning

Brian was woken by an approaching rumble again. He quickly glanced at his watch. 1.45am. This time he knew it wasn't thunder. The bikes were back.

He was wide awake in an instant and shuffling off the bed, quickly pulling on underpants and jeans as he went. Seconds later he was outside, unzipping the awning and stepping out as the motorbikes tore through the entrance gate. The sound of airhorns filled the air and echoed off the surrounding trees. Mark fell out of Olivia's motorhome, zipping up his jeans and yelping. He rushed over to Brian in a pained, lopsided way. Tel leapt out of his caravan, looking around, spotting them both and running over, shouting, "Not again!" above the noise. They watched from the middle of the gravel driveway as several scramblers, four, maybe five, possibly even six, started careering across the grass on the field, kicking out at tent ropes and tables, screaming and yelling and holding the air horns high above their heads. Inside the tents, children started to scream in terror.

Mark raced in a painful way to his van, parked behind his caravan, and pulled open the doors. "HERE!" he shouted, taking out brooms and spades and hoes, "Prod them in the wheels! Try not to die doing it!" They grabbed one each and hurried onto the field. The women watched from the driveway, huddled together in a frightened group.

Scramblers shrieked past and they jabbed at the wheels with their poles like lances. The riders kicked out in protest. Tel swung at them, missing a couple of helmets by millimetres. Mark started jabbing at the riders' bodies. They all missed, the bikes were just too quick. Men came out of their tents, shining torches, illuminating the field of high-pitched engines. The bikers blew the air horns in their faces as they passed. Two scramblers skidded behind them and into the caravan area. The women had to quickly jump out of the way. The scramblers skidded and blasted them with gravel and they all screamed. Brian spun round and raced back, positioning himself at the entrance, half crouching, the pole of a hoe held out in front of him. "COME ON THEN!" he hollered.

The scramblers skidded to a stop outside Olivia's motorhome and their helmets glanced at each other. Then they both revved up and peppered the motorhome with gravel, moving their rear tyres back and forth to pick up more stones, then circling round on the spot, hitting the awning and making the women cry out in alarm. Brian grunted and stood his ground, waiting for them to come to him. Mark joined him. Tel was running around the field furiously waving his pole, shouting in frustration at not being able to hit a single one of them. Men followed him with a variety of implements.

The riders came speeding up the driveway. Mark crouched and winced and held his pole tight. Brian didn't move. Mark almost lost his nerve and jumped out of the way as the bikes approached at speed, but stuck with Brian. Brian raised his pole to the side of his head, ready to swing like a baseball player. The first bike ploughed into him and he threw down the pole and grabbed onto the handlebars, tipping the rider off. The rider cried out as he crashed onto the ground. Brian heaved the bike to one side and lunged for him.

The rider leapt to his feet as the other rider crashed sideways into Brian, making Faye cry out, which incensed Brian enough to ignore the pain in his side and grab the first rider by the arm. The rider slipped free as the other bike continued to try to push them out of the way with its front wheel. Brian lunged at him again but wasn't quick enough to grab him before the rider picked up his fallen bike and jumped onto it.

Mark was swinging his pole, making contact with helmets and leather. Unable to escape, the bikes spun around and zoomed down to the water tap at the bottom of the caravan area, spinning round again until the two factions were at opposite ends. The engines idled. The riders looked at them and at each other. Then one nodded and they both took off through the hedge on the right and between the other caravans. Dogs barked and children cried as the bikes skidded down the other driveway and back onto the field.

"YOU OKAY?" Brian yelled at the women huddled together inside the awning. They nodded. He ran towards the entrance gates. Tel was nearby, still swinging his pole at riders. "TEL! SHUT THE GATE!"

Tel immediately sprinted towards the gate. The bikes were coming up the field, revving and roaring and blowing the air horns. Tel started to swing the gate shut but was met with sudden resistance when a car on the other side shot forward and held the gate open with its front bumper. Tel jumped when it blew its horn twice. The bikes poured past it in a quick, single file, and the car reversed, spun round on the pub car park, spraying both Brian and Tel, and followed the bikers out onto the lane, their headlights illuminating the trees as they sped through the countryside and out of sight.

Brian and Tel gasped for air. Mark rushed up and joined their heavy breathing, as did several men. Jim wandered over, dishevelled and sleepy-eyed and rubbing at his face. "Bloody bikers," he said.

"Yeah, thanks for your help!" Tel snapped.

"What could I do? I only have cushions and a set of fairy lights!"

The other men were talking in raised voices, angry and frustrated. Two small dogs that had chased after the bikers on the field were yapping at their feet. Women and children were shouting to each other on the field. Chelsea came running out of the pub, almost hysterical. "Why are they doing this?" she wailed. "I'm so sorry, everyone, I – "

"Not your fault, love," someone said.

"Just some bleeding hooligans," said another.

"I'd like a refund," a tall chap at the back demanded, and they all turned to glare at him.

"I'll be leaving in the morning," said a man with two hysterical children clinging to his legs, "I can't have my family terrorised like this."

"I totally understand," Chelsea sobbed, as Brian wrapped a comforting arm across her shoulders, "And of course we'll be offering full refunds to anyone who wants to leave."

The women came rushing over. "Are you okay, Bri?"

"Aye, love, just wished I could have got my hands on them."

"Me too," Tel said, hugging Sophie.

"Oh Chelsea!" Olivia cried, wrapping the sobbing woman in her arms, "I'm so, so sorry."

"I've called the police," she sniffed, just as one blue flashing light pulled onto the pub car park and another sped off in chase down the lane. Two officers languidly got out of their car.

"You were quick," Brian said.

"We were just round the corner on a drugs raid."

The campers were interviewed. None of whom could describe bikes or faces, or even the make or colour of the car that held the gate open. The officers said they'd do what they could but didn't sound particularly enthusiastic about it.

"If they come again," Brian growled, when they eventually wandered back to their caravans, "I'm going to be ready to fight back."

"Me too," Mark and Tel said in unison.

Jim said nothing.

Brian looked at Mark, limping along besides him. "Why you walking like that?" he asked.

"I'd rather not say."

"Pulled muscle?"

"No."

"Are you injured?"

"Not in battle, no."

"In what way, then?"

Mark hesitated, then said, "Pulled the zip on my jeans up too fast. No underpants."

Brian and Tel sucked in air as Jim burst out laughing. Mark turned to Olivia and said, "I may need some assistance taking my jeans off."

"Of course, darling. Poor you."

"Quick and firm, like pulling off a plaster," Jim said.

"I don't need advice from someone who couldn't be bothered to leave his shed on wheels during a – "

"Here, let me," Jim cried, desperate to be part of the group again and lunging at Mark's jeans.

"GERROFF!"

"It'll just take a sec!"

"GET O- AAARGH!!"

"There, see? All done."

Mark pushed him away. Jim fell backwards onto the grass, still laughing. The others tried not to look at the gaping hole in Mark's jeans.

"GIT!" Mark hissed, cupping himself and mincing off.

"You're welcome!"

"We should decide what to do in case they come back tomorrow," Tel said.

"I think we should all go to bed," Sophie said, leading him away, "And think about this in the morning, when testosterone levels aren't quite so high."

"I concur," Brian said.

But Brian hardly slept that night, tossing and turning in bed, making plans in his head.

* * *

"Is that your alarm?"

Faye snuffled awake and grunted, "Yes."

"Why have you set your alarm on holiday?"

"So we wouldn't be late."

"For?"

"Whatever plans Chelsea has for us this morning."

"Oh God."

They shuffled up to the pub at 10.15, all yawning and baggy-eyed. Jim immediately lay down on a bench seat and went back to sleep. There was a new banner hanging outside The Woodsman reading TUESDAY NIGHT IS CURRY NIGHT.

Chelsea came out and wouldn't stop apologising. She didn't look like she'd had much sleep either, her eyes were puffy and as red as her hair. "You don't have to do it if you don't want to," she said.

"Do what?" Brian asked, "We don't know what 'it' is yet."

"I've arranged a trip out for you all today, to see if it's something we could offer campers in the future."

"What kind of trip?"

"It's …"

A large van pulled onto the pub car park. Several bicycles were strapped to racks on either side.

"No," said Brian.

"You don't know what it is yet," said Faye.

"A wild guess is it's something to do with cycling."

"It's better than that," Chelsea said.

"What could be better than cycling?" Brian drawled, already deciding he wasn't going to do it, he'd look like an elephant on a wire coat hanger.

"Electric bikes!"

"Oh!" cried Olivia, clapping her hands together, then stopping when she looked at her friends' tired and unimpressed faces. "I think it might be quite fun."

"I think it will be exhausting," said Tel, himself awake half the night making fighting plans, "I don't think my exhaustion could take any more exhaustion."

"Come on," Sophie said, slapping him on the back,

"Where's your sense of adventure?"

"Still in bed, sleeping."

A man jumped out of the van. "Are you my group today?" he asked cheerfully.

"No," said Brian, "They just ran screaming off down the road when they saw you coming."

"Brian!"

"These are they," Chelsea said.

"Good, good. My name is Callum and I run an electric bike touring company. Now it was short notice," he said, glancing at Chelsea, who shrugged, "And we don't normally work in this area, but we've done a quick circular route for you to follow which takes you through some scenic points of interest."

"Seen all the scenic points of interest from the comfort of my car," Brian said.

"Yes, well, cycling in the fresh air and listening to the birds is a whole new experience."

"I can hear the birds right here," Brian said, holding up a finger and listening.

"Brian!"

"I don't want to," he whined.

A younger man opened up the back of the van and started handing out helmets.

"Not wearing one of those," Brian said firmly, "You won't have one big enough for my head anyway."

"Biggest one we do," the young man said, handing him what looked like a plastic colander. Brian growled and took it.

"Now, is anyone over eighteen stones, or 250 pounds?"

They all shook their heads, except for Brian.

"Sir?"

"Yes?"

"Are you over eighteen stones or 250 pounds?"

"I'd rather not say."

"John," Callum said to the younger man, "Help me get the big Bosch bike out the back."

It took two of them to lift it down. Brian surveyed it through suspicious eyes. "I'll do myself an injury with that saddle, it may never see the light of day again."

"Put the ultra-padded seat on, John."

A bit of excitement rippled through the group when they were given their bikes, each with a wicker basket on the front, and a laminated A5 map.

"Bit basic," Brian said, looking at it.

"Looks like a Jackson Pollock," Tel laughed, "During his 'scribble on canvas' period."

"Did a toddler do this?" Mark asked.

"Like I said, we prepared this tour at short notice, but you should be able to follow it easy enough. The round trip will take you about two hours."

"Two hours!" Brian cried.

"Stop moaning," Faye said, "You're getting on my nerves."

"Ridiculous," Brian muttered under his breath, "I'll never survive two hours perched on a bike."

Callum gave them simple instructions on how to use them. "You shouldn't have any trouble, but our number is on the bottom of the map if you need any help, like if you get a puncture or anything like that."

"Or to rescue anyone who's fallen headfirst into a ditch," Tel laughed.

Olivia giggled and said, "That'll probably be me."

"I'll rescue you," Mark said.

"Oh, thank you, darling."

"Any time."

"Bleurgh," Tel heaved, which made Mark heave. "Oh! I'd forgotten all about your sensitive gag reflex." He heaved again, as did Mark. "This is going to be fun."

"Stop it."

"Bleurgh!"

"Stop … ugh … it."

"Pack it in, you two," said Sophie. "Any more

misbehaving and you'll both be grounded for the rest of the week."

"Bleurgh!"

"Ugh!"

They started mounting up, except for Brian, who glared at both the helmet in his hand and the bike, huffing. Bill's bright red BMW came through the campsite gate. Flo scrambled out and hugged Faye. "I'm off now, thank you for a fan*tas*tic time, I've really enjoyed myself, but I have a cat to rescue and look after. Thanks, Brian," she said, unwrapping herself from Faye and leaping up to hang from his neck in a hug, "You've been fan*tas*tic too, thank you for putting up with me, I bet you'll be glad to see the back of me now." She cackled as Brian attempted to shake his head and say, "It's been lovely having you and – "

"See you all again soon, I hope," she said to the others, jumping down from Brian's neck, "Have fun."

She eased herself back into the car and Bill gave a wave through the windscreen before pulling away.

"Did you tell her she could pop in whenever she wants?" Brian asked his wife, suddenly awash with guilt. Faye nodded and smiled.

"Mount your cycles," Callum announced dramatically.

They did. Except Brian, who, despite having a step-through frame, found it difficult to manoeuvre himself onto the saddle. "It's a bit high," he said.

John dashed over with a tool and lowered it.

"It's a big low now."

Brian had to step off while the saddle was raised again. When he got back on it was higher than it had been before and his feet barely reached the ground, but he didn't like to say anything, he just wanted it over with.

Chelsea and Melissa came running out of the pub carrying large paper bags and a cardboard box. "Wait!" she cried, "We've done snacks to keep you going."

"Ooh," Brian said, suddenly excited as he peered into the

bags. "An assortment of savoury goodies."

"And energy bars," Mark said, pulling a face.

"There's chocolate bars at the bottom," said Tel.

"Is there?"

"You're like a couple of kids on a school trip," Sophie tutted.

Melissa handed out plastic bottles of water from a box and they loaded up their wicker baskets.

The van drove off. They straddled their bikes and set off in a wobbly 'Ooh' kind of way, with Mark in the lead and Brian at the rear, feeling like an elephant balanced on a wire coat hanger, wearing a stupidly tight bowl on his head.

They got as far as the end of the lane, where there was a T-junction. It took ten minutes of deep discussion and much scouring of the Pollock line drawing before they decided to turn left.

Shortly after, Sophie suddenly stopped her bike, turned round in her saddle to the others and cried, "We forgot Jim!"

"Probably for the best," Mark said.

"Poor Jim," Olivia said, "He said he was feeling left out of the group last night and now we've gone and left him behind."

"Lucky Jim," Brian mumbled, sweating and puffing and turning the pedals with the tips of his toes as they came to the first hill.

* * *

"I am *literally* dying."

"You have *literally* been peddling for fifteen minutes."

"Is that all?" Brian whimpered. "It seems like a lifetime. Me and exercise have never got on, and you don't use your legs in a steelworks, only your arms, so rowing would probably be more my thing."

"It was just one hill," Sophie said.

"That wasn't a hill, it was a *mountain*."

"We could get off and have a quick rest?" Tel suggested.

"I would get off," Brian said, "Except my feet don't reach the ground and me and the bike have now become as one. If I get off there's no way I'm getting back on again. I might call a taxi. Can I borrow someone's phone?"

"I thought you'd brought yours, so I haven't brought mine," Faye said.

"Chelsea said not to bring anything," Sophie said, "So I didn't."

"I've left mine in the motorhome," Olivia said, "Daddy kept calling so I threw it in a drawer."

"I forgot mine," Mark said.

"Panic not," declared Tel, pulling his phone out of, Faye noticed, a pair of quite tight jeans, "I've got mine." He glanced at the screen and held the phone above his head. "Oh, no service."

"Joking!" Brian gasped.

"Not."

"So, we have one phone between all of us," Mark said, "And no service."

"And I forgot to charge it. 15% battery left."

"Kill me now," Brian whined, "We're never getting out of here alive."

"It's a bit like a horror film, isn't it," said Faye, who was quite partial to a good horror film, "Where the group gets lost in the woods at night and are murdered by rednecks."

"Exactly like that," Brian said, "Except it's daytime, we're in the middle of the English countryside, and the only rednecks round here are people who didn't put on enough sun tan lotion."

Tel was still waving his phone above his head. "Should have a signal at the top of the hill."

"Mountain."

"HEY!" came a voice, and they all peered down the hill. Another cyclist was peddling up, the old-fashioned way, without the aid of electricity. "HEY, YOU LOT! YOU BLOODY WELL LEFT ME AT THE PUB, YOU GITS!"

"We're so sorry," Olivia gushed.

"We're not," Mark said, "It's been very peaceful."

"Apart from Brian gasping and complaining."

"How did you know where we were?" Sophie asked.

"And how did you manage to catch us up so fast?"

"Chelsea had a spare map, and a bike in the basement, and it's taken less than ten minutes to catch you up. You haven't got very far, have you."

Brian pretended to cry. Jim straddled his bike up to him and pushed him in a jovial, 'get a grip' kind of way. Brian slowly leaned sideways, his left foot scrabbling for the ground. His bike toppled sideways, taking him with it. He crashed onto the grass verge and lay there like a bike lane sign painted into tarmac.

"You okay, Bri?"

"Do I look okay? Help me."

They all dismounted and tried to pull him up, but he was too heavy.

"Lift your leg up and we'll pull the bike out," Tel suggested.

"As previously mentioned, me and the bike are now as one, and my leg muscles died about ten miles back."

"We haven't done ten miles, Bri."

Brian pretended to cry again. Faye lifted up his right leg, assisted by Olivia, while Mark and Tel pulled the bike out. "No, no," he cried, "Just leave me here to die, save yourselves. I'm sure a council truck will pick me up at some point and take me to the tip."

"Stop being such a drama queen," Faye said.

"I'm in hell, I'm allowed to whinge and whine."

"When was the last time you rode a bike, Bri?"

"Junior school."

"Blimey."

Now free of the bike, Brian slowly rolled onto his front and got to his knees, then unsteadily to his feet, gasping and groaning the whole time. Jutting out his chin, he started walking back down the hill, saying, "I'm going back to the campsite."

"Don't give up so easily," Sophie teased. "Besides, it'll be faster going down the hill on the bike."

"I'm not getting back on the thing."

"How are we going to get the bike back then?"

"I don't care. Throw it in the hedge. Give it to a passing masochist."

"Chelsea said she paid a £150 deposit," Olivia said, "For each bike."

Brian stopped walking. He was hot and sweaty, he was tired and his buttocks hurt, a *lot*, but he was, through and through, a Yorkshireman. "£150?"

"Yes. If they have to come and retrieve it they'll charge extra. If it's stolen you'll have to pay for the bike."

"And your sturdy steed doesn't look cheap," Tel added.

Brian turned back round and surveyed the bike on the ground. "I'm not sitting on that saddle."

"Stand on one pedal and coast down, like you did when you were a kid," Mark said.

"It's the easiest way," said Sophie.

Brian looked at Faye, who gave a resigned nod. With a huff, Brian snatched the bike up, checked traffic, and crossed the road. He tentatively tested the 'balance on one pedal' theory. It felt very unsteady. He looked down the mountain they'd just cycled up. It was long, and steep. The others gathered behind him.

"You can do this, Bri."

"Come on, big man."

"Kids do it," Jim said, "How hard can it be?"

As it turned out, very hard indeed.

* * *

"Wow," said Chelsea, collecting glasses from the front tables as the first two cycled into the pub car park, "That didn't take long. Did you do the whole route? Callum said it would take at least two – "

"First hill," Mark said, "We made it as far as the first hill."

Brian came staggering into the car park, leaning heavily on the handlebars, his t-shirt soaked in sweat. "Take it!" he gasped, and Tel ran over to put the bike on its stand. Brian staggered to a bench and fell front first across the table.

"First hill?" Chelsea said, "You mean the slight incline after the T-junction?"

"Yep."

"That's as far as you got?"

"Yep."

"What happened?"

"Brian wanted to come back but he didn't want to get back on the saddle," Sophie said, "So he stood on one pedal to coast down and kept … crashing."

"Repeatedly," said Tel, "I've never known anyone with such a poor sense of balance."

"He was doing at least fifty-five miles an hour," Faye said.

"He'd be less injured if he'd thrown himself off the top of the hill and rolled back to camp."

"It was pretty funny though," Jim laughed.

"It bloody wasn't!" Brian grunted from the table.

"At one point," Jim said, still tickled, "This truck flew past and just blew him into the bushes, and then we got to a bend and he didn't even attempt to turn, just went straight up the embankment and flew headfirst over the handlebars."

"It was a near-death experience," Brian growled.

"Took us ages to find him, we had to follow the sound of his groaning."

"Water," Brian croaked, rolling off the bench and onto the seat. "I need water."

Olivia fished a bottle out of her wicker basket and brought it to him. He downed it in one. Chelsea dashed into the pub and came back out with the large pitcher of iced water they used for whiskies. Brian took it and poured it over his red, sweaty head.

"Take this stupid hat off before it chokes me," he said, and Faye fiddled with the straps, and fiddled some more. Then Sophie stepped in for a bit of a fiddle, followed by Olivia. Brian sat there, covered in scratches and various forms of foliage, and stared straight ahead, his hairy chin jutting, his eyes bulging like a frog. Eventually, the helmet was removed. It left deep ruts on either side of his face that disappeared into his beard.

Melissa came out with a first aid box, which Faye opened and, using water from a bottle, started cleaning off Brians scratches, his cuts, the slowly forming bruises, and the stinger rash all down one side of his body. There was foliage stuck in his hair and in his beard. Olivia started picking them out, while Mark, for some reason, took off his trainers. Just for a second, through his pain, Brian thought it was quite a nice feeling to be pampered, but then the agony slammed back into gear again and he groaned.,

Sore, humiliated and in a great deal of pain, he attempted to stand up, maybe storm off to lick his wounds in the sanctuary of his caravan, but found his muscles burned and his bones ached. He fell back onto the seat, groaning, and they all stood around him, looking concerned. He looked up at Chelsea. "My good woman, would you be so kind as to fetch me a very large whisky, purely for medicinal purposes." He sensed Faye struggling to not look at her watch as Chelsea dashed off.

Tel and Sophie started lining up the bikes on the edge of the car park. Brian watched and grumbled, until Chelsea brought his whisky out. "We're out of water," she said, watching the ice cubes melt on the ground around his feet.

Brian downed it in one and handed it back.

"You okay, Bri?" Mark asked, "You don't think anything's broken, do you?"

"Only my pride, my dignity, and my sense of balance."

"Do you think you need an ambulance?" Chelsea asked.

"Fell off the shed roof once," he said, staring off into the distance. "Knocked myself out. Faye was hysterical, called an ambulance. They couldn't lift me onto the trolley, they kind of rolled me onto some tarpaulin I had in the shed and dragged me down the side of the house to the ambulance. Faye had to get a couple of neighbours round and it took all five of them to lift me off the tarpaulin and onto the trolley. Then they couldn't get me in the ambulance, they pushed and pushed but the trolley legs wouldn't fold because of the weight, until yet another neighbour came round to help. Good job I was semi-conscious or I'd have died of humiliation. They eventually got me in, except my feet hung over the end of the trolley and my head hung over the top. They had to fold me up like a concertina before they could close the doors. At the hospital they said I was lucky to have such a thick head."

"Is he delirious?" Olivia asked Mark. "*Should* we call an ambulance, just in case?"

"No," Brian said, "I'll be fine, I'm just traumatised." He turned to Chelsea. "I would not," he said, and she visibly braced herself, "recommend the electric bike tour to future campsite visitors unless you have extremely good liability insurance and some very fit campers who've had some military training."

"No," said Chelsea, pausing a beat before adding, "You're not going to sue us, are you?"

Brian shook his head. "No, of course not. I will, however, take another shot of that very fine whisky."

"Brian!"

"Silence, lass, I've looked death in the face, I *deserve it.*"

* * *

They helped Brian stagger back to his caravan – straight through the two lines of hedges, Mark noted. They lowered him onto a lounger and Faye padded him out with a variety of cushions. She tried to throw a blanket over him, it was what you did with sick people at the care home, but Brian cried, "It's nearly ninety degrees, woman!"

"Alright, there's no need to snap."

"Sorry, I'm just in a great deal of pain."

She dashed back into the caravan to get paracetamol.

They stood around him, looking at his ever-darkening bruises, including a spectacular black eye and two purple knees.

"Great advertisement for the bike tour," Mark laughed.

"Beat up hobo in bare feet," Jim laughed.

"Who looks like he's been run over by several trucks," Tel added.

"Leave him alone," Faye said, handing him tablets and a glass of water, then hugging his big head, "Poor baby."

Brian wriggled his eyebrows at them and grinned. "I could get used to being pampered. Bring me my coolbox, wife, I'm dehydrated and in need of a cool drink."

"I've got some ice cubes in the microscopic freezer, I'll do you a nice glass of orange juice."

"With a shot of vodka in it, for the shock."

"It's barely midday!"

"It's five o'clock somewhere."

Tel glanced at his watch, then at Sophie. "You know, we might be able to do the route in less than two hours."

Sophie immediately jumped to her feet and started running through the hedge. "Race you!"

Tel leapt up and bolted through the hedge after her.

"Oi!" Mark cried, "Mind my hedges! Oh, Liv?"

"Come on!" she cried, giving chase, "We can take them!"

"I didn't realise you were so competitive," he laughed, trotting through the hedge after her.

"*Come on!*"

"Hey, wait for me!" Jim yelled, "You're not leaving me behind again!"

Suddenly there was silence, except for the birds, the gentle breeze rustling through the trees, children playing, dogs panting, a radio, the sound of someone playing tennis on the camping field, and a child in the shower block screaming absolute blue murder to the sound of running water.

* * *

"So, where are they?" Callum asked Chelsea.

"I don't know."

"What time did they leave?"

"About midday."

"And now it's ..." Callum checked his watch for the tenth time in as many minutes, "... half-past two."

"Yes. I've tried calling Liv but there's no answer. I got the big bloke to call Tel, the only one with a phone, apparently, but he didn't answer either."

"So, where are they?"

CHAPTER 11

"Where are we?"

Tel looked at the laminated map, squinting in the bright sun. Sweat drizzled from beneath his helmet and into his eyes. He turned the map upside-down and it still made no sense.

"Maybe we should have turned left at the crossroads back there?" Mark said, leaning forward to rest against the handlebars, panting. "Each turn seems to take us down a narrower lane. Are you sure we're not just going round in circles?"

"You do know how to read a map, don't you?" Jim asked.

"Yes, of course!"

"So how come we're not back at the campsite yet?"

"Because this isn't a *map*, it's a line drawing with no points of reference on it! It's literally a squiggly circle with some random lines coming off it."

"We'll come across civilisation at some point," Sophie said, pausing for a beat before adding, "Won't we?"

Tel turned the map around again. None of it made sense. "I think we should carry on."

"We've *been* carrying on," Mark snapped, "We haven't seen another living soul for over an hour, and I might die from heat exhaustion at any minute."

"No cars either," Jim said, looking around, "Bit worrying."

"It's a weekday," Tel said, "That's why it's so quiet."

"Or maybe these roads haven't seen traffic since the horse-drawn days," Mark gasped. He could no longer feel his buttocks, and his knees were absolutely killing him. He was just a giant bag of sweat and aching muscles, and the sun was boiling his brains under the stupid helmet. Next to him, Olivia looked equally knackered; still lovely, though, utterly lovely.

"We should carry on."

"Yeah, no point turning back," Mark scoffed, "We don't know where we've been, where we are now, or how we get back. Let's just carry on and see what happens, maybe we'll get lucky and come across some rednecks who are willing to *put us out of our misery*!"

"I think I read a Stephen King story like this once," Jim said, "Only they didn't have bikes, they were walking."

"You *read* something?" Mark gasped.

"How did that end?" Sophie dared to ask.

"I think they all died. I can't remember now."

"Helpful."

"I was just saying."

"Say less," said Mark.

"Are you okay, darling?"

"Bit thirsty, is there any more water left?"

"No, I'm afraid we drank all the water when we stopped for a picnic with the packed lunches."

"About a thousand miles ago," Jim said, running a hand down his dripping face, "When we were happy and didn't know about the horrors that lay ahead. Do you think they'll eventually find our bodies?"

"Shut up, Jim."

"Come on," Tel said, "Let's see what's round the corner."

"Probably another corner and another narrow lane."

Tel set off. He was trying to be calm for the others, but inside he did wonder if they'd gone through some kind of time warp into another dimension, it was unnatural and a bit alarming to see no houses or cars at all – the countryside was unnervingly quiet and seemingly endless.

"Oh," Mark said, looking down at his handlebars, "My battery's run out."

Jim tried his and lurched forward. "Mine still works. Maybe yours has run out because you're so fat."

"I'm not fat!"

"He's not fat," Olivia said. "You're not fat, darling, you're just well padded."

"Heavily padded with an exhausted battery."

Up ahead, Tel stopped at the side of the road and turned in his seat. "Are you lot coming?"

"What choice do we have?" Jim said, cycling off, followed by Sophie.

Mark started to pedal without electrical assistance. After a few turns of the pedals he stopped and pulled a face. "Hard and heavy to cycle without the battery," he said, "And, of course, it would be uphill. You go with them, Liv, I'll walk back."

"No, I'm staying with you, we've spent too much time apart already."

"Are you sure?"

"Yes, darling."

"We'll catch you up!" Mark yelled. He got off his bike and started pushing. Olivia did the same. They were both stiff and tired and hot, very, very hot. The others nodded and quickly disappeared round the bend.

"The electric bike man was right," Mark breathed, "It is very peaceful. Fancy a quick snog?"

"Ooh, yes please."

* * *

"So, where are they?"

They all turned in their seats to stare off down the hill they'd just pedalled up. Nothing.

"They're not going to like pushing their bikes up this hill," Sophie said, "It was bad enough on dwindling battery power."

"I can hear something?" Jim said.

"Your brain bubbling from the heat?" Tel asked, feeling the top of his hot helmet.

"No, I hear cars."

They all looked ahead. Another bend in yet another

narrow lane. They quickly cycled on. There was a road beyond, a proper road with proper traffic. Jim let out a whoop of joy and cycled straight into it. A car blew its horn as it veered around him, missing him by millimetres. "Good to see you, too!" he called after it.

"Come on," Tel said, merging less dramatically into the road, "There's a sign ahead. We'll be home soon."

When Sophie didn't answer, he stopped and turned. She was still on the side road, pointing at her handlebars.

Her battery had run out.

* * *

"Which way do you think they went?"

Mark and Olivia were at a crossroads. All three lanes looked narrower than the one they were on. There was nothing around them except vast yellow fields and hedges. They felt very lost, and hot.

Mark looked at the ground, hoping to see wheel ruts in the dirt. There were none. There was, however, something even better. A paper bag fluttered underneath a stone at the side of the lane straight ahead, the same lunch bag they'd been given at the pub.

"How lovely," Olivia said, "They've left us markers."

They trudged on.

* * *

Three knackered cyclists strenuously pedalled dead electric bikes down the side of the dual carriageway, following the signs to WOODSTOCK 5 MILES. A van pulled up in front of them and screeched to a halt. Callum and John jumped out, both looking more than a little peeved.

"Uh-oh," said Jim, "We're in for it now."

"Where have you been?" Callum raged. "We've been searching for you for over an hour!"

"What the hell is *this*?" Tel snapped, taking the

laminated 'map' out of the wicker basket and shaking it in front of him, "It was about as useful as a kid's drawing!"

A lorry roared past, blasting its horn at the crowd at the side of the road.

"All our batteries ran out," Sophie said.

"I'm not surprised, they only last three hours and you've been gone for four and a half! Why didn't you call for assistance, or at least let us know where you were?"

"Dead phone," Jim said.

Callum huffed, "Get in."

They slowly and painfully pushed their bikes over to the van and John loaded them up. Then they got into the back and braced themselves against the walls.

"There's two missing," Callum said, "Where are they?"

Jim shrugged. "Your guess is as good as ours, mate."

"One of their batteries ran out first," Sophie said, "So we … left them. Sounds bad now I've said it out loud, doesn't it."

"They did insist."

"We should have stuck together, isn't that what all the survival guides say, to stick together and not leave anyone behind?"

"We'll find them, Soph."

"I hope so."

"There were a lot of yellow fields," Tel said to Callum, "Then we came to a big hill, and then onto this dual carriageway. We've been cycling for about twenty-five minutes, all of it uphill. Does that help?"

"I'm not familiar with this area," Callum snapped, "I'm not even sure if we're still in the Cotswolds."

"Chelsea might know," Jim said, "Ring her, or Melissa, she's a local."

"You're not completely useless then, you've got …" Tel did air quotes with his fingers, "contacts."

Jim flipped him the bird, then said, "Sorry, Sophie."

"That's okay, I've seen fingers before."

Callum stood on the grass verge talking to Chelsea on

the phone. Sophie looked at Tel and said, "We will find them, won't we? You don't think anything's happened to them, do you?"

"They'll be fine," Tel said, patting her hand and hoping he was right.

Callum came back to the van door and said, "I've got a probable ten-mile radius to search."

"Please find them," Sophie said.

"We will. Those bikes are expensive."

* * *

The van was scratching its way down a narrow lane when they saw them, sitting on a wooden fence with their bikes lying on the grass in front of them. They slithered off with some effort when the van stopped and hobbled over to it. The side door opened and Jim slowly got out, followed by the others, all bent and groaning. They hugged weakly.

Mark gasped, "Water! Has anyone got any water?"

"No," Tel said, licking his dry lips.

"I'm so glad we found you," Sophie cried.

"So am I," Callum said, loading up their bikes, "Bloody expensive, these are."

"Yes, so you've said, repeatedly."

They all groaned their way into the back of the van.

By the time they reached the campsite they were as stiff as boards. Chelsea came running out of the pub, crying, "Oh thank God! I was so worried!"

"Water!" Mark gasped, and Chelsea mimed 'drink' through the window at Sue, the barmaid.

Tel and Sophie staggered to a wooden picnic bench, both surprised they weren't as fit as they thought they were. Olivia groaned with each step she took, and Mark's knees were just pulsing points of pain. Jim seemed alright.

Sue came out with a tray of glasses filled with iced water. Mark grabbed one and drank it down in one. The others slurped thirstily. Sue went back for more.

"If there's any damage to the bikes I'll have to charge you," Callum snapped.

"It was your stupid map!" Tel snapped back. "It made no sense at all! If anything, I should charge you for pain and suffering. I'm a lawyer, you know."

"We said we'd never do that," Sophie whispered to him, "Use our jobs to threaten people."

Callum looked taken aback. "Like I said, it was a last-minute booking and I did the best I could under the time constraints."

"I *told* you to photocopy a map and highlight the route," John said.

"Shut up, John."

Jim nodded at him, kindred souls.

"Thank you for saving our lives," Olivia said, shifting tentatively on the wooden seat.

"He put our lives in danger!" Tel said, "It's all his fault! I could sue you!"

Callum's eyes widened and his mouth fell open.

Sophie whispered, "Bit extreme, don't you think? It is only the Cotswolds, not the middle of the Australian desert. We were never in any real danger."

Tel dropped his head. "I'm just tired and everything aches. Extortionate gym fees seem a waste now if we can't do a simple bike ride."

"Simple?" Mark snorted, "It was like a triathlon!"

"I think the bikes are alright anyway."

"Except for the reinforced Bosch the big bloke was riding," said Callum, looking down at it, "The pedal's bent and the paint's chipped."

"A bit like my coccyx," Mark said, wincing. "I think my bum cheeks have actually fallen off somewhere."

"I can't feel my bum at all," Olivia groaned.

"I'll massage it back to life for you," Mark winked, and she flushed.

When the bikes were loaded, Callum and John jumped into the van and drove off, glaring at them all through the window as they passed.

"I need a shower," Sophie said, standing up and groaning.

"Me too."

"Me three."

"I wouldn't recommend it, Chelsea," Tel said, staggering off.

"Worst experience of my life," Mark added, "I may never ride a bike again."

* * *

Brian, lounging in a lounger, burst out laughing when they hobbled down the driveway. "Where the hell have you lot been?" he howled.

"Oh, you know, touring the scenic countryside." Mark shrugged, instantly regretting it as pain shot across his shoulders, "Taking in the sights and listening to the birds singing in the *endless bloody trees*!"

"Enjoyed it, then?"

"No."

"It was torture."

"Never again."

"I quite liked it," Olivia said brightly, "It was only the last two hours that were an excruciating nightmare."

Faye came running out of the caravan, immediately opening and arranging chairs on the grass for them. "He hasn't moved all day," she said, nodding her head towards Brian. "Here, sit yourselves down, I'll bring you something cold to drink."

"We need a shower first," Sophie said, limping towards their caravan, "We're just human-shaped balls of sweat and misery."

"Bri," Mark said, peering down at him, "Why are you

green all down one side?"

"It was the wife. Stinger rash was killing me, even after I struggled to have a shower, so Faye ran off into the woods and brought back a huge bouquet of dock leaves, insisted on rubbing them into the side of my face, one arm and a leg. It was quite pleasant, actually, like half a massage."

"You look like the Incredible Hulk," Olivia laughed, as she followed Mark to the motorhome.

As she closed the door behind her, she dialled a number on her phone and said, "I have an idea."

* * *

Washed and marginally refreshed, they slowly regrouped like the merging of zombies outside Brian and Faye's caravan.

"Well, would you look at the time!" Brian announced, "Five o'clock already! Jim, bring me my coolbox."

"Can I have one if I do?"

"Yes, help yourself, then fill it up from the back of the car."

"Exactly how much beer have you brought?" Faye asked.

"Never you mind, woman. I don't ask about the contents of your handbag and you don't ask about the contents of my car, it's an unwritten rule."

"From your Little Book of Men's Answers?" Mark laughed.

"Absolutely." He dropped an arm over his lounger, took cans one by one out of the coolbox and handed them out. The women popped corks on a couple of bottles of prosecco.

"Jim."

"What?"

"Do your thing."

"What thing?"

"Memory of a goldfish," Mark tutted.

"Fill 'er up, lad."

Jim dragged the coolbox to the back of Brian's car and opened up the boot. "Can't see any cans, Bri."

"They're ..." He glanced at his wife, who raised a questioning eyebrow. "They're under the canvas sheet."

"Got 'em. Blimey!" he cried.

"What?" said Faye.

"Say nothing, Jim, or I may be in big trouble."

Faye got up and marched over to the car. Brian shouted, "Shut the boot, Jim! Shut the boot!"

Jim slammed the boot shut. Faye opened it again, looked inside, and shouted, "Brian!"

"For emergency purposes only."

"What emergency requires you to have eight cases of beer in the car? And there's twelve cans in each box! That's ..."

"Ninety-six," Brian muttered under his breath, as the others stifled giggles.

"That's ..."

"Ninety-six," he mumbled again.

"That's a lot of cans, Brian."

"Yes, dear. Shall we count how many cushions and blankets you have in the caravan now?"

She gave him the evil eye as she stormed back and threw herself down into her lounger. He reached out and patted her hand. She tried not to smile.

"We're okay for beer then," Jim grinned, dragging the filled coolbox back.

"You will be expected to contribute towards said stash at some point," Brian said.

"Yeah, yeah."

"Yeah," Mark said firmly.

"So, tell me about this scenic little trip then?" said Brian.

They did, and his howling laughter echoed across the campsite.

* * *

A small red car came down the driveway and pulled onto the grass right next to them. Chelsea got out.

"Bit lazy!" Jim laughed.

She winked at them, then went into Brian and Faye's awning and removed the halogen oven and Teppanyaki grill from the plastic camping table, placing them carefully on the groundsheet underneath. She lifted it up.

"You'd make a crap burglar," Brian shouted, "We can all see you, you haven't even *attempted* to camouflage yourself."

With a big smile, Chelsea carried the table over to them. "I thought," she said, placing it in the middle of their ragged circle, "You should rest after your exertions today, so I've brought you spicy sustenance."

"Ooh, lovely!"

Tel hurried to empty the other camping table and carry it over. They all 'oohed' as Chelsea opened up the boot of her car and pulled out a huge catering bowl covered in tin foil. "Basmati rice," she announced, setting it down on one table. She pulled out another bowl and said, "Hope you all like curry, it's the chef's special recipe, chicken, spinach and potato."

"Ooh!"

Brian drooled as he took the foil off the bowls. "Oh, it smells delicious!"

"Offended," Faye snapped.

"I apologise for my insensitivity, my little anosmiac. The aroma of herbs and spices in a rich creamy sauce is *divine*, shame you can smell it."

"Oh yeah," Tel laughed, "You can't smell, can you, Faye. Remember last year when you helped us with our toilet cassette?"

"Let's not revisit that scenario just before we eat a curry," Sophie said.

"Naan breads and poppadoms," Chelsea announced, putting down trays of both. "An assortment of dips, bhajis and samosas."

"Oh wow," Faye gasped, as the sound of rumbling tummies filled the air.

"Serving spoons, plates, cutlery, and two bottles of chilled prosecco, compliments of the management, who ask that you don't sue us."

"Perfect," Brian gasped.

"Are two bottles enough?" Chelsea frowned.

"Should be plenty," said Faye, "We've got our own stashes too."

"Exactly how many bottles of prosecco did you bring?" Brian asked pointedly.

"Enough," she grinned, "For emergency purposes only, like when we run out."

Faces peered over the hedge at them from the neighbouring caravan area. A man asked, "Can we order the same?"

"Of course," Chelsea beamed, "It's all available at the pub."

"You don't do deliveries?"

"They've got a delivery," someone whined.

"They're a special case," she told them, "They've been injured in the course of duty."

"We're special," Jim grinned.

"Special needs," Mark laughed.

"Will you stop picking on me?"

"You're so easy to pick on."

"It's getting a bit boring."

"Yes, you're right, I'll stop, at some point, around the time you actually buy some beer."

There was a lot of muttering from behind the hedge, and then the faces disappeared. Through the gaps in the hedge they saw a small crowd hurrying over to the pub, walking quickly, then breaking into a run in their haste to be the first to order at the bar.

"What a good idea!" Olivia said, and Brian noticed a look pass between her and Chelsea which he found intriguing. "A takeaway service for campers!"

"Put it in the suggestion box on the survey," Mark said.

"Yes, I will."

"And might I suggest," Brian drawled, "That you maybe have an electrified fence and coils of barbed wire erected around the whole campsite, with several armed guards in sentry towers to keep out marauders and rampaging motorbikes?"

"And soundproof domes to cover our caravans for when the snorer comes," someone shouted over the hedge.

Chelsea laughed and said, "We'll take all suggestions under careful consideration." She slammed her boot shut and stood at the end of the tables, giving a little cough to get their attention. "The management of The Woodsman pub apologises for the unfortunate series of events today. You'll be pleased to hear that we won't be offering the bike tour to any future campers, but we may," she said, nodding at Olivia, "be offering a takeaway service. We hope you enjoy your food, and if you need anything else just call me, Liv has my number. Bon appetite."

They thanked her and she climbed into her car and drove off.

"This reminds me of when we had that Indian takeaway last year," Olivia said.

Tel laughed. "Hope you're all well stocked up on toiletries."

"It's burned into my memory as well as burning my – "

"No toilet talk at the table," Faye swiftly cut in.

They all stared at their curry, forks poised.

"How hot do you think it is?" Mark asked.

"Doesn't smell especially spicy," Tel said, sniffing.

Sophie tentatively licked at the curry balanced on her fork and shrugged. "Hard to tell."

"I'll take one for the team," Brian said, pushing a forkful into his mouth. They all watched him chew. He rolled his eyes from side to side and declared, "It's *delicious*."

They all tucked in, passing bowls and spoons to each other.

"We're going to be so stiff tomorrow," Sophie said, "We'll hardly be able to move, and I go to the gym three times a week."

Brian – his sixth sense possibly heightened by heat stroke, or maybe stinger rash – noticed the way Tel quickly glanced at Olivia. He suspected they knew what plans Chelsea might have for them the next day but didn't dare ask, he wasn't sure he wanted to know.

"So," Tel said between mouthfuls, "What are we going to do if the scramblers come back again tonight?"

"I've had a few ideas," Brian said.

They discussed plans. When they'd finished, leaning back in their chairs as full as eggs, they got Jim to earn his beers by running around for them. He fetched things from the back of Brian's car, checked the contents of Mark's van, and opened the fridges in each of their mobile homes to do a quick count.

"How many?" Olivia asked, when he came back.

"Brian and Faye, eight. Tel and Sophie, nil points. Olivia, three, I think."

"Oh, I thought I had more than that."

"I'll check." He raced back to the motorhome. Olivia called after him, "Could you bring my phone out of the drawer at the front, in case we need to call Chelsea for anything?"

He came hurrying back. "Twelve," he puffed, handing Olivia her phone.

"So that's twenty altogether," Brian said.

"Well done," Faye giggled, stretching across the table to refill glasses.

"Yeah?" said Brian, "This from the woman who couldn't work out eight cases times twelve cans?"

She gave him a droll look.

"Will twenty be enough?" Tel asked.

"It'll have to be."

"Jim, nip to the shop and get some more."

"I'm skint," he whined.

Mark huffed, and was about to reach into his jeans pocket for his wallet when Olivia gasped out loud. "It's been in the drawer," she said, frantically flicking at the screen on her phone, "I haven't looked at it since ... Sunday! 74 messages and 105 missed calls."

"Who from?" Sophie asked.

"Daddy. They're all from daddy. He's ..." Olivia scrolled through the messages, her cute, overbite smile fading with anxiety. Mark put an arm across her shoulders and peered at the screen. "He's furious, absolutely furious. He said ... he said they're both staying in the village until I come to my senses. They're still in the village!"

"We saw them yesterday," Faye said, glancing at Brian.

"Don't you worry about them, Liv," he boomed. "They won't try anything while we're here."

"And your lawyers will be on the case by the time we're not," Tel said.

Olivia held the phone out to Mark and he took it, started reading out the messages. "Call me. Call me right this instant. Call me when you get this. Olivia, I will not be disobeyed, call me immediately. Olivia, I need to speak to you urgently. You MUST – capital letters – call me. Call me, call me, call me ..." Mark scrolled through them quickly, his face hardening. "They start to get a bit nasty after that."

Olivia took the phone off him. "You will not win this," she read in a tiny voice. "I will make you pay for ignoring me. You will regret treating your father in this despicable manner." Tears stung her eyes and she couldn't read anymore. Mark took it from her and looked through them silently.

"He can't do this to you," Sophie said, "You should contact your lawyer and arrange to get an injunction to stop your father from harassing you. Call them first thing in the morning. You have to do this, Liv."

Olivia nodded her head. "It's a fair settlement. Mummy and I wanted to be fair and our lawyers said we were being more than generous."

"Some people are just never satisfied," Sophie soothed, as Faye squeezed her hand. "They'll always want more. You can't give in to them, Liv. You have to draw the line."

Mark pulled her close to him, still reading through the texts.

"Spoilt, is what they are," Tel said. "They've had it good for so long, I don't think either of them like losing control."

"I know a bloke who'd be willing to take their kneecaps off," Jim said, "I could get in touch and – "

"No," Olivia sniffed, wiping her eyes. "They just need time to get used to the idea that they can't bully us anymore."

"Christ," Mark said.

"What is it?" Olivia leaned over, trying to read the screen.

"I've deleted them," he said, "You don't need to read stuff like that."

She looked at him in horror for a second, and then nodded. "You're right, he can be really horrible when he's angry. He once threatened to shoot our dog when mummy upset him once."

Mark looked at Brian with wide eyes as he passed the phone back. Sophie went to stand up and made a pained noise.

"It's okay," Olivia said, forcing a smile, "I can feel your hug from here. I can feel all your hugs. I'm very lucky to have you as my friends."

"We love you, Liv, but we can't do anything except advise you. Only you can stop this."

"I know."

"First thing in the morning?"

"Yes."

There were long moments of silence, broken only when Jim said, "So, do you want me to go to the shop then?"

He went, while the women cleared the tables and put everything in the back of Brian's car. Faye drove it up to the pub, helped unload it, and drove back again, pulling up just as Jim was getting back from the shop with the eggs and Brian was saying, "I can hold it no longer, lad, I need your assistance in getting t'toilet."

"Why me?" he asked, handing the eggs to Olivia.

"You're the only one who's unaffected by today's events."

"Lucky me. Here, use this instead." Jim picked up an empty bottle of prosecco and handed it to him.

Brian looked at it and drawled, "And what do you expect me to do with *this*?"

"You know," Jim said with a wink, "Think of it as a posh bed pan."

"Have you seen the aperture on the thing?"

"The what?"

"The hole," Mark said, "The mouth."

"Mouth?"

"And you wonder why I make fun of you!"

Jim looked at the bottle and said, "Oh, you don't have to put it *in*."

"In?" said Brian, as Mark exploded with laughter and Faye sucked her lips in to stifle hers. Sophie was literally crying.

"Yeah, you know, just hold it near the 'mouth'."

"Stop it!" cried Tel, "You're making my aches ache."

Brian remained stone-faced. Jim huffed and stood up, took one giant arm while Mark took the other, and together they hauled him out of the lounger, into the caravan, waited outside for a bit until Brian had finished, then helped him back again. He groaned the entire time.

"Are we all set for tonight then, if the bikes come back?" Tel asked.

"Rigor mortis might hinder us a bit," Mark said, "But yeah, I think so."

"Should I go through it again?"

"No, we've got it."

"What am I supposed to do again?" Jim asked.

They all sighed. "Weren't you listening?"

"Yeah. Well, no, I was texting Beth."
Tel went through the plan again. "Clear?"
Jim nodded.
They were ready.

CHAPTER 12

Day 6: Early hours of Wednesday morning

None of them could sleep that night, each of them lying painfully and pensively in bed, waiting for the bikes to come.

Faye had just started drifting off when she suddenly sat bolt upright in bed. "FLO!" she cried.

Brian shot up next to her. "Where?"

"No," Faye cried, "She's not here, and I don't remember Bill's car coming back either, do you?"

"He probably stayed over."

"Flo doesn't have *men* staying over."

"Well, he's quite a *safe* man, if you think about it."

"Not if he's a thief or a fraudster who just wants to get his hands on her savings, he's not."

Faye scrambled off the bed and lifted the back window blind. It was too dark to see if Bill's car was outside his caravan, so she slipped into the awning, unzipped it, and looked over the hedge. "It's not there," she whispered back to Brian, now standing in the doorway in jeans and t-shirt, ready to do battle at a moment's notice. "She hasn't rung me either to say she got home safely and I asked her to. I asked her to call me, didn't I?"

"I'm too tired to remember."

"Oh Brian, do you think something's happened?"

"No."

"You don't know that! They could have had an accident on the way back. He could have kidnapped her. He seemed nice but maybe – "

"Faye, stop panicking."

Faye shook her hands in front of her, fighting off the rising panic. "I'll call her," she said.

"Yeah, I'm sure she'll appreciate being woke up at – " Brian glanced at his wrist, but he'd taken his watch off. He tried to look at the clock on the wall above the TV set, but it was too dark to see. He picked his phone up but it was dead, he'd meant to put it on charge earlier but forgot about it. "Late," he said.

Faye squeezed passed to snatch up her phone and dialled Flo. She held it anxiously to her ear as it rang out. "There's no answer," she whimpered, "She's not answering. Oh Brian, what shall - ? Oh, Flo! You're alive! Yes, I know it's late, sorry, I just suddenly started worrying about you and if you got home okay. You did? He did? Is it? No, as long as you're okay, and Bill's sleeping on the sofa, is he? Oh good. I have to go, Brian's tapping on the back of his wrist and looking at me funny. Talk soon. Love you, bye."

"Can we possibly get some sleep now?"

"Yes," she beamed, clambering back into the caravan and slipping under the duvet, "I can sleep now."

"Oh good."

Brian climbed back into bed, lay on his back, arranged his pillows behind his head, and was just about to drift off into blissful unconsciousness when he heard them. The scramblers. Approaching down the lane, getting louder and closer.

Groaning, he crawled down the bed, Faye crawling next to him.

"Be careful," she said, following him outside.

They all met on the driveway, just as the bikes screamed across the pub car park and through the entrance gate to the campsite. Air horns started almost immediately, along with the laughter and the kicking of tent lines. Brian picked up a baseball bat from the table in the awning. Mark raced to the back of his van and handed a hoe to Tel, taking out a broom and a length of rope.

"Where the hell is Jim?" Mark cried above the noise.

Three bikes came screaming straight into the caravan

area, skidding along the driveway and showering them all with stones. Brian immediately started swinging at the tyres like a giant wielding a club, missing them all. He tried running after them, then stopped, realising his back was frozen and his arms were killing him.

At the water tap end, Mark and Tel turned as one from the back of the van and started jabbing at the tyres and the riders with their wooden poles ("Try not to kill anyone," Brian had said earlier). The bikes spun round and round in front of them, peppering them with stones and laughing. They started spinning on Olivia's pitch, spraying her motorhome again. She peered through the window looking terrified. Mark was spurred into action, screaming out loud as he raised his pole in the air and brought it down hard on a helmet. The rider looked round in surprise, and Mark swung at the helmet again, so hard it broke the handle. The biker roared off. Mark dashed back to his van for a spade. Tel tried to hit them but mostly just jumped out of the way as they careered towards him.

Brian was trying to get close enough to maim a tyre but was held back by the spinning wheels. Tel was jabbing like a swordsman on speed but didn't even come close to making contact.

"Pretend it's shorter than it is!" Brian yelled at him, and Tel stepped forward but still couldn't hit anything, as the bikes spun round in front of them all.

One rider threw out an arm and they all skidded off towards the entrance of the caravan area. The three men ran after them, Mark shouting, "Jim! Jim!" as they passed the shepherd's hut. The bikes spun round at the entrance, facing in, revving their engines. Just as the men reached them and started raising their weapons, the bikes roared down to the motorhome again, where they stopped, each rider unzipping their leather jackets and pulling out what looked like white tomato sauce squeezy bottles. They popped the lids as the three men ran towards them and quickly squirted the contents of the bottles at the motorhome. White goo oozed down the windows and side panel. When the bottles stopped squirting the riders tossed them aside.

Olivia threw open the door and stood there with an open box of eggs in one hand. She quickly started lobbing them one by one at the bikers, shouting, "Leave … us … alone!" with each egg. She had a good aim. One struck the front of a helmet and the rider had to lift up his visor. Mark, rushing up with his spade, only caught a brief glimpse of the face beneath, not enough to identify him in a line-up.

Tel cracked the hoe handle down on a leather-clad back. Brian charged with his baseball bat, hollering like a madman. Olivia continued to lob eggs, screaming, "Get away from my motorhome!"

"Bloody 'ell!" the egged biker cried, spying two more women racing towards them with egg boxes, "Bloody nutters! Let's get outta here!"

The bikes roared off. The trio lumbered up the driveway after them. The women ran through the hedges towards the entrance gate.

"JIM!" Mark yelled, as they ran past his hut, "JIM!"

"JIM!" Brian bellowed, and inside the shepherd's hut they heard Jim scream out in alarm. "GET OUT HERE, NOW!"

"Christ!" Mark gasped, "That's some gob you've got on you there, Bri."

"I work in a steelworks, you have to shout to be heard."

"I think my eardrums have exploded," Tel said.

"JIM!"

Jim fell out of the shepherd's hut door wearing nothing but a very small pair of briefs. His eyes were wide but clearly not focusing. "What?" he cried, scrambling unsteadily to his feet.

"What do you think?" Mark shouted as he ran, "Bloody bikes, you moron!"

"Oh." Jim reached inside his wooden box and pulled on his jeans. "Yeah, ready."

"Here." Mark threw the length of rope at him.

The scramblers rampaged across the field, kicking out at tents and barbecues, howling with laughter and blowing the air horns. Children screamed. Men shouted. Women got all high-pitched with panic.

Jim ran a hand through his untidy hair as he looked down at the rope on the ground in front of him. "What was I supposed to do again?"

Mark swore, before following Brian and Tel as they raced onto the field. A group of campers were scrambling out of their tents with cricket bats and poles and, worryingly, peg mallets and wheel braces. Brian had a horrible feeling that things could easily get out of hand. He glanced over his shoulder. Jim was meandering out of the caravan area.

"HURRY UP!"

Jim jumped and hurried towards the now closed gate, where the women stood with their egg boxes, looking ready.

"ROUND THEM UP LIKE SHEEP!" Brian

bawled at all the people bearing weapons on the field, "EVERYBODY ON THE LEFT AND WORK YOUR WAY RIGHT! DON'T LET THEM PAST YOU."

The bikers, seeing the crowd gathering on the left side and herding them like a pack of sheepdogs, stopped blowing their airhorns. As one, they took off towards the entrance, where Jim was slowly tying the rope around the gate and the post so it couldn't be opened, and the women stood ready with their boxes of eggs.

Brian, Mark and Tel ran towards the gate. People raced across the field and came out of the other caravan area. There were at least thirty people chasing after them as the scramblers scrambled for the exit.

Olivia led the egg-throwing with excellent arm throws, hitting bikers as they roared up towards her, not flinching from her position as they got closer and closer. Sophie and Faye were less accurate but made up for it with pumped-up enthusiasm. The bikers were hit over and over again the closer they got. They lifted their egg-smeared visors to see and pulled back the throttles as they sped towards the gate.

Jim had almost tied a second knot in the rope when, through the mayhem, he heard a car start up on the car park behind him. Turning, he saw a car lurch towards him and the women. It hit the gate, unravelling the rope and breaking the latch. It swung open with some force and the women had to jump out of the way. The car skidded to a stop, holding the gate open. The women threw the last of their eggs at the windscreen. The wipers came on, smearing the eggs across the glass. The bikers filed through the narrow gap, across the car park, and out onto the lane.

The car reversed. Mark lunged at the driver's door and pulled it open. Behind the wheel sat a skinny bloke wearing a peaked cap and a blue Covid face mask. Mark grabbed the sleeve of his jacket, intending to pull him out and give him a good slap, when the face looked up at him. He'd seen those eyes before, though not quite as wide and as terrified as they were now.

"Danny?" he gasped.

The driver frantically pulled the door out of his hands and slammed it shut, reversing furiously and spinning the car round until he faced the right direction, then gunning it out of the car park, windscreen wipers still on. A few seconds later they heard a dull thud, like an egg-blinded car hitting a tree. Tel ran out onto the lane just in time to see the car reversing away from a tree and roaring off.

A crowd of campers gathered in the car park, looking angry and frustrated.

"ANYBODY HURT?" Brian yelled.

There was no answer, just a lot of puffing and panting.

"Is everyone accounted for?"

Again, no answer, just a lot of swearing and testosterone talk.

Mark stood there, looking shocked.

"You okay, Mark?"

He turned to look up at Brian and said, "I know him. I know the kid driving the car."

* * *

The police came again. Mark gave a statement, including the name and address of the driver. They said they'd look into it.

"It was a kid called Danny in the car," Mark said, as they slowly made their way back to the caravans. "He lives with his mom and dad at the pub in the village and works at my nursery on Saturdays. I asked him to do Sundays once and he said he couldn't because he did *motocross* on Sundays on his *dirt bike*."

"Maybe we should pay him a little visit," Jim said.

Faye shook her head. "Leave it to the police."

"He's only nineteen," Mark continued, "Good kid, would never have dreamt he was capable of something like this." He stopped dead at the entrance to the caravan area. "Oh Liv," he sighed.

Olivia's motorhome was dripping down one side with a white substance.

"The buggers!" she snapped, running up to it and touching the white stuff with a finger. "Paint! They squirted my motorhome with *paint*!"

Brian touched it and rubbed it between finger and thumb, giving it a quick sniff. "Get the hosepipe," he said to Mark.

"Paint won't come off with water, Bri."

"I think it's emulsion."

Mark dashed for the hosepipe, fixed it to the tap, turned

the water on and dragged it over, spraying the side of the motorhome. The paint washed off in white waves. Faye hurried over with a soft broom and started rubbing at the windows.

"Oh, thank goodness," Olivia cried, rubbing at the door with a short-handled brush, as Faye did broad strokes with her broom and Mark aimed the jet of water.

Brian suddenly leapt in front of Faye with his arms wide and boomed, "Nobody look at my wife!"

Everyone looked at Faye, furiously brushing at the motorhome in her cotton nightie. She spotted them staring at her and said, "What?"

Brian stood with his arms outstretched. "Gorgeous woman," he said, peering down at her, "Do you remember the picture of Princess Diana holding a child on her hip with the sunlight shining through her skirt?"

"What's that got to do with anything? Why are you talking to me about Princess Diana, can't you see I'm busy?"

"You're *drenched*," he said.

She shook her head. "I'm washing down a motorhome!"

"Your thin, cotton nightie is *soaking wet*."

"Because I'm washing down a motorhome!"

Sophie said, "Your nightie's *clingy*, Faye."

Faye looked down at the nightie, now transparent where it was glued to her body, and screamed. Dropping the broom, she threw one arm across her chest and one hand down in front of her. The hand moved to the back as she turned and bolted for the caravan, with Brian sidestepping next to her, his arms still outstretched.

"I didn't look," Tel said, to no one in particular.

"Me neither," said Mark.

"I did," Jim shrugged. "Am I doomed now?"

"Probably."

"Shut up."

"Good figure for a woman of her age," Sophie said.

"I think it's all off," Olivia said, brushing back her

curly hair with a wet wrist as she surveyed the side of her motorhome.

"We'll be able to see better in the morning." Mark dragged the hosepipe back and turned off the water.

"Wonder why they picked on Liv's motorhome in particular," Tel said, frowning.

"I don't think they attacked anyone else's caravan." Sophie glanced over the hedge at the others but couldn't see much in the dark.

Mark looked at Olivia. "You don't think …?"

"No, no, he wouldn't. He couldn't. Could he?"

"Who wouldn't or couldn't?" asked Tel.

"Her dad."

"Or Richard," Olivia said, looking worried.

"Or both," said Jim.

"You definitely need to call your lawyer in the morning and tell them," Sophie said.

"I will, I will."

Brian ambled back. "Faye says she's mortally embarrassed and will never be able to face any of you again. She sends her love and says it was lovely knowing you."

"You've got nothing to be ashamed of," Sophie yelled at the caravan.

"I didn't see a thing," Tel shouted.

"Me neither," said Mark.

Jim said nothing.

"Liars, the lot of you," came Faye's muffled cry.

"Don't you think we've suffered enough for one night?" came a man's voice from over the hedge. "I'd like to get *some* sleep on my holiday!"

"YEAH, SHURRUP!"

Brian pulled a face and whispered, "See you in the morning."

They sloped off to their beds.

* * *

"You okay?" Mark asked.

Olivia snuggled up to him in bed. "I think so."

"Do you think it was them who instigated this, your dad and Richard?"

"I don't know. I guess we'll find out eventually."

"Trying to terrorise you!" he growled. "Still trying to bully you! Makes my blood boil. Who do they think they are?"

"They're just angry."

"Stop making excuses for them, Liv. If it is them, what they're doing is inexcusable."

"I guess I'm more used to it than you are."

"Get unused to it, you'll never be treated like that again, not while I'm around."

"My hero," she said, raising her head to kiss his cheek. "I don't need protecting, I just need to toughen up a bit."

"I'll look after you." He held her tight in his arms.

"I don't need looking after." She heard him huff and added, "I could incapacitate you with one finger." She held up a finger. "One finger."

"I doubt that," he laughed.

"You don't think so?"

"I know so."

She lowered her finger and prodded him in his side. He cried out and started laughing, and she did it again, and again. "No, stop! Stop! You know I'm ticklish."

"One finger," she laughed, prodding him as he writhed for escape across the bed.

The finger followed.

* * *

Sunlight woke Sophie. She stretched out in bed and realised Tel wasn't there. She lifted her head but couldn't see him inside the caravan. She sat up and peered through the window. He was outside on the driveway, talking to Olivia.

She made coffee.

* * *

"I can't go out there and face them after … after last night."

"Of course you can."

"I can't, Bri! I was practically naked!"

"No, you weren't."

"I was!"

"Your nightie was a bit clingy is all."

"It was *see-through*!"

"It wasn't."

"I was virtually standing there stark naked in front of everyone! I'll never live it down. I'm mortified. I'm not going out there."

"Pull yourself together, woman, nobody saw anything. What are you going to do, stay inside the caravan until it's time to go home?"

"Yes."

"Don't be silly. Nobody will care. They're our friends, they won't say anything."

"They might not say anything but they'll *know*, Brian, and I'll know they'll know. I can't face them, I just can't."

"You can, and you will."

* * *

"Is everything ready?" Tel whispered to Olivia, out on the driveway.

"Yes."

"Are you sure?"

"If you ask me that one more time I may have to rugby tackle you to the ground and put you in an arm lock. Don't think I can't, I've had self-defence lessons."

"Okay, if you're sure."

"I'm sure. What time do you have to be there?"

"Eleven o'clock." He glanced at his Rolex. "Better get a

move on."

"Everything will be ready by the time you *arrive*."

Tel grinned, then stop grinning. "I hope it goes okay. I can think of a million different ways it could go wrong, death being one of them."

"Stop worrying, it'll be fine."

"I've never done it before. Sophie's always wanted to, I'm hoping she'll be impressed, not furious or terrified. Oh," he groaned, "My stomach's in knots. I think I'm going to be sick."

"Just stay calm and focus on the end goal."

He nodded, his face hanging with anxiety as he shuffled nervously from one foot to the other, rubbing his sweaty palms together.

"Mummy and I did it in … oh, can't remember where now, but we loved it. If we can do it, you certainly can. Good luck."

"Thanks, I think I'm going to need it."

"We'll be here when you *get back*."

"Thanks for doing this, Liv."

"It's totally my pleasure." She clapped her hands together. "Oh, it's so exciting!"

"Petrifying. Horrifying. I wish I'd never thought of it in the first place, what was I thinking?"

"Go on, you don't want to be late."

* * *

"What were you two scheming about?" Sophie smirked when he came in. "I saw you out there, whispering to each other in a conspiratorial way."

"Oh, nothing."

"Didn't look like nothing to me."

"Liv's just … helping me with something."

She handed him a mug of coffee. "Helping you with what?"

"Oh, just something."

"Something that makes you this nervous?" She noticed he couldn't keep still, leaning against a counter, then unleaning and leaning again, all the while shifting his feet and rubbing his palms together. "Now I'm worried. Didn't you conspire with Liv about coming here on Saturday? And your 'surprise' last year was a week spent in a tin can."

"That worked out well though, didn't it? We have our own caravan now."

"And very lovely it is too." She kissed his moist cheek. He was definitely nervous, which made her nervous. "So, what's the plan for today?"

"It's a surprise. You like surprises, don't you?"

"I like *nice* surprises, I like flowers and jewellery and chocolates, mostly jewellery, it has to be said. What's the surprise?"

"Well," he said, trying to smile and failing miserably, which worried her even more, "It wouldn't be a surprise if I told you, now would it?"

She gave him a side-eye, but decided not to interrogate him further. She did like surprises, although not ones that made her normally calm boyfriend sweat so much. "Toast?" she asked, "Or a full English at the pub?"

"We'll grab some croissants on the way out."

"On the way out to where?"

He tapped the side of his nose and tried to laugh, but it came out dry and humourless, like a donkey with a cough. "You'll see." He glanced at his watch. "We have to leave."

"What, now?"

"Yes."

"I'll get dressed then."

She did, hoping that what lay ahead, wherever they were going, wasn't too terrible.

* * *

Olivia sat in front of her motorhome, waiting for Mark

to come back from the showers, when her phone rang. 'Daddy' came up on the screen. She hesitated before answering.

"Finally!" he snapped. "Are you ready to talk to me now?"

"I've said all I wanted to say, daddy."

"You've not changed your mind then?"

"About?"

He sighed impatiently. "About the divorce settlement, of course!"

In the background she heard Richard say, "And mine, too."

"Have you spoken to your mother yet?"

"No, I haven't, she's away."

"I know she's away! Call her and tell her I'm not the least bit happy about it."

"Me neither," Richard said, "I'm not happy either."

"Daddy, I don't want to talk about this anymore, and I certainly don't want to bother mummy with it. It was all agreed between the lawyers. Your lawyers sanctioned it."

"I never agreed to what's in that miserly, spiteful settlement. I want more, I *deserve* more. Call your mother immediately, get her to call me as soon as possible."

"No, daddy."

"No? You're little Miss High and Mighty now, aren't you, thinking you can do whatever you like."

"I *can* do whatever I like, daddy, I'm a grown up."

"Show me some respect!"

"I am, as much as I can."

"It's that farmer who's making you do this, isn't it. He wants the money all for himself."

"Mark isn't the least bit interested in my money."

Harry laughed nastily. "Oh Olivia, poor, naïve Olivia."

"Not everyone's like you and Richard."

"Aren't they?" A silence hung heavy between them, broken when Harry snapped, "Call your mother, we need to sit down and thrash this out."

"Thrash mummy, you mean? Browbeat her into submission, like you always did?"

"Watch your tone, Olivia!"

"I won't. I'm not calling mummy and I don't want to speak about this anymore. Just sign the papers, daddy."

"I'm not signing *that*! I never agreed to *that*!"

Olivia sighed and rubbed at her forehead.

Harry said, "I thought you would have changed your mind by now."

"Did you? Why?"

"Oh, I don't know, I just wondered if maybe something had happened to make you come to your senses."

Olivia sat up straight in her chair, suddenly alert. "What do you mean by 'something', daddy?"

"I said there'd be consequences to your actions, Olivia. You can't treat your father in this manner without there being repercussions."

"Are you threatening me, daddy?"

"No, no, not threatening, merely pointing out the obvious. For every action there is a reaction."

"Daddy." She took a deep breath and gulped hard. "Did you send the motorbikes?"

"Motorbikes? What motorbikes?" She could hear the grin in his voice. "I don't know anything about any motorbikes."

In the background she could hear Richard stifling a laugh. And she knew, she knew then, at that moment.

She stood up, angry, strong. "I'm calling my lawyer," she said.

"Good girl. I knew you'd come round in the end."

"I'm taking out an injunction against you to stop you contacting me, and then I'm calling the police."

"The police?" He gave a little laugh. "I haven't done anything, Olivia. I know nothing. And there's no proof, you have no proof."

"Goodbye, daddy."

She pressed the red button to end the call, and scrolled through her list of contacts.

* * *

"Are you alright, Liv? You look a bit pale."

Mark had come back from the showers wearing only a towel, a pile of clothes over one arm and a big smile, which vanished when he saw her sitting outside the motorhome looking upset.

"I've just spoken to daddy," she said.

"Oh, you shouldn't have answered."

It was a spur of the moment thing, despite feeling instantly guilty. She felt compelled to do it, not for herself – well, maybe a little bit for herself – but to prove a point; not that she had anything to prove, especially not to daddy, but nonetheless, she needed to know.

"I … I might lose all the money," she blurted quickly, as self-loathing washed over her. She felt cruel and deceitful, but she couldn't stop herself. "All of it, everything."

"You can fight him, fight them both." Mark sat on the camping steps next to her and took her hand. "The law's on your side, Liv. They can't take it all."

"But if they can, if they did, how … how would you feel about that?" She'd never hated herself more. "How would you feel about *me* if I lost everything?"

Mark looked at her curiously. "We'll manage. I make a good living with the nursery, we'll get by." He lifted her chin with his fingers. "I love you, Liv, I love you because you're beautiful, inside and out. I love you because of your cute, overbite smile and the tinkly way you laugh, the way your eyes light up when you look at me, and the joy you carry with you everywhere. I love you more than I've ever loved anything in my life, including the garden centre." She laughed, and he pulled her onto his lap, into his arms. "I love you, Olivia Harrison. I love you rich or poor, thin or fat, young or old. I love you, I love you, I love you, and nothing will ever change that, nothing."

"I love you more," she said, bending her head to kiss him.

"Not possible."

"Clearly is."

"Bleurgh!" Brian shouted, coming out of the caravan and pulling a very reluctant Faye along behind him. "Could you hold back on the gushiness a bit, I haven't had any caffeine yet."

Olivia laughed, then wriggled in Mark's lap. "Your towel's wet," she said.

"Yes, I should take it off."

"I think you should."

Tel stepped out of his caravan, looking anxious and glancing at his watch. "Come on, Soph!"

"I'm coming! Blimey, bit of a rushed surprise, isn't it?" She waved at them all as she rushed to the car.

Tel glanced over at them. Brian lifted a hand. Faye, held by Brian on the grass outside their awning, quickly turned her head and looked awkward. Olivia raised two thumbs and then blew him a kiss.

"Hey, what's going on?" Mark asked her. "I sense a conspiracy."

"I'll tell you when they've gone. I'm going to need your help anyway."

"Sounds interesting."

"It is, I'm so excited."

"Keep wriggling like that and I'll be excited too."

Tel took a final glance at his watch before getting into the car and driving away.

"Liv seems very excited about something," Sophie said.

"Liv gets excited about everything."

"Yes, but she seems especially excited about us leaving. She's in on it, whatever it is, isn't she?"

"My lips are sealed."

"This surprise had better be good."

* * *

"It was them," Olivia said. They were sitting in the pub garden, eating breakfast. "Daddy sent the bikes."

"Are you sure?" Brian asked.

"He more or less admitted it. It's my punishment for not doing as I'm told, for daring to disobey him, for not giving him what he wants."

"That's why they only targeted Liv's motorhome," Mark said.

"I assume Richard's in on it too?"

"Yes, I could hear him in the background."

"Are they still at the pub in the village?" Brian asked.

"Don't get any ideas," Faye told him, "Leave it to the police."

"Did you call the police, Liv?"

"Yes, and my lawyer, and mummy, telling her not to take any calls or read any texts from daddy."

"They're little sods, aren't they," Faye growled.

"I can think of more appropriate words to describe them," Mark said.

"Steady, lad, don't let the testosterone lead you astray, it'll get sorted."

They glanced at Jim, gluttonously chomping through his full English as though he'd never eaten before. "What?" he said.

"Are you not the slightest bit interested in what's going on around you?"

Jim looked around the garden. "Why, what's going on?"

"Liv's just told us her dad and Dick sent the motorbikes."

"I could have told you that," he said, slashing a sausage in half.

"Funny, you never mentioned it," Mark said.

"I thought you all knew. Who else could it have been?" He pushed both halves of the sausage into his mouth and grinned.

Faye, still acutely embarrassed by the nightie episode but keen to lighten the atmosphere, said, "Does anyone know where Tel and Sophie have gone rushing off to today?"

Olivia slowly raised her hand, biting her lower lip. Mark grinned excitedly.

"Do tell!" Brian said.

So she did.

* * *

"What?" said Sophie. "Why are we here?"

They'd just driven through a set of gates, next to a sign reading COTWOLDS AIRPLANE CLUB.

Tel thew a smile at her, hoping to gauge her impression, good or bad, but she just looked surprised and confused. His nerves suddenly ramped up tenfold. His hands actually shook on the steering wheel. Suddenly, now he was here, he wasn't sure it was such a good idea after all.

"What do you think?" he asked.

"I don't think anything yet, unless you actually want to tell me why we're here?"

"Not yet, but soon, very soon."

"Come on, Tel, the suspense is killing me. Why have you brought me to an airport? Have you bought me a plane, or flying lessons, or are you going to push me out of a plane at 15,000 feet?" She laughed, then stopped suddenly when she saw the look on his face. "You're going to push me out of a plane at 15,000 feet, aren't you."

He glanced over at her. "Not on your own," he said, "There'll be a man strapped to your back. You said you'd like to try parachute jumping."

She stared resolutely through the windscreen and didn't speak as he drove towards a hangar next to a small runway and pulled up.

"Soph? Say something."

She jutted her chin out. "Parachute jumping?"

"Well, it's called tandem skydiving."

"And that's supposed to make it sound better, does it, 'skydiving', rather than 'falling to your death from a great height'."

"You said you wanted to try it."

"I did. I regret saying it now."

"Do you want me to turn around? I can turn around. I put a lot of time and effort into this, but I can cancel everything if you want, I can just call them and say – "

"No." She took a deep breath and turned to look at him. She looked as terrified as he felt. "You're supposed to do something every day that scares you."

"Eleanor Roosevelt."

"I think 'skydiving' from 15,000 feet should cover me for, oh, the next five years or so."

They were both quiet for a moment.

"You okay?" he asked.

"Yes, I'm just very … scared."

"Me too."

They laughed nervously and got out of the car onto weak, trembling legs.

A man greeted them at the entrance to the hanger, inside which were several small airplanes.

"They look like remote-controlled toys," Sophie whispered, following the man inside.

"I'm sure they've got some proper ones somewhere."

They both gulped.

CHAPTER 13

They'd just completed their training session and the trainer said, "We'll fit you up with your harnesses now."

"Wait, what?" Tel gasped, "Is that it? Twenty minutes preparation before we launch ourselves into the air thousands of feet above solid ground?"

"That's everything you need to know," the trainer said. "Your tandem instructors will do most of the work, you just have to hang there and enjoy it."

The other four other people in the group laughed, but Tel didn't. "What if the instructor passes out or has a heart attack or something as soon as we leave the plane, what are we supposed to do then?"

"Calm down," Sophie breathed, "They know what they're doing."

"Have you had many losses?" Tel blurted, petrified to the very core of his soul, "You know, any deaths?"

"Tel!" Sophie hissed, "I'm not sure you should be saying the word 'death' right now."

"Any serious injuries?"

Everyone looked at the trainer, excitement nose-diving into abject fear.

"No," the instructor said, "Not even close."

"But you wouldn't tell us if you did, would you."

"Tel!"

"We mostly bring our guests back alive," the trainer said.

"Mostly?" Tel's eyes were bulging out of his face like pickled onions.

"He's joking," Sophie hissed, "Remember when you used

to have a sense of humour?"

"Yes, before I stared death in the face."

"Come on, put your harness on. I like mine," she said, glancing over her shoulder at her handsome tandem instructor, who was called James. "Tel?"

He was running across the hanger to the toilets with his hand over his mouth.

* * *

"Is that them?" Faye asked.

"That's a jumbo jet," Brian drawled.

"Well, what's a small plane look like?"

"Small."

"Sounds like a lawnmower," Jim said.

"Looks like a cardboard cut-out you'd get with a box of cereal," Mark said, shuddering at the memory of his one and only flight in a Cessna years before.

They were trying to casually sit outside their caravans enjoying the sun, but they were all jittery, their necks cricked back on their chairs to stare up at the blue, cloudless sky. Everything was ready. Chelsea and the bar staff were on high alert. Faces kept peering out of the top floor windows of The Woodsman, and everyone on the campsite was staring up, like they were expecting aliens to land at any moment.

They just needed Tel and Sophie now.

"That one?" Faye asked.

"That's a jet plane."

"Well, what's the difference?"

Brian rolled his eyes.

* * *

The trainer held a piece of paper in his hand and spoke directly to the tandem instructors. "Package A," he said, nodding at the first couple, "Package B, and Package C."

"What's Package C?" Sophie asked.

The trainer patiently pointed at a poster on the wall,

listing the different packages. "Package A is jumping at 7,000 feet with ten seconds of freefall."

"I think I know and I'm too scared to process it," she said, "But just to be clear, what is freefall?"

The trainer sighed. "Did you not read your information sheets?"

"Haven't had sight of any information sheets," she said, glaring at Tel, who was paler than she'd ever seen him before, almost ashen. "Knew about this less than an hour ago. A 'surprise' from my boyfriend, and I have to say, I've never been more surprised in my life."

"Life," Tel breathed softly, "I want to live, please let me live."

"Freefall is what happens *before* the parachute opens," the trainer said.

"When you're plummeting to earth with the tandem instructor hopefully still on your back," Tel said, "Before, fingers crossed, the parachute opens in time."

"Can somebody shut him up?" said a woman in a high-pitched voice.

"Yeah, mate, we're looking forward to this and you're dragging us down."

"Down," Tel said, "Falling down from a great height."

"Package B is jumping at 10,000 feet with thirty seconds of freefall," the trainer continued, eager to get rid of the lot of them, "And Package C is jumping at 15,000 feet with sixty seconds of freefall."

"I see," Sophie said, feeling dizzy as she turned to Tel. "You booked us on Package C, one whole minute of freefall?" Tel's face was totally blank. His lips were slack and his eyes weren't focused on anything, least of all her. "Tel? Tel?"

"Your instructors are equipped with cameras on poles to record your experience," the trainer continued, "And you'll be landing back here at the airport ... except for you two."

"Us two?" Sophie said, pointing at herself. "Where are we landing?"

"Somewhere else," the trainer winked.

Sophie sighed long and hard. "This just keeps getting better and better. Tel, what have you got us into?"

Tel raised his arms an inch from his sides and mumbled something inaudible as his eyes stared off into nothingness.

"Follow your tandem instructors outside, and enjoy your experience."

The group trudged out onto the tarmac, their harnesses rattling. Tel took one look at the Cessna on the tiny runway and stopped dead. "No," he gasped, "I want a proper plane! I want a plane that doesn't look like it's made out of balsa wood and will fall to bits if you cough!"

"Come on," Sophie said, nudging him quite fiercely as she walked past, "You got us into this and you're bloody well going to see it through to the end."

Tel started whimpering as he scuttled after her.

* * *

They were sitting on the floor of the plane with Tel still whimpering, ranging from short, high-pitched whining like a dog, to a single, extended note of misery. They'd been climbing steadily for three minutes. "It's too steep!" he wailed, "It's too high!"

"If you don't shut up!" said a bloke sitting next to a silently sobbing woman, "I'm going to unclip your harness and throw you out myself!"

Sophie threw out a protective arm. Tel stopped whimpering and went still and silent, slumped in catatonia. When the clear shutter door on the side of the plane was lifted and the first couple to jump shuffled on their bums into the gaping hole, he threw a fist into his mouth and started hyperventilating.

"Three, two, one, *jump*!"

Tel started chanting random bits of prayers as the four skydivers slipped out and were gone. Sophie held his hand. "I think you have vertigo," she said, "I didn't know you suffered from vertigo."

"Neither ... did ... I," he gasped, "I've never been ... up ... this high ... before."

"We're going higher," said his instructor.

"Yes, thank you," Sophie said, giving him the evil eye.

The plane flew higher. Tel was now non-responsive. Sophie patted his hand and tried to get him to focus on her, to no avail.

"He'll be fine once he gets out the door," his instructor told her, "I've seen it plenty of times."

"Are you sure?"

The instructor nodded as he watched the other couple shuffle into position. The door was raised and Tel squeaked, "Don't go. Don't jump."

And then they too were gone. Tel tried to shuffle further back, away from the door, but was halted by the weight of the instructor strapped behind him. "Sophie," he whined, "Sophie."

"I'm here, Tel. Do you want to go back to the airport? You don't have to do this if you don't want to."

He started nodding. Then stopped and patted the breast pocket of his skydiving suit. A semblance of sanity crept into his head. He *had* to do this, he'd been planning it for weeks. Today was the day. He had to pull himself together. He couldn't be afraid, not now.

"I-I-I'll be f-f-fine," he spluttered.

"Are you sure? We can go back if you want?"

"N-n-no, I'll d-d-do it."

"Told you," the instructor on his back said, "He'll be fine once we leave the airplane."

Tel cringed and held onto the straps of his harness with a vice-like grip. His hands trembled, his whole body shook.

"Okay, get ready," the pilot shouted back.

Sophie forced a smile onto her face, holding Tel's limp, moist hand as the instructors shuffled them to the side of the plane and lifted the shutter door. They sat together on the edge with their legs hanging out, buffeted by the wind. Tel looked at her with wide, terrified eyes. Sophie wondered if his bulging eyeballs might actually fall out on the way down and be lost for all time. Wind whistled past them. The ground below seemed very, very far away. The instructor on Sophie's back said, "Three, two – "

"NO!" Tel screamed in heart-pounding, sphincter twitching horror, in a pitch that Sarah Brightman would have been proud of, "I'VE CHANGED MY MIND! I DON'T WANT TO DO IT! I DON'T WANT TO DIE!"

" – one, *jump!*"

His instructor forced him off the ledge of the plane and suddenly he was falling. The wind was like a roaring tornado in his ears, pulling his face into stretchy expressions. He tried to open his mouth to scream, but air filled it and silenced him.

He was falling!

He was going to die!

Sophie, thrilled beyond expression and beaming with exhilaration, looked across at Tel, falling through the air on her left, and saw his twisting, open-mouthed, silently screaming face and his wildly rotating arms. She'd never seen a living soul look that scared before. She was just wondering if he was going to be okay when his arms stopped windmilling, his eyes closed, and he hung limp, pressed by the power of the wind against his instructor.

He'd passed out.

* * *

"There they are!" Faye squealed, jumping up and down as two dots jumped out of a tiny plane high up in the sky.

Mark brought up his binoculars and peered through them. "Yeah, I think it's them."

"Who else could it be?" Brian laughed.

"Their parachutes haven't opened!" Jim cried, jumping

up from the grass. "Shouldn't their parachutes have opened by now?"

"They're freefalling," Olivia said.

Faye turned to look at her with a wry smile. "You sneaky thing, keeping this a secret."

Olivia turned her eyes to Mark, who was about to shrug when he noticed Brian looking at them both with a strange expression. A smile bloomed behind his beard and an eyebrow was raised. Mark quickly lifted his binoculars and hid behind them. "Oh," he said, "They're still freefalling and ... one of them looks a bit ... limp."

"Let me see," Brian said, taking the binoculars from him. Mark suddenly thudded into his side, grasping at his neck and choking. "Oh sorry," Brian said, releasing them, "Didn't realise there was a strap. You okay?"

"Yeah, yeah, bit of garrotting never hurt anyone."

"Strangle victims the world over would disagree."

Unstrapped now, Brian lifted the binoculars. "Yes, one of them just seems to be ... hanging there."

"Is it Sophie?" Faye asked.

"Can't see."

"Is it Tel?"

"Still can't see."

Jim said, "The parachutes aren't opening, Bri."

"They will."

"They're not opening, Bri!"

"They will, you'll see."

"Not seeing it, Bri! Bri! Oh, they've opened." Jim flopped back onto the grass in relief. "Thank God for that!"

* * *

Tel made a *humphing* noise as the parachutes opened, fiercely yanking them upwards, and opened his eyes. "Where - ?" He looked down and started screaming, clutching onto the straps of his harness and hysterically kicking his legs out.

"Tel!" Sophie yelled, "Tel! It's okay, Tel!"

"Okay?" His voice was incredibly high, almost soprano. "We're thousands of miles above the – " He promptly vomited, most of it down his flying suit, some over his shoulder and into the face of his instructor, who casually wiped it away with his free hand, the other holding a camera on a stick, recording it all for posterity.

"Better?" Sophie shouted.

Tel looked at her and started crying.

"It'll soon be over, Tel."

The parachutes moved away from each other. Tel reached out. "Sophie! Sophie!"

"I'm here, Tel."

"Go … after … her," he panted over his shoulder, "Don't let her … get away."

The instructor pulled on the parachute and they came close together again, Sophie grinning and laughing and enjoying every second, Tel terrified and sobbing.

"Sophie," he yelled, "Will you - ?"

"What?"

"Sophie, will you - ?"

"I can't hear you, Tel."

"Get closer," he said to his instructor.

"This is as close as we can get without the parachutes tangling up."

"Tangling," Tel shuddered, screwing up his face and then shouting, "Sophie, will you - ?"

A sudden gust of wind grabbed them and tossed them sideways. Tel cried out once, and promptly passed out again.

* * *

Everyone was standing around the edge of the camping field, eagerly waiting for them to land. A man came up to Brian and said, "Shall I light a celebratory firework?"

Brian looked down at him. "Rocket, is it?"

"Yeah, I've got about a dozen for my kid's birthday tomorrow, he's ten."

"Yes, of course, send a few rockets into the sky, set fire to one of the parachutes and watch them plummet to the ground in front of your son, make his birthday really one to remember."

The man frowned and walked off. Olivia and Mark sidled up to him.

"You know, don't you," Mark said.

"Might do."

"What do you think you know?"

"What do you think I know?"

"You tell me."

Brian lowered his eyes and looked at them both.

"He knows," Olivia said.

"Or he thinks he knows."

"I know," Brian said.

"How do you know?" Olivia asked.

Brian tapped the side of his nose.

"Does anyone else know?"

"Not that I know of."

"Can you … not tell them?"

Brian sucked his lips in, mimed pulling a zip across them and locking it, then threw the invisible key over his shoulder.

"Thank you." Olivia glanced at her feet. "Do you think me very deceptive and horrid?"

Brian pulled off the invisible lock and quickly unzipped his mouth. "No one would ever think that about you, Liv."

"See," said Mark, "I told you."

"Perfectly understandable why you did it," Brian said.

"Is it?"

"Aye, it is." He gave her a wink. "Worry not, lass they'll understand too."

"I hope so."

"I know so."

* * *

Tel came round again a few feet from the ground and burst into tears of joy. Then, as the instructor expertly landed them both on their feet in the camping field, Tel noticed the crowds all around him, clapping and whistling. He wiped his tear-stained, vomit-blotched face, and stamped on the ground to make sure it was real.

"Oh my God!" Sophie screeched, jumping up and down as her tandem straps were unclipped, "That was the best thing ever! That was amazing! Awesome! Amazing!" She hugged her instructor tightly. "You were brilliant, totally brilliant! Can we do it again?"

Tel quickly tried to compose himself as he saw Brian and the others racing down the field towards them. His instructor unclipped him and he wavered unsteadily on his feet. He brushed vaguely at the vomit down his front. Sophie stopped bouncing and rushed over to him, about to hug him, then, noticing the vomit, rubbed his back instead. "You did it, Tel! Well done. Wasn't it *amazing*? Are you okay?"

"Tel!" boomed Brian, "You okay, lad?"

Tel doubled over, balancing himself with his hands on his knees, feeling incredibly pumped up with adrenalin, and nausea and emotion, and feeling really, really grateful to be alive. He raised a hand at Brian and Faye and Jim, shaking his head. Brian instantly turned and shouted, "Abort! Abort!" to Olivia and Mark, who were running down the field with a bottle and several glasses in their hands. They stopped, glanced at each other, and hid the bottle and glasses in a hedge.

"You okay, Tel?"

"Did you do it?" Jim blurted.

"Of course they did it," Brian said, piercing him with a death stare, "You just watched them do it."

"No, I meant – "

"I know what you meant."

"Time to shut up now," said Mark.

"Tel?"

He stood up straight. "I'm okay." He took a deep, calming breath. "Better now I'm on terra firma."

Jim looked confused for a moment, then said, "He's hallucinating, thinks he's somewhere else. Oh, looks like you've had a little accident, Tel."

"Shut up, Jim," Mark hissed. Then, focusing and comprehending the stain on the front of Tel's skydiving suit, he started gagging. "You enjoyed ..." He gagged again. "... it then?"

"It was brilliant," Sophie said, her eyes blazing and her smile enormous. "Poor Tel wasn't a fan though."

"Well done you!" Faye hugged her, followed by Olivia.

Jim and Brian patted Tel's shoulder. Mark stayed back, looking everywhere except at Tel's suit and holding back the urge to heave at the smell coming off him.

"We'll wait for you in the car park," Sophie's instructor said. "Our van should be there to pick us up."

"Thank you," she beamed, "Thank you so much."

"See if you can give the suit a quick hose down before we take it back," Tel's instructor said, slapping him on the back as he passed.

"Come on," said Brian, gently guiding him up the field, "Let's get you washed off. Skydiving not your thing then, eh?"

"Scariest thing I've ever done, Bri. I didn't think I'd survive. I thought I was going to die."

"I'd better cancel the wingsuit flying experience I booked for your birthday then."

"Don't even joke."

The others were up ahead. Brian bent to Tel's ear and whispered, "You didn't do it then?"

Tel shook his head. "Between the screaming, the crying, the vomiting and the unconsciousness, I didn't really get a chance."

"Never mind, you can go up again and get it right next

time."

"Again? NO!"

Brian laughed and gave him a sideways hug.

* * *

He stood at the bottom of the caravan area, ashamed and embarrassed, as Brian gently hosed down his flying suit and harness. Sophie helped him to peel it off, and he cringed and held his hands down in front of his darkened jeans. Brian hastily hosed the area down to blend it in. Tel pulled off his now wet t-shirt, exposing his toned torso, and there was a sudden gasp from somewhere.

"Someone catch my wife as she topples," Brian said.

"How do you know it was me?" Faye snapped, embarrassed.

"Were you thinking of Colin Firth coming out of the water?"

"No," she mumbled.

Sophie rushed to their caravan and came back with his dressing gown, a towel, and a bag of toiletries. "Put this on and go shower," she said softly.

"Soph," he breathed.

"Yes, Tel?"

"Are you ashamed of me?"

She kissed the side of his face. "No, of course not."

He turned to look at her. "Are you sure?"

"I'm sure. You did it, Tel, and I'm proud of you. I love you, a bit of fainting and screaming and vomiting and yellow belly cowardice won't change that."

They laughed, and he shuffled off to the showers, Sophie next to him, carrying their harnesses and flying suits.

While she chatted to the instructors in the car park, Faye went to Brian and said, "Did he do it?"

"No."

"So, what do we do about the pub?"

"The pub?"

"Yes, the pub."

"Ah, the pub. Liv?"

"Yes, Bri?"

"The pub?"

"Oh my goodness, I'd forgotten about that. I guess we'll have to eat al fresco tonight."

"Al fresco," he said to Faye.

"Al fresco," she nodded.

"Is that a pasta dish?" Jim asked.

"All that buffet food," Olivia fretted. "Do you think he'll do it tonight, or should Chelsea just give it away to customers?"

"Leave it with me," Brian said.

* * *

"How you feeling now, Tel?"

They were all sitting outside Brian and Faye's caravan, chatting. After his shower and a change of clothes, Sophie had given him a large glass of brandy for the shock, and he clutched it in his still trembling hands, sipping at it constantly. Faye gave him a couple of Kalms tablets she kept for emergencies. He was starting to look normal again.

"Better," he sighed, managing a weak smile.

"Good."

"In fact, I think I'm actually hungry." Four faces froze with rictus smiles. "Are we going to the pub to eat?"

"Great, I'm starving," Jim said, jumping up.

"Nah," Brian said.

"It's such a nice night," said Faye, "I thought we could eat out here tonight."

Jim crumpled into his chair again.

"Oh," said Sophie, "We ate out here last night, and I was quite looking forward to the carbonara."

"Carbonara's off," Mark said, "Pasta's … off."

"Off?"

"Or they're out of pasta, I can't remember what Chelsea said now."

"Oh."

Brian glared at Tel as Faye started talking about pasta dishes with the girls. Tel glared back and frowned, shrugged. Brian mimed, "Need to talk."

"You couldn't fetch me a drop more brandy, could you, Soph?"

"Did your legs shatter on landing?" she laughed. "Anyway, you haven't finished that one yet."

Tel necked the brandy in the glass, coughing on the fumes. Sophie got up and took his glass to the caravan for a refill. "Don't expect this kind of service all the time," she called over her shoulder, "It's only until you recover."

Brian immediately leaned forward in his chair. "The pub," he whispered to Tel.

"The pub?"

"Yes, the pub full of decorations and celebration champagne and – "

"Oh God, I forgot about that!"

"What should we do with it all?" Olivia asked.

"What's happening about the pub?" said Jim.

"Try to keep up," Mark said.

"How can I keep up when nobody tells me anything. I'm like a mushroom, kept in the dark and fed sh-"

"Do you think you might do it tonight, while everything's ready?" Brian asked. "I don't mean to pressure you or anything, but it would be kind of nice doing it here, in front of the gang in the sunshine, it'll make a nice memory."

"Do what?" Jim asked.

"I suppose I could." Tel was clearly warming to the idea. "Much better than screaming it at 15,000 feet. 15,000 feet, can you believe it? I didn't think you could even breathe that high up, let alone – "

"So, what do you think?" Brian whispered, as Sophie came walking across the driveway with a half-filled glass.

"Yes." Tel was smiling now. "I think you're right. It's the perfect moment, here, in front of friends, on holiday, in the sunshine."

"What holiday in the sunshine?" Sophie asked, handing him his brandy and sitting down again.

"This holiday in the sunshine," Tel winked.

"What about it?"

"Are you enjoying it?"

"Surrounded by friends, what's not to like?"

"I'm glad you say that, because – " Tel patted his shirt pocket and his face dropped. He leapt up from his chair, patting at his jeans pockets, and raced back to the caravan.

"Oh, so now you're capable of getting things yourself, are you?" Sophie laughed.

Noises came from the caravan, the sound of doors and drawers being pulled open and slammed shut, before Tel jumped out again. "Sophie!" he cried, "What did you do with my clothes after the jump from hell?"

"I put them in to wash in the utility shed."

Tel bolted through the hedge, across the neighbouring caravan area, narrowly avoiding a small child who was wandering around aimlessly, and through the other hedge. Sophie stood up. "What's got into him?"

Brian stood up and watched Tel run into the utility shed. "Delayed reaction to trauma?"

Mark stood up. "Clearly doesn't want his clothes pinched, they must be expensive."

Tel came out of the utility shed, holding his head in both hands. He looked over at them, looking at him, and yelled, "BRIAN!"

* * *

"S'up?"

"Brian! Brian!" Tel's eyes were as big as saucers. "The ring! It's gone! I've lost it! I've lost the bloody ring!"

A hole appeared in Brian's beard as his jaw dropped. "You've *lost* it!"

"I … I … I …"

"Deep breaths, lad."

"I took it out of my shirt pocket at the airport and put it in the front of the flying suit." He tapped his chest, reliving the moment. "I planned to present it to her after we'd landed but … it didn't turn out like that."

"Did it fall out?"

"I-I don't know, I wasn't awake the entire time. Oh, oh, what if it did?"

"You've checked the clothes you were wearing?"

"Yes, yes, not there." He was furiously rubbing his head.

"You bent forward after you'd landed, maybe it slipped out then."

"Pockets were velcroed, but yes, possibly, and then …" He stared blankly, remembering. "Then I took the suit off while you were hosing me down at the water tap." He took off towards the water tap.

"I'll check the field!" Brian called after him.

Tel was rifling through the tall grass around the water tap stand. Sophie wandered over to him. "Have you actually lost your mind?" she asked casually.

"No, no, I've mislaid something."

"What kind of something?"

"Just … a thing."

Tel starting turning round on the spot, his eyeballs on the ground scouring the area

"What is the thing?"

"It's … I mean … I … it would look out of place if you saw it on the ground," he said cryptically, "You'd look at it and think, 'That doesn't belong there'."

"You're being very vague, Tel."

"I know. I'm sorry, I can't tell you, but I've lost something, something important."

She gasped, "Not the Rolex I bought you for Christmas?"

"No, no, but … similar."

"Similar to a Rolex?"

"No."

"Tel, you're not making any sense."

Tel stared off down the field, where Brian was wandering around with his head bent. "I have to go."

Brian, having searched the ground in the middle of the field, stood up straight and bellowed, "HAS ANYONE FOUND AN UNUSUAL ITEM AROUND HERE?" He paused. Several people looked at him, but there was no response. "THERE'S A SUBSTANTIAL REWARD!"

"How much?" someone asked.

"Have you found something?"

"No, I was just curious."

Brian was looking down at his feet as he walked, prodding clumps of grass with his sandals, when Tel rushed up to him. "Anything?"

"No."

"Oh God."

"It's probably still in the flying suit."

"What do I do, Bri? I can't think! I can't believe I lost it!"

"Deep breath."

"What should I do, what should I - ?"

Brian clamped a hand down on his shoulder. "Suck in air," he boomed. Tel did. "Hold it." Tel did. "Let it out, *slowly*." Tel did. "And again. Better?"

"Dizzy from ... excess oxygen."

"Ring the airport."

"Yes, yes, of course." Tel pulled out his phone and tapped the screen with trembling fingers. "Hello, this is Tel Okenado. Yes, I was there this afternoon. Oh, you remember me? Yes, but probably not the worst customer you've ever had, right? Oh, I am? By far? I see. I apologise." Brian nudged his shoulder. "Help me!" he cried, "I've lost the engagement ring! Can you check the flying suit I was wearing? Can you do it -? What, it was picked up by the cleaners?" Tel stared up at Brian, aghast. "Yes, of course, the vomit, and the ... I understand. Can you call the cleaners and - ? They're closed for the day? You'll

do it first thing in the morning?" Tel fell to his haunches.
"You'll call me? Yes, thank you. Bye." He slowly stood up again.
"I'm screwed. I've ruined everything.

"Sorry, lad."

"I just hope it's still in the suit."

"It will be."

"But what if it isn't?"

Brian saw the gang walking down the field towards
them. "What are you going to tell - ?"

Tel's phone rang. "Hello?" He listened for a moment,
then ran up the field, straight past the others, with Brian
lumbering along after him.

"Bri," Faye cried, "What - ?"

"I'll tell you when I get back."

"Where are you - ? Brian!"

Tel leapt into his car and skidded to the entrance of the
caravan area, where he picked Brian up.

"Is this like a Don't Tell the Wife themed campsite?"
Faye huffed, as they drove off.

"Mystery and Intrigue," Mark said.

"I'm getting really fed up of not being told anything
when my husband inexplicably rushes off."

"Another woman," Jim said, and Mark slapped the back
of his head. "Oi! That hurt!"

"It was meant to."

Jim shoved Mark, who shoved him back. Sophie stepped
between them and drawled, "Fisticuffs at dawn if you want to
fight."

"What time is dawn?" Jim asked.

"5am, I think."

"I'm not getting up at 5am!"

"Then *stop fighting*!" She walked back towards the
caravans. Jim and Mark looked at each other, then followed,
nudging at each other with their shoulders.

* * *

They raced to the office at the far end of the hangar. There was no one behind the counter. Brian pounded heavily on a bell, and a young man sauntered from behind a partitioned area. He took one look at Tel and laughed. "Not you again. You haven't come to book another jump, have you, because I don't think any of the instructors will take you."

"You called me about a ring," Tel gasped.

"Did we?"

"Yes!"

"I don't know anything about a ring, I just know that your face is on our wall of fame as the worst skydiving customer we've ever had." He pointed at a noticeboard on the wall next to the counter. Tel's corporate portrait was pinned to it.

"Just me?" he asked.

"We took the others off, they didn't come anywhere as close."

"Focus," Brian nudged.

"The trainer who was here earlier, he called and said he'd found my ring."

"I don't know anything about that."

"Could you tell him I'm here?"

"Boss ain't around."

"He's not here?"

"No, he's just nipped out."

"Out where?"

"I don't know, he didn't say."

Tel slumped against the counter, then said, "Can you call him?"

"I could," the man said, lifting up a mobile from behind the counter, "But this is his phone."

Tel dropped his head onto the counter and groaned.

"Any idea how long he'll be?" Brian asked.

"I'll see if James knows," and he wandered behind the partition.

"He's run off with it," Tel said, standing up again.

"You don't know that."

"I do. It's a very expensive ring, he's taken one look at it and done a bunk."

"Legal term, is it, 'done a bunk'?"

"Theft of personal property is the legal term, Bri, or theft through stupidity, for which I'm wholly culpable. How could I have been so *stupid*!"

"When you say 'expensive'," Brian said, as casually as he could, "Are we talking eye-watering or stratospheric?"

"Expensive enough to make a man leave his old life and start a new one on a Caribbean Island."

"Blimey."

Tel started pacing up and down, running his hands over his head. "He's gone. The ring's gone. I've got nothing for Sophie except my undying love and a Haribo jelly ring from the packet in my car."

"I like Haribos."

"So does Sophie, but I have an inkling she'd prefer, and would be expecting, something a little more substantial, like a diamond set in platinum."

"Insurance job?" Brian asked.

Tel shook his head. "I didn't bother in case she didn't like it and I had to take it back."

"Oh. Stuffed, then."

"Appears so."

The young man came back. He brought James with him. "You're looking for a ring?" he asked.

"Yes, I left it in my skydiving suit."

"Bit of a silly thing to do."

"Yes, it was, for which I shall give myself a severe thrashing at the earliest opportunity."

"We sent the suits off for cleaning."

"I know, your boss told me over the phone. Do you know where he's gone or how long he'll be?"

"No. Sorry."

Tel gave a strangled cry and turned to Brian. "It's gone. It's all ruined. I've forked out an absolute fortune, and she's worth every single penny, and then lost the bloody engagement ring! I mean, it takes a certain skill set to screw up so impeccably." He gave another strangled cry, just as Brian said, "It'll be alright, lad."

"It won't! It won't!"

"It will, it will. Look."

Brian nodded towards the hangar entrance. Tel spun round and let out a long sigh of relief. The trainer was walking towards them.

"You got here fast," he shouted over.

"Seventy-five miles an hour down country lanes will do that," Brian said.

"I called the cleaners and they searched the jumpsuits."

"And?" Tel said nervously.

"They found it."

"Oh, thank God!"

"They called me and said they didn't want the responsibility of keeping such an expensive item in their shop overnight, their insurance didn't cover it, and told me to come and fetch it."

Tel was making strange noises, a cross between a laugh and a cry. "Thank you," he gasped.

"So I did, and ..." The man reached into his jacket pocket and pulled out a turquoise Tiffany box, placing it on the counter between them. "... here it is."

Tel was definitely laughing now. "Thank you, a thousand times, thank you." He picked it up and opened the lid. Brian put a hand in front of his face against the glare. The two young men leaned over to take a peek. "Nice," James said. The mouth on the other man just dropped open.

"Do you think she'll like it?" Tel asked Brian, and James piped up, "For a ring like that, mate, I'd agree to marry you."

They laughed.

Tel mockingly wiped his brow and exhaled. "Here," he

said, taking his wallet from his jeans pocket and opening it up, "Take this for your troubles." He placed a couple of notes down on the counter, then, glancing at the ring, put another two down. "And this is for the cleaning expenses." He put more notes down. "And this," he said, placing another couple of notes down, "Is for being a genuinely honest man."

The man picked up all the notes with a wary eye, shuffled them into a neat pile, then counted three out. "That should cover the cleaning, and the twenty I slipped the cleaner for staying over. The rest," he said, handing them back to Tel, "Is my wedding gift to you."

Tel reached out and wrapped his arms around the man's neck, pulling his head across the counter. "Thank you," he said, "Thank you, thank you, thank you."

"No problem at all," he said, unravelling himself. "You take care of that ring now, y'hear?"

"Oh, I will."

"Good luck."

"Thanks."

As they walked out of the hangar Brian said, "Are you crying, Tel?"

"I am, Bri."

* * *

"So," Faye asked, when they got back to the campsite, "Where have you been this time? Another caravan trapped in a farmyard? Some unknown damsel in distress? Off saving the planet with your FBI mates?"

"Tel left something at the airport."

"You couldn't have told me before rushing off again?"

"I suppose I could have, but where's the fun in that?"

Faye tutted and gave him the evil eye.

Tel sat down and finished off his glass of brandy in one gulp, coughing again. They all sat in silence, smiling and staring at each other.

"What's going on?" Sophie asked, "I sense an atmosphere of anticipation."

Her eyes settled on Tel. He smiled, his eyes soft as he slid off his seat and got down on one knee in front of her.

"Oh no!" she gasped, her hands rushing to her face.

"Is that her answer?" Jim asked. "Bit of an anti-climax if you – "

"Shut up, Jim!"

"Sophie."

"Yes, Tel?"

"I love you very much. You are perfect in almost every way, except for your cooking, but I can overlook that." There was a murmur of laughter. "I'm so grateful to have found you, you make my life complete. You make me very, very happy, and I hope I make you happy too."

"You do, Tel, you do, very much so." Tears slipped down her face.

"You're my everything, Soph, I am nothing without you." Brian reached out for Faye's hand and squeezed it. Tel reached into his jeans pocket and pulled out a small turquoise box with Tiffany inscribed on the lid. As he opened it, he said, "Sophie Forbes, would you do me the very great honour of agreeing to be my wife?"

Sophie screamed at the ring glittering in the box, falling forward and wrapping her arms around his neck. The women cooed over the sparkles, while the men pretended to shade their eyes from the glare.

Jim whispered, "She's not answered yet, isn't she supposed to give him an answer?"

"Just enjoy the moment, Jim. These things can't be rushed."

Sophie pulled back and held Tel's handsome, nervous face in her hands. "Yes!" she breathed, "A thousand times yes!"

They all cheered and clapped.

Tel stood up, taking her with him, and they kissed passionately. Then he stepped back and gently put the ring on her finger. Sophie sobbed and stared at it in awe. Everyone hugged them and admired the cluster of diamonds. The joy was tangible. People looked over the hedge to see what was happening, clapping when they realised what was going on.

"It's so beautiful," Olivia gushed.

"Beautiful ring for a beautiful lady," said Faye, giving her another hug

"Blimey, that's brighter than the Airstream you stayed in last year," Brian laughed, holding Sophie's delicate fingers in his giant paw.

"Lazer beams," Mark cried, "Don't aim it at anyone, Soph, they'll be zapped out of existence."

"Your children are going to be *gorgeous*!"

"One thing at a time, Faye." Snuggling up to Tel, she said, "Is this what the skydiving was about?"

"I wanted the proposal to be spectacular."

"It was."

"I wanted it to be memorable."

"Oh, it was certainly that."

"In my head it played out differently."

"I'll bet."

"There was no screaming or passing out – "

"Or vomiting," Mark said, heaving a little.

"No, none of that."

"I liked it better this way, with all our friends around us."

They all hugged again.

"Right!" Brian boomed, winking at Olivia before disappearing through the hedge, "T'pub t'celebrate!"

CHAPTER 14

"When did you do all this?" Sophie gasped, as they entered the pub to the sound of applause and cheering from everyone inside. "Oh my gosh, I'm going to cry again!"

There was heart-shaped bunting everywhere, and sparkly red hearts on the walls. Cliff Richard was singing Congratulations through the speakers. Above the bar a banner proclaimed CONGRATULATIONS TEL AND SOPHIE! Bar staff came from behind with trays of champagne and started handing them out. When everyone in the pub had a glass, Brian boomed, "To Tel and Sophie, wishing you every happiness in your new life together." Glasses were raised in a toast, and Sophie burst into tears.

"Tears of joy?" Tel asked, "Not tears of regret?"

She pushed him with a shoulder. "Of course tears of joy!"

"Just checking to make sure you didn't feel under any pressure to accept."

"I've been waiting ages," she giggled.

"Have you indeed!"

Jim suddenly said, "Oh, there's a buffet, just like last year!"

They all turned towards the tables lined up against one wall, heaving with food, with two bains marie steaming at the end.

"Exactly like last year," Tel said. "The pub's certainly catered to our needs in a very spooky way."

"Very déjà vu," said Faye.

Jim immediately headed off towards the plates. Brian winked at Olivia, who widened her eyes, just as Chelsea leaned over the bar counter and held out a phone. "Liv, it's the police."

"Oh!" Escaping the tinkling of glasses and chatter, Olivia hurried into the back garden with the phone. Mark went with her, and the others followed.

"Hello? Yes, this is Olivia Harrison." They were gathered at the end of the patio, where it was quietest, just a couple of occupied tables. "Yes, I have an emergency injunction against my father, Harry Britton, and my ex-husband, Richard Harrison. Yes, to stop them harassing me. Oh really?" She looked at them, and they tried to figure out if it was good news or bad from her ever-changing expression. "Yes, I see. Oh dear, was it? Yes, of course I'll come down and make a statement, is tomorrow morning okay? Lovely. Thank you for calling, I really appreciate it."

She hung up, beaming her cute, overbite smile. "They've arrested them!" she said, "Both daddy and Dick. They talked to Danny, the driver of the car, and he admitted taking money off them to rampage across the campsite and pay special attention to my motorhome. Danny got his mates from his motocross club to help him."

"Blimey!"

"The little sods!"

"What's going to happen to them?" Faye asked.

Olivia leaned against Mark and said, "I don't know. I don't care. I'm just glad it's over, finally over."

Mark wrapped his arms around her and kissed the top of her head. "They were trying to terrorise you into submission, to get what they wanted."

"Their modus operandi," said Brian.

"They'll probably serve a prison sentence," Sophie said.

"It's what they deserve."

Chelsea came hurrying out. "Everything alright, Liv?"

"Everything's fine. They've got the bikers and the perpetrators."

"Richard, was it?"

"And daddy."

"Wow, double whammy. At least it's over now, for you

and for the pub. I couldn't have taken another sleepless night."

"A double celebration," Brian said.

"Yes!" Olivia cried. She climbed up onto the nearest table, occupied by four people, who seemed a bit surprised to have her standing above them. "Drinks are on the house," she cried, in her tiny, high-pitched voice.

Nothing. The people at the table stared at each other, then up at her, wondering what was going on.

"DRINKS ARE ON THE HOUSE!" Brian boomed, and suddenly there was a crowd running towards the pub doors.

"You do know what 'on the house' means, don't you, Liv?" Tel said, as Mark helped her down from the table.

"Drinks are on me."

"Drinks are on the house, on the pub."

"Oh." Olivia looked at Chelsea, who smiled and nodded.

Tel leaned towards Chelsea and whispered, "Put it on my tab." He took out his wallet and discretely held out a credit card, which she didn't take. "Your money's no good here," she whispered.

"Oh?"

"Oh!" Olivia cried, "I'm not hijacking your celebration, am I, Sophie? Oh gosh, I never thought of that, I was just – "

"Absolutely fine, Liv, don't worry. Two celebrations are better than one." She raised her champagne glass and said, "To new lives, for both of us."

"Glad to participate in your happy ending," Tel added.

She snuggled up to Mark and said, "It is a happy ending, isn't it, darling."

"Not for Dick and Harry it isn't."

Jim wandered out of the pub holding a steaming plate, eating while he walked. "Where'd you all go?" he asked. "You're always leaving me behind!"

"It's 'cos we don't like you," Mark laughed.

"Don't be mean," Olivia said, tearing herself from his arms and hurrying over to give Jim a hug. "We love you, Jim."

Sophie went over to hug him too, as did Faye. The men

looked at each other, then joined the group huddle in a manly, jovial way. Some people in the garden started clapping, despite not knowing why.

"Feel the love," Tel cried. He unhugged the gang to grab hold of Sophie, who squealed as he spun her round and dipped her backwards over one arm. "Sophie Forbes," he breathed, staring down at her beautiful face, "I love you."

"I love you."

"Woman!" Brian hollered, "Come hug me now!"

Faye rushed over to him, laughing as he enveloped her in his giant arms.

Mark and Olivia embraced. "To freedom," he said.

"And love."

"All you need is love."

"Love is all you need."

Jim stood there, plate still in one hand, alone and unhugged. "Knew it wouldn't last," he said, and carried on eating.

* * *

"Mummy."

"Darling, how lovely to hear from you. Daddy's not still troubling you, is he?"

"No, mummy, it's over. They've been arrested."

"Arrested?"

"Daddy's being charged with conspiracy to harm, and Richard for aiding and abetting and for deliberate breach of an injunction. Sophie's going to explain it all to me later."

"Oh my goodness! Are you okay, darling?"

"Yes, mummy, I'm fine. Better than fine. I'm free, we both are."

"Oh, I'm so pleased. I felt dreadful that daddy was coming after you because he couldn't get to me, I've been so worried."

"I know, mummy, but you don't have to worry anymore."

"Such a weight off my shoulders. Colin," she called out, "They've been arrested, both of them. Yes, isn't it wonderful? Well, not wonderful, but they did dig their own hole. Colin's putting two thumbs up, darling, and now he's blowing kisses. It's such good news, I couldn't be happier."

"I've been thinking about the divorce settlements."

"Have they signed them?"

"No, they refused, they said it wasn't enough."

"Wasn't enough? But our lawyers said we were being more than generous."

"I know, that's why I wanted to talk to you. I hope I'm not being spiteful or vindictive – "

"Darling, you've never been spiteful or vindictive a moment in your life. You don't have a mean bone in your body."

"I think the lawyers might be right, mummy. I think you should keep the villa in Spain, you love it there and we could fly out together for girlie weekends, just the two of us."

"That sounds lovely. Maybe the odd party, too." She giggled, just the way Olivia giggled.

"And you should sell the flat in Bristol, why should daddy get to keep it when he used it to ...?" She trailed off, unable to say the words. Mummy had been so hurt and upset when she'd found out about it, and his succession of women.

There was a moment's silence, and then Elizabeth said, "I think you're right, darling. I'm not sure I want to be fair or generous anymore. I'll get onto the lawyers first thing in the morning and tell them we want to go with the original settlements that they suggested. It's time to stop being good girls, darling, and start putting ourselves first for a change. Leave it with me."

"I'll call them tomorrow too and adjust Richard's settlement. He's not going to be happy."

"Good, I never liked him anyway. How's it going with your young chap?"

Olivia laughed. "I'm happy, mummy. I'm really, really

happy."

"Good for you. We'll all get together when we get back and I can finally meet him, run his details through Interpol, and get the baby photos out."

* * *

They were inside the pub, partaking of the delicious food, when Melissa, behind the bar, suddenly cried, "Oh my God!" She looked up from her phone and stared straight across at them. "It's online!"

"What's online?"

"Liv's dad and the dick."

Everyone whipped out their phones.

"Where?" someone shouted.

"YouTube, search for 'Cotswolds arrests.' It's all over Facebook and Twitter!"

Chelsea snatched the remote from under the bar and turned on the TV on the far wall, quickly navigating to YouTube. The whole place fell silent as there, up on the screen, appeared the pub in Woodstock in ultra-HD. Out of the doors came two police officers, followed by two men in handcuffs, who were being guided by two more police officers. The camera was wobbly, but they could all see the anger and the fury on the arrested men's faces.

"Unhand me at once!" Harry spat, yanking his arm away from the policeman's grip. "How dare you treat me like a common criminal!"

"It wasn't me!" Richard whined from behind, "It was all *his* idea!"

"Shut up, Richard!"

"I should never have listened to you! I knew it was a mistake!"

"Just keep your mouth – " Harry suddenly stared straight into the camera. "Are you filming this? You don't have my permission to film me! Delete that video immediately!

Officer, arrest that man for breach of privacy at once!"

Harry lunged at the camera but was held back by the police officers. A voice behind the camera said, "It's a free country, mate."

"I forbid you to film me!"

"Public area, pal, I can film what I like."

Harry's face suddenly filled the screen, his eyes blazing with fury, spit coming out of his mouth. "This is all your fault, Olivia!" he barked, and, in the Woodsman, Olivia flinched. Mark pulled her close. "*You* caused this! Conspiring with your mother to cheat me out of what was *rightfully* mine!" The police officer pulled him back towards the squad car. As he bundled him into the back Harry yelled, "Take these handcuffs off immediately or I'll sue you for false arrest!"

A third, younger man came out of the pub wearing handcuffs.

"Danny," Mark sighed, "You stupid bugger."

Richard started struggling. "Let me go! I'm not a criminal! It was *him*, not me! I had nothing to do with it!" He was still protesting his innocence as he was put into the back of another police car.

The video ended. The silence remained. Olivia broke it by saying, "That's that then," and the pub exploded with excited chatter.

"You okay, Liv?"

"Yes, I'm fine. Bit relieved actually." She gave a nervous, high-pitched giggle, and said, "Not sure they're going to like prison much."

"Don't do the crime if you can't do the time," Tel laughed.

"Serves them both right," Faye said. "Here, let's toast to freedom and new beginnings."

They all raised their glasses.

Chelsea came running over to their table. "Liv," she said, looking awkward as she held out the mobile phone again, "There's a call for you. I think it's your father?"

"My father?"

"He wouldn't!" Tel gasped.

Olivia took the phone and put it on loudspeaker on the table. Conversations all around them faded as people pretended not to listen.

"Hello?"

"Olivia! For Christ's sake, put your bloody phone on, I've been trying to call you for over an hour! What the hell are you doing to me? This whole fiasco is entirely your fault."

"Why are you calling me, daddy?" Her face was set, emotionless, hard.

Mark reached out to the phone, but, to his surprise, Oliva gently but firmly moved his hand away without looking at him.

"Why the bloody hell do you think I'm calling you?"

"I have no idea."

"To get me a lawyer, of course! Don't you understand the implications of what's going on? *This is serious.*"

"You probably shouldn't have done it then."

"They're taking it way out of context, they're charging me with all sorts. It was just a joke."

"It wasn't funny."

"It was just a little prank to nudge you in the right direction."

"Daddy," she said, "Why have the police let you call me? I have an emergency injunction to prevent you from contacting me, the police know about it, so why did they - ?"

"I told them I was calling my lawyer," he whispered.

"So why aren't you calling your lawyer?"

"Because I can't bloody afford it, thanks to you and your mother! You'll have to use your lawyers. Just get me out of here."

Olivia was silent for long moments, a frown creasing her brow.

"Olivia, are you still there?"

"Daddy, can I put you on hold for just a moment?"

Before he answered, she pressed the mute button, and stared straight ahead. They all watched her, alarmed and concerned.

Mark leaned towards Brian and, glancing back at Olivia, breathed, "I've never seen that expression on her face before."

"She's having a lightbulb moment," Brian said. "What you see there, lad, is determination, rising empowerment, and little bits of anger. You ever see that expression directed at you, you run and hide."

"Gotcha, Bri."

Olivia unmuted the phone. Very slowly she said, "Just so I have this clear, daddy, you want me to contact *my* lawyers, who you previously fired, to get you out of custody, for charges of harassment and intimidation against *me*?"

"Yes! This isn't difficult, Olivia!"

"Do you know how ridiculous that sounds?"

"Don't you take that tone with me! Call them now, the quicker they're on the case the quicker I get out of here."

"No," she said. "Absolutely not. You sent bikers to attack me!"

"Not *attack*! Don't be so dramatic. It's not my fault they took it too far, they went way beyond my remit."

"Admission," Tel whispered, "You all heard it, right?"

They all nodded, including the couple at the next table.

"Olivia, call them now, this minute, do you hear me?"

Olivia turned her face to Mark, still frowning. "Am I going mad?" she asked.

"No, Liv, you're not."

"Classic case of antagonistic narcissism," Tel said, and Sophie nodded, as did the woman at the next table. "It's not you, Liv, it's him, it's them, gaslighting you."

"Olivia? Answer me!"

"I'm sorry, daddy," she said, and Harry breathed a huge sigh of relief, saying, "Well thank goodness, I thought I was banging my head against a brick wall for a – "

"I'm having a hard time comprehending what you're asking me to do."

"It's perfectly *simple*. Call your lawyers and tell them to – "

"No, I mean, I can't believe you're asking me to do this, after everything you've done."

"It was just a few bikes! I'd call my own lawyers, except they're not accepting my calls, some confusion over payment or – "

"The answer's no, daddy. Absolutely, categorically, no. No with bells on. A platinum 'no' studded with diamonds in a filigree setting." She glanced down at Sophie's ring and winked. "The audacity of you, daddy. You got yourself into this mess by your own actions, and you can get yourself out of it. If you try to contact me again I will involve the police and I shall insist on prosecution." She glanced at Sophie and pulled a face. Sophie nodded. "Goodbye, daddy."

She pressed the end call button and stared at the phone. There were long seconds of silence, before the woman at the next table said, "Well done, love. What a git!"

"Oh my God!" Olivia suddenly cried, and they stared at her, unable to tell if she was about to burst out laughing or burst into tears, "The cheek of the man! Who does he think he is?"

Mark hugged her. The girls patted her hand on the table. Brian said, "Well done, Liv."

"Proud of you," Mark said.

"Oh, it was easy," she grinned, rolling her big eyes, "I don't know why I didn't do it ages ago. Now, if you'll excuse me for a moment, I have to call the police and make a formal complaint." She wandered out into the garden with the phone at her ear.

"Celebratory drink, methinks. CHELSEA!" Brian boomed, and the whole pub instantly fell silent. "Do you have more champagne, love?"

She nodded.

"Bring it forth and keep it coming."

"Don't you think you've had enough?" Faye said.

"Hassle me not, woman."

"Are you drunk?"

"Has anyone drunk ever admitted that they're drunk?"

"You're drunk."

"I'm happy, don't try to steal it away from me. Our lovely Liv has *finally* connected with her soulmate and got rid of her evil tyrant of a father and moron of a husband." He winked at Mark. "Our obscenely gorgeous legal types have faced death and gotten engaged, yay!" Tel and Sophie kissed each other. "And we, my naggy little wife – "

"I'm five foot seven and I *don't* nag."

" – have patched up our differences and are living a quiet, sister-free existence, and thank Odin for that. So, we should celebrate our good fortune and offer up a token of our appreciation to the gods."

"And by 'token' you mean 'booze', and by 'offer up' you mean 'chug down'."

"It worked for the Vikings."

"You're not a Viking."

"I have Viking blood in me," he said, puffing out his chest, "No doubt about it. I'm constantly fighting the urge to plunder and pillage."

"I can see you as Thor," Mark nodded, and Brian threw up his biceps.

"Phwoar," Sophie laughed, "I think I might be marrying the wrong man."

"Hey!" Tel cried, as Faye threw herself across Brian and snapped, "He's taken, love."

Chelsea put two open bottles and fresh glasses on the table. Tel leaned into her and whispered, "We can't expect the management, whoever they are, to put up with our champagne swilling habits." He discretely held out his credit card again. She looked at him and said, "I've already told you, your money's no good here. Enjoy."

She passed Olivia, on her way back to the table, and smiled.

"Very generous management they have here," Tel said, raising his glass. "To our lovely Liv and Mark!"

"To Tel and Sophie!"

"To us," Brian whispered to Faye, clinking her glass. "Love you, lass."

"You are drunk," she laughed. "Love you too, big man."

"Oh the love!" he cried, "Feel the love!"

"All you need is love," Tel wailed, waving his hands in the air, until Sophie pulled them down again. "Cramping me style, woman!" he cried, "Put a ring on ya finger and you go all *wifey* on me."

"I haven't even started yet."

"Be afraid," Brian said, "Be very afraid."

"Where's Jim?" Olivia suddenly said.

"When did we last see him?"

"Outside in the garden, before we came in to eat."

"On it," Mark said, taking out his phone. "Let's videocall him on WhatsApp to identify his whereabouts."

They all huddled round the screen as the call rang out.

A hair-ruffled Jim appeared. "Yeah?"

"We were wondering where you'd gone." Mark peered closer at the screen. "Are you in bed?"

"I certainly am."

"You really are an idiot! Will you never learn? Beth's going to kill you!"

The picture moved. Beth's equally hair-ruffled face filled the screen. "I am gonna to kill 'im," she cackled, "But not in the way you think."

Jim reappeared. "You all buggered off for food and I'd already eaten, so I thought I'd nip home and see the wife, and – ooh!" he laughed, looking down. "I'm busy, bye!" And he was gone.

"Well, wonders will never cease," Mark said. "I actually think they might make it."

"They will," Olivia said, resting her head on his shoulder, "We all will."

* * *

There were no rampaging scramblers that night, just the sound of Brian's deep and thunderous snoring, which kept quite a few people awake until the early hours of the morning.

"SUFFOCATE HIM WITH A PILLOW!" someone screamed from a neighbouring caravan.

"Stick a sock in it!" cried another.

Faye, wearing her earplugs, was oblivious to it all.

CHAPTER 15

Day 7 - Thursday

Tel and Sophie emerged from their caravan holding steaming mugs, dragging their camping chairs across the driveway to where everyone else was sitting outside Brian and Faye's caravan.

"Have you seen my engagement ring?" Sophie laughed, moving her hand so it caught the light and blinded everyone.

"Ooh!" Faye cried, "Show me again."

Sophie did, saying, "I can't get used to the weight of it on my finger."

"Rich folk problems," Mark drawled.

"It's gorgeous, Soph!"

"I know, I can't stop looking at it!"

Mark took a pair of sunglasses from his shirt pocket and put them on.

Sophie sat down, her hand inadvertently slipping off the armrest. "Help Sophie with her hand, Tel," Brian quipped, "She seems to be having trouble with the weight of her rock."

Tel laughed, sitting down next to her. "So, what shall we do today?"

"Doing it," Brian said, leaning back in his zero-gravity chair and basking in the sun with an open book on his chest.

"It's our last day," Sophie said, "We should do something memorable on our last day."

"Memorable?" Brian drawled, briefly lifting his head. "We've survived the flow of Flo, fought off marauding bikers, survived a bike tour to hell and back, watched Tel and Sophie jump from 15,000 feet, observed Tel having some sort of nervous breakdown and losing a vastly expensive ring – "

"Losing?" Sophie gasped. "You lost it?"

"Tell you about it later."

" – and seen Harry and Richard arrested. Pray tell, how much more memorable do you want this holiday to be?"

"Yeah, you're right."

"Of course I'm right," Brian said, closing his eyes, "I'm always right."

Faye mimed 'He's not' and rolled her eyes.

A small, white Transit rolled into the caravan area and parked next to the shepherd's hut. Jim got out and sauntered round to where they were all sitting. "Whatsuuuuuuup!" he cried.

"Jim!" cried Sophie, "How lovely to see you!"

"Oh Jim!" Faye said, jumping up. "Sit down. Here, have my chair and I'll make you a nice cup of coffee."

"Croissants?" Mark asked.

"What?" Jim looked perturbed.

"Can I get you some fresh croissants from the camp shop?"

"Well, I'd rather go to the pub for a full English, if it's all the same to you, but thanks for the offer, strange though it was."

"Suit yourself."

"Ta, I will."

"How you feeling, Jim?" Sophie asked, sidling behind him and reclining his chair, where she proceeded to gently massage his shoulders.

"Nervous, I'm feeling very nervous. Why are you all being nice to me?"

"We like you," Tel said, bringing a plastic side table over to him, onto which Faye, all smiles, placed a mug of coffee.

"What's going on?"

"We want to make you feel welcome and part of our gang," Sophie said. "We think we've been a bit mean to you."

"Well, Mark has."

Mark tutted.

"You help yourself to beers from the coolbox whenever

you want," Brian said with a wink. "Not now, obviously, it's far too early, but later, when the sun is over the yardarm."

"The sun is where?"

"That's noon, isn't it?" Tel said.

"Oh, well if it's good enough for sailors it's good enough for – "

"No," Faye snapped, "Don't you touch that coolbox."

Brian started humming, "It's five o'clock somewhere."

"It's eleven in the morning, Bri!"

"Ah, just another hour to go before the sun is over – "

"Try it and see what happens. You okay there, Jim?"

"Yes, very comfortable, very caffeinated, very … anxious about all the attention."

"Don't be anxious," Sophie whispered eerily in his ear, "You're amongst friends."

Jim shot up in his chair. "Okay, your behaviour is making me edgy."

"Don't be edgy," Tel said, displaying all his perfect white teeth, "We want you to feel comfortable."

Jim jumped to his feet. "What is this, The Twilight Zone? Have I slipped into another dimension where you're all nice to me? I don't like it."

"Don't like being pampered?" Faye asked.

"No, not like this. I feel like one of you is going to kick me off the chair or slap the back of my head at any moment."

"All that's in the past," Tel breathed.

"Stop it, you're scaring me."

"Okay, Operation Be Nicer to Jim has failed," Brian said. "Sit yourself down, lad."

Jim moved towards Faye's chair, and she said, "Gerroff, that's mine."

"Well that didn't last long, did it! Where should I sit then?"

"On the grass."

"Like a dog?"

"No," Sophie said, "Like a friend who hasn't brought his

own chair."

"Hasn't brought anything at all," Mark laughed. "It's like he left his house empty-handed on Friday morning and suddenly decided to go camping."

"Mark, insulting me," Jim said, smiling as he grabbed his coffee from the table next to Faye. "I can relax now."

"Olivia not up yet?" Tel asked.

"She's gone to the police station to make a statement, insisted on going alone."

"Good," Sophie said, "That will put an end to it all."

* * *

Olivia had finished making her statement and was just leaving the tiny interview room when she bumped into Harry and Richard coming down the corridor. They looked tired and dishevelled, and were still wearing handcuffs.

"Olivia!" Richard cried, actually smiling at her, looking pleased to see her; things he hadn't done in years. "Have you come to get us out? It's been dreadful, absolutely – "

"No," she said, "I've ... I've just given my statement."

"Against us?" Harry snarled.

"Just the facts, daddy."

"The facts *against* us."

"The facts you created. I had nothing to do with what happened."

"Didn't you? It was that ridiculous divorce settlement that started all this, and you definitely had something to do with that. You're the instigator of this, Olivia, remember that. They're going to lock us up and it's *all your fault*."

"No, it's not, this is all down to you and him." She glanced at Richard, who frowned. "You have no one to blame but yourselves. Don't contact me again unless it's through the lawyers, either of you."

Harry glared at her as she walked past. She glared back, unblinking, unflinching. She saw a glimmer of surprise in his eyes, and then she walked away.

"Olivia?" Richard called after her. "What about me? I didn't do anything, it was all – "

"Shut up, Richard!"

Olivia didn't stop. Mark and her new life were waiting for her.

The slamming of a cell door somewhere in the building was like the death knell on her old life.

"Bring on the new," she said to herself, as she walked out into the sunlight, smiling.

* * *

"Ooh, there's a market on the High Street in Witney on Thursdays," Tel said, reading from his phone.

Brian groaned loudly.

"More details," Faye snapped.

"It's been going since the medieval times and sells everything from street food to gifts."

Faye jumped up out of her chair and cried, "I'll get my purse! Brian, put your sandals on, we're going out."

"I haven't had breakfast yet!"

"Me neither," Jim said.

"We'll grab croissants on the way out."

"Ugh, croissants," said Tel, "Made me ill yesterday."

Sophie burst out laughing. "It was the croissants that made you throw up like that girl in The Exorcist, was it?"

"Must have been."

"It wasn't anything to do with freefalling from 15,000 feet, mostly unconscious?"

"Nah," Tel grinned, "Nothing to do with that."

"You and your big mouth," Brian grumbled at Tel, clambering out of his chair.

"I was just saying," he laughed.

"I can feel my credit score dropping like a rock from a great height already. She loses all control at markets, her eyes take on this feverish look, and the hunter-gatherer instinct kicks in big time." He gave them a feverish look, then shuffled off to find his sandals.

"Fancy it, Mark?"

"I'll stay here and wait for Liv to come back."

Jim scrambled to his feet. "Who's buying the croissants then?"

"Not me, can't stand the things now, make me ..." Tel glanced at Mark, grinning. Mark said, "Don't do it. Don't you –"

"Bleurgh." Tel splayed his fingers in front of his face, making Mark dry wretch. "Bleurgh, bleurgh, bleurgh."

"Stop it," Sophie said, nudging him with her shoulder as Mark rested forward on his knees with a hand over his mouth. "Stop being mean."

"Taste of your own medicine," Jim laughed.

"Bleurgh," Tel went, and Mark heaved again, gasping, "Stop it!"

"Okay."

"We all ready?" Faye asked, coming out of the caravan with her shoulder bag and locking the door behind her. "Do we have enough bags-for-life in the car, Bri?"

Brian's eyes widened. "Why, how much are you planning to buy?"

"Whatever takes my fancy," she grinned.

"Oh God."

* * *

They went in Brian's black Kia and found the market at Witney *heaving* with people. Brian followed Faye around, saying, "We don't need it. It's too expensive. We already have three of those," to no avail. Faye dawdled from one stall to the next, in her element, touching things, touching everything.

"Is a man, sitting on a chair, made entirely out of nuts and bolts, strictly necessary in our lives?"

"You're cramping my style, Bri."

"I'm keeping an eye on our financial stability."

His eye was briefly distracted by a craft beer stall and he suddenly had a hankering to try some Elvis Juice, or maybe a Red Welsh ale, or even a caffeine-infused porter, but when looked to see how bored Faye was she had already made a bolt for it. He frantically searched the crowds, spotting her two stalls down, and hurried over, just in time to stop her purchasing an ostrich egg.

"I've never had one," she whined, when he took it from her and placed it back on its stand.

"We don't have a frying pan big enough."

Tel and Sophie had been captured by a vegan seller, despite them not being vegans. "Organic is so much better for you," the seller was telling them, "No artificial chemicals, naturally grown with care and attention on our biocyclic agricultural farm."

"I could buy a massive Wagyu steak for the price of those carrots," Tel whispered to Sophie.

"Buy some, and then we can escape."

Jim poked his head between their shoulders. "Occurring? Oh, veg, uber-bore. Christ, expensive much!"

"So much better for you," the seller began.

"Not at those prices, love."

"No artificial chemicals – "

"I quite like chemicals."

The seller looked aghast. While the mouth hung open in aghastment, they made their escape and bought steak and ale pasties at the next stall.

"Cushions, Faye? Really? We have a plethora of the things in the caravan, I'm sure they're breeding like Tribbles in Star Trek."

"We don't have any blue ones like this."

"Put it down, Faye."

"No, I can't."

"Put it down and step away from the cushions!"

"Is that you trying to be firm?" she grinned up at him.

"It is."

"It's not working."

Brian sighed.

"Faye!" Sophie called through the crowds.

"What?"

"Come and look at this!"

Faye dashed off, with Brian in hot pursuit, hoping the 'this' wasn't unbearably expensive.

Sophie, Tel and Jim were standing in front of a jewellery stall. Brian's heart pounded in his chest and he gave a little groaning noise at the back of his throat when he saw the prices for 'hand crafted silver'. Tel handed both him and Faye a paper-wrapped pastie, and his heartbeat calmed a little.

Sophie pointed at something. "What do you think of that?"

"Ooh, for Liv?"

"Yes. Isn't it perfect?"

"It is."

"I think I'll get it."

"We can all club together as a joint gift," Faye suggested, and Brian flinched.

"That's a really good idea," said Sophie.

"I'm skint," Jim said.

Brian and his pastie leaned forward. "Which shiny object are we talking about?"

"That one."

"Oh." Brian nodded as he went back to his pastie. Pricey, he thought, but not eye-wateringly catastrophic.

"Ooh," Faye cried, pushing a twenty into Sophie's hand and rushing off again.

* * *

"How was it?" Mark asked.

"It was okay. I gave my statement and they said they'd be in touch if they needed anything else from me. Saw daddy and Richard on the way out."

"No!"

"They send their love."

Mark laughed and hugged her. They were in the motorhome, lying on the bed. "Are you going to tell them today?" he asked.

"Yes, tonight. I'm amazed I lasted nearly a week, there were so many times I nearly slipped up."

"You've done well, my little sneaky one."

"Couldn't fool Brian though, he knows."

"He does, but he's equally good at keeping secrets."

"Do you think they'll hate me?"

"I keep telling you, they'll understand."

"I hope so. I've written a short speech which starts, 'Please don't hate me'."

"Stop worrying, Liv, they'll be fine with it."

"Where are they anyway?"

"They've all gone shopping at a village market."

"Have they?" Olivia snuggled up closer to him. "How long do you think they'll be?"

"Oh," he grinned, leaning in for a kiss, "Ages."

* * *

"Faye, you have to stop now!"

"There's still some stalls left."

"I'm tired, my feet are killing me, my back has caved in on itself, and I need a beer."

"Nearly done." She skipped to the next stall.

"Show some self-control, woman!"

"I can't!"

He huffed. "One more stall, and then that's it."

"One?"

"One!"

"Oh." Faye stepped away from the display of Wiccan accessories to look down at the row of stalls she hadn't yet visited. There were so many of them, she couldn't decide.

"I'm getting into the car and leaving in five minutes, Faye."

"Oh."

Brian stood there as Faye hurried off towards one stall, then changed her mind and headed to another, walking passed it as she was drawn to yet a different one.

The others came and stood next to him.

"Get much?" Brian asked, hanging onto the four bags-for-life Faye had managed to fill.

"Just Olivia's present and a card," Sophie said.

"Nothing," said Jim, "Skint."

"You?" Tel asked.

"Everything," Brian sighed, "And then some."

"Is she always like this?" Sophie watched Faye flitting to and fro amongst the crowds, frantically picking things up and reluctantly putting them down again.

"Only at open-air markets, craft fairs, bookshops and garden centres. FAYE!" he suddenly boomed, making them all jump, "I'M OFF!"

She came running up the road. "I haven't found my last stall yet!" Frantic, she picked up the nearest item from the Wiccan table and looked at it.

"Why," said Brian, "do you need an ornately engraved chalice?"

"For my prosecco."

"Put it down, Faye."

She did, then shot off to a stall on the other side of the road. Brian sighed heavily as he watched her rifling through rails of clothing. Her face suddenly lit up and money was exchanged. She sauntered back looking happy with her final purchase, pushing it into her bag.

"Come on, lass, let's go home."

* * *

As they passed The Woodsman they saw a banner hanging at the front reading THURSDAY NIGHT IS KARAOKE NIGHT.

"That's our evening sorted then," Tel said. "Haven't been to a karaoke for years."

"You've done karaoke?" Sophie laughed. "I mean, I know you have a good voice, I've heard it in the shower, but standing up in front of people?"

"Not that different from standing up in court."

"Except we don't sing in court."

"We could start a trend."

"I'll look into Johnny Cash's back catalogue immediately," she laughed.

Brian was hauling the last of the bags from the car and Faye was popping a prosecco cork when Mark and Olivia emerged from the motorhome looking ever so slightly dishevelled.

"Way-hay!" Jim cried, "Haven't disturbed you, have we?"

"Afternoon nap," Mark said.

"Good nap, was it?"

"All our naps are good," he said, and Olivia turned puce.

"Here," Faye said, handing her a glass, "Have some of this to cool your cheeks down."

"Ooh, quite parched myself," Jim said, jumping up from Faye's chair and heading towards Brian's coolbox.

"Oi!" Brian cried, "Where do you think you're going?"

"You said I could help myself."

"That was when we were being nice to you, before you threw our kindness back in our faces." Brian tossed his head sideways in a dramatic 'hurt' pose, then said, "Ow, cricked my bloody neck."

Jim hovered over the coolbox, his hands itching to lift the lid.

"Go on, help yourself."

"Bring me one, Jim."

"And me."

"Does no one actually contribute to the group's alcoholic stash?" Brian sighed, as his beer was generously handed out. All he heard in response was the cracking of can tabs. He sighed again and said to Faye, who was pushing Jim out of her chair, "Don't know where we're going to sleep tonight, wife, the sofas are piled high with impulse buys."

"None of them were impulse buys, Bri."

"There's an Arabian hookah pipe in one of the bags, Faye."

"I didn't buy a pipe, Bri."

"What's a hookah?" Jim asked.

"It's a tall thing with a pipe for smoking tobacco ... or cannabis. Are you planning on becoming a pothead, Faye?"

"I didn't buy anything like that."

"Tall, purple, glass ball with a rubber pipe coming out of it, ring any bells?"

Faye looked at him and huffed. "It's a lamp," she said, "I bought a lamp. Pretty, isn't it. I'll have to find a matching shade and a bulb to – "

Brian exploded with laughter, so hard he had to clutch at his aching belly.

"I don't see what's so funny," Faye tutted. "It's just a lamp."

"Stop, I'm going to be sick!"

Mark dry heaved.

"I thought it would look nice in the bedroom."

Brain could barely catch his breath. When he did, he gasped, "Yeah, Faye, put it in the bedroom so the police can easily find it when we get raided."

"It's just a lamp, Bri!"

Brian struggled to control himself. The others were giggling.

"I can't wait to see you plug it in," Brian gasped, dragging the coolbox out onto the grass. "Anybody got any ginga?"

"Any what?" Jim asked.

"Genga, ganga?"

"If you can't pronounce it you probably shouldn't smoke it."

"I think we have enough trouble with our alcohol consumption," Sophie said, swigging at her prosecco, "I don't think we should be adding drugs to the mix too."

"There's a karaoke at the pub tonight," Tel said, looking at Mark and Olivia, who had their heads together, whispering sweet nothings. "Hello, earth calling Markol, come in, Markol."

"Markol?" Jim grinned, "That's terrible."

"Short notice."

"What?" said Mark.

"Hi, I can see you're busy in your little cocoon of love, but I was just saying there's a karaoke at the pub tonight."

"I know."

"Can you sing?"

"Like a galloping cowboy with haemorrhoids."

"Nice image."

Olivia glanced at her watch, "It starts in half an hour." A warbling, high-pitched wail drifted over the campsite as an amplified voice attempted to sing something vaguely familiar. "Blimey, they're keen, they've started already."

"Have they? Or did a cat get caught on the microphone."

Brian chugged the contents of his can down and stood up. "Let us depart and astonish the audience with our dulcet tones, just as soon as we've eaten, I'm starving."

"You're always starving," Faye said, finishing her prosecco.

"I'm a growing boy."

"Time to stop growing, you take up too much bed space."

They wandered off through the hedges.

The others followed.

* * *

Once again the pub was filled to capacity when they walked in. In front of the fireplace at the far end a man stood behind a music desk, and a woman on a microphone in front was totally torturing a Whitney Houston song, failing to make the high notes and seemingly incapable of reading the lyrics on the autocue.

"There's a prize for the best and the worst singer tonight," Sue laughed as she served them. "So far we've got three candidates for worst and none for best. Nobody can sing around here."

"I intend to change all that," Brian said.

"Confident, eh?"

"I don't hear any serious competition." Brian winced as the woman finished screeching her oohs at the end of the song.

A young girl immediately leapt behind the microphone. Familiar piano music started and Faye said, "Oh, this one's hard."

"What is it?" Tel asked.

"This is Me from The Greatest Showman. She'll never be able to pull it – "

The girl started singing, in perfect pitch, and the whole pub went silent, enthralled by her voice. Even the bar staff stopped serving. When she'd finished, the pub exploded with cheers and applause, and the girl took a bow.

"Confidence rating now?" Sue laughed.

"I'm assuming you'll have a male and a female best singer?"

"Nope, just the one."

"Ah."

"We've reserved your usual table for you."

The others went over with their drinks, while Mark and Brian stayed at the bar waiting for their pints to be pulled.

"I see you and Faye are back on track now," Mark said.

"See?"

"Yeah, you were flirting with Sue and Faye didn't bat an

eyelid."

"She's happy. Watch." He turned to the table and yelled, "FAYE!"

"WHAT?"

"I'M FLIRTING WITH SUE!"

"POOR SUE!"

"You call that flirting?" Sue said, when he turned back, "I thought you were spasming or in some kind of pain."

"Funny!" He turned to Mark. "Happy wife – "

"Happy life."

"You remember that, lad."

"I will."

* * *

They ordered from the menu, ate it to the sounds of various howls and diabolical shrieks, and then read through a laminated list of karaoke songs.

"Found it," Brian cried, standing up and lumbering off.

"This should be good," Tel said.

Faye smiled.

He spoke to the man behind the music desk, who nodded, and then turned and gripped the microphone. "Hello, I'm Brian."

"Hi, Brian!" everyone yelled.

"I'd like to sing you a little song, and it goes something like this." Guitar music started, quite slow, and Brian, in a deep baritone, started singing about the woman he loves. He stared at Faye the entire time, and she had to dab at her eyes with a napkin. It was perfect, and when he finished the audience gave him a rapturous applause. "More!" someone shouted, and Brian held out an encouraging hand. "Faye?"

"What?"

"Will you join me?"

"The heck I will!"

"Come on, wife."

"No!"

There was laughter. A man at a table near the bar drunkenly yelled, "Get up there, you old tart."

Brian said into the microphone, "That's no tart, that's my wife."

"Better luck next time, mate."

The other man at the table quickly shut him up with a firm nudge and a fierce look.

"Come on, lass, you know you want to."

"I don't, I really don't!"

The pub started chanting, "Fa-ye! Fa-ye!" Sophie gently pushed her off her chair, while the others urged her on. Faye rolled her eyes, stood up reluctantly, and joined Brian behind the microphone.

"Number 157," Brian said to the man in charge, and he nodded. Brian grabbed the microphone again and said to the audience, "I think you'll like this one."

"Which one is it?" Faye whispered.

"You'll see." To the pub he said, "Feel free to join in."

The music started. Faye looked shocked for a moment, then rushed to the microphone next to Brian and they both started singing about getting married in a fever. The pub cheered and clapped along. Mark looked at Tel and said, "Bloody brilliant!"

"Aren't they!"

"They're both really good," Sophie cried. "I think the fake Texan drawl mixed with a Yorkshire twang and a thick Brummie brogue really give it an edge."

Brian and Faye did a spot of line dancing between solos, which went down well with the already excited crowd. When they finished people stood up to whoop and applaud, and they walked back to their table to the cries of, "More! More!"

As they passed the bar, Brian winked at Sue and said, "Confidence level, restored."

The drunken man cheered the loudest.

As they sat down, Tel and Sophie were arguing.

"Come on, Soph."

"Absolutely not."

"Faye did it."

"It's alright once you're up there," Faye said.

"Not in a million, trillion years."

Tel lifted her left hand. "Look at this lovely ring I got for you, don't I deserve a little song in return?"

"You're using my engagement ring as a bribe?"

"Yes. Come on, you'll love it."

"You're overlooking the fact that I can't actually sing."

Behind the microphone a woman was murdering a Janis Joplin song.

"People don't care if you can sing or not, it's all about the fun, Soph."

"I won't be having fun, Tel."

"Give it a go, I swear I'll have to drag you off afterwards."

"Which one?" she pouted, glaring at the karaoke list.

Tel pointed at one. She considered it for a moment, sighing. Then, just as Janis Joplin's assault on the eardrums mercifully ended, she grabbed Mark's tumbler of whisky, gulped it down, and stood up.

"That's my girl!"

"Woman, Tel, I'm a woman, about to be chronically humiliated in the name of *fun*."

They stood behind the microphone, Tel looking excited, Sophie looking terrified. The music started and everyone cheered in recognition. Tel leaned towards the mic and sang about having chills and they were multiplying.

"Wow, he can really sing!" Jim gasped.

"And wriggle those hips," Faye sighed.

"Take your eyes off our friend's wriggle, woman."

Sophie missed her cue and came in late, softly murmuring about needing a man.

"Louder!" Tel cried.

"Give it some wellie!" Brian boomed.

"Terrible!" screamed the drunken man, "Get off!"

Tel gripped Sophie's arm to stop her running, and she unwillingly wailed that her heart was set on him. The pub, who had been clapping along with Tel, suddenly went quiet as they struggled to catch the rhythm of someone who seemingly didn't have any sense of beat at all. Sophie's face took on an extremely pained expression as she continued to sing along, very badly.

"She sounds like an untuned violin," Jim said.

Mark pulled a face and said, "Oh, that is awful."

"Poor Sophie," said Olivia.

"Is she tone deaf?" Brian asked. "I didn't think it was possible to sing that flat."

Behind the mic, Tel motioned the man to stop the music and the pub suddenly went quiet. He pulled Sophie away from the mic and whispered, "Just pretend you're in court with a really obnoxious judge, who's deaf."

"I can't do this, Tel."

"If I can jump from 15,000 feet, you can sing in front of a few people."

"A few?" She glanced around the crowded room. "There's hundreds!"

"You can do this, Soph, you really can, and you'll be so proud of yourself afterwards, and I will too. Do something every day that scares you."

"I've filled my allocation for that."

"Face your fears. Come on, Soph."

"O-okay."

Tel nodded at the karaoke man and the music started again. "Deaf judge," Tel said, leading her back to the microphone.

This time, Sophie didn't even attempt to sing. She stood behind the mic, her chin in the air, and loudly spoke about shaping up in the poshest voice anyone in the room had ever heard, postulating to the crowds as if giving a closing speech.

"Very Baz Luhrmann's Sunscreen," Brian said.

"Ingenious," Mark laughed, clapping and whistling.

The crowds loved it and gave rapturous applause when they'd finished. Tel bounced back to the table, exhilarated. Sophie stomped, her face like thunder. "Say nothing," she told them as she sat down. To Tel she growled, "Never, but *never*, make me do that again!"

He vigorously shook his head.

Someone suddenly appeared next their table and screamed, "KARAOKE TIME!" They turned as one and saw Beth standing there, already dancing along to a group of girls singing a Spice Girls song.

Jim jumped up and kissed her. "Glad you could make it," he said.

"Weren't gonna miss this, was I, babe. I love singing, *love* it." She threw her handbag down on the table and cried, "Watch that, it cost an arm and a leg and a promissory note for my organs in the event of my death. I'm going up!"

"She's not even had a drink yet!" Sophie gasped in awe, her fingers nonchalantly stroking the Louis Vuitton bag.

Jim watched with some pride as his wife sashayed through the crowds and up to the karaoke man. The music started and Beth began to sing Someone Like You. The pub fell totally silent, except for the drunken man, who was loudly cheering.

Her voice was staggering.

"Are you sure," Brian said to Jim, "Absolutely positive, that you haven't inadvertently married Adele?"

Jim, beaming from ear to ear, said, "She's good, isn't she."

"Good? Her voice is stunning."

"Tel," Sophie said, unable to tear her eyes off Beth, "Is Beth ... Adele?"

"I'm ... I'm not sure."

Beth finished and took a bow before rushing back to the table. "Bloody parched," she cried, "Go get me a drink, Jim."

He bounced off, proud as punch. The others just stared at her.

"What?" she laughed.

"Is your real name Adele?" Tel asked.

"No! I sound like 'er though, don't I."

"You're amazing," Faye said.

"Outstanding," said Brian.

"Thanks. You should 'ear my Paloma Faith impersonation, makes people cry."

"I can do that," Sophie said.

"What, sing like Paloma Faith?"

"No, make people cry with my voice."

Jim came back with a drink and another big kiss for his talented wife.

"Your turn to wow us with your vocals," Brian said to him.

"Me?" Jim laughed, "I can't sing, mate, I'm worse than Sophie, and that's saying something."

"Thanks," Sophie snapped beneath hooded eyes.

"No offence, Soph."

"*Loads* taken."

The drunken man near the bar shouted across, "Oi, fat bird, sing us another song."

Jim visibly prickled and half turned, but Beth nudged him and said, "I can take care of this, babes."

She walked back towards the mic, all smiles. The man cheered and clapped and made lewd noises. She kicked the leg of his chair as she walked past and he crashed to the floor. The other man had to help him up again.

Beth grabbed the mic and said, "This is my favourite song, hope you like it." She sang Changing, by Paloma Faith, faultlessly. The crowds were enthralled. When she finished, the pub was silent in breath-held amazement before people stood up at their tables and clapped wildly. "Thanks," she said, as they cried out for more. "Gotta have a drink with me mates now," and walked off.

The drunken man made a grab for her as she passed. She deftly avoided his hands and whacked him on his head with her elbow.

"Nicely done," Brian said.

"Thanks, I get lots of practice." They shuffled round to make space for her at the table.

"I don't know what you do for a living," Tel said, "But quit and take up singing."

"Oh no," she cackled, "I just sing for fun. And I don't do nuffin' for a living, me dad won the lottery and moved us all here, bought a house, hated the countryside, and moved back to London. I liked it so I stayed."

"And I'm so glad you did," Jim said, hugging her.

"Mark?" said Brian. "You and Olivia getting up to sing?"

"When hell freezes over." Olivia nodded her fervent agreement.

Singers came and went, some good, some bad, some dreadful enough to make ears bleed. Olivia was just coming back from the loo to the warbling twang of a Dolly Parton song when the drunken man suddenly started swearing at the other man at his table. He jumped up, pushing Olivia back against the bar, and she gave a surprised cry. Mark immediately raced towards her, impeded by people and chairs.

Everything that happened next he saw as if in slow motion.

The man, still swearing, started waving his arms about. A glass fell off the table and crashed to the floor. Chelsea darted around the bar and, just as she reached the table, the man, still swearing and wildly swinging his arms about, struck her across the face with a stray hand. She cried out and fell back, clutching her face. Olivia immediately leapt forward, grabbing hold of the man's wrist and twisting it up his back in one smooth movement. With her other hand she pushed the man's head down, like a police officer apprehending a suspect. Holding him in that position she marched him towards the open door and took him outside.

The gang flew after her.

Olivia shoved the man onto the car park and growled,

"You're banned! Don't ever show your face in this pub again!"

The man staggered towards her, yelling, "Don't tell me what I can and can't do, you little - " Brian stepped out, his arms crossed across his vast chest. Mark stood next to him, his lips twitching in fury. Tel joined them. The man stopped shouting.

"Clear off!" Olivia shouted. "We don't want your type here."

"My mate's inside!"

"I don't care, get off my property!"

"I ain't got no car, my mate's got the car."

"Then walk!"

"Start walking, pal," Mark growled.

The man pouted and staggered out of the car park onto the lane, where a passing car blasted a horn at his sudden appearance.

Olivia stood dead still, her back to them, feeling the realisation of her actions washing over her. She continued to stare after the man as her mind whirled. She felt everyone's eyes upon her. She didn't turn or look back, but she could sense their confusion.

She'd blown it.

Mark was instantly at her side, holding her hand.

"Liv?" Sophie said.

Olivia felt frozen to the spot. "Yes, Sophie?"

"Why did you tell that man to stay off your property?"

"Because … because he was causing a nuisance."

"On *your* property?"

"And how can a customer ban another customer?" Tel asked.

Olivia slowly turned round, giggling nervously. They were all staring at her, frowning, not understanding. "I was going to tell you."

"Tell us what, Liv?"

A large group at one of the tables out front started getting up and leaving, chatting animatedly. She pointed towards it with an open hand and they sat down.

"What's going on?" Tel asked.

She smiled her cute, overbite smile, as Mark rubbed her back and said, "Tell them, Liv."

"Well." She exhaled and gripped Mark's hand tightly. "It's ... it's my pub, my campsite. The sale went through in January. That's why I haven't seen much of you this year, I've been busy getting it ready, making improvements, organising ... things."

They glanced fleetingly at each other, and then back at Olivia. "Why didn't you tell us?"

Olivia rifled frantically through the bag on her shoulder, pulling out several pieces of paper. "I have a speech," she said, smoothing out the pages and reading, "'Please don't hate me - '"

Brian pushed down the papers and said, "Just talk to us, Liv."

"You bought the place?"

"Wow."

"I ... I just wanted your honest feedback. I value your opinions and I didn't want to sway you either way."

"We would have been honest," Sophie said.

"I know, but ... I wanted unbiased honesty from people I respect." She felt very nervous. "Do you think me terribly deceitful and dishonest?"

"No," Tel shrugged, "I think we're all just ... a bit shocked, actually."

"You bought the pub and the campsite?"

"Yes. It's a special place, where I found my freedom and an amazing group of friends. I made Ant, the previous landlord, an offer, and he practically bit my hand off."

"I bet he did," Mark laughed, then, to the others, "I only found out myself a couple of days ago."

"I've been working on it all year," Olivia continued. "I wanted to make this a special place for other people, too."

"I think you've achieved that," Faye said, looking around

at all the happy, smiling people on the benches around them, the crowds having a good time inside the pub, and those laughing and playing in the camping field.

"And I love it, I really love it," Olivia continued. "Chelsea does all the hard work, I couldn't have done this without her, but I get to create, to make a place where people can forge their own happy memories, and I'm actually good at it too, it's turning a profit. It's *so* satisfying and I'm having so much fun with it." She paused. "You don't all … hate me, do you?"

"Hate you?" Sophie cried, "Oh my God, Liv, of course not! We love you and we're behind you one hundred percent in anything you choose to do."

"You've done an *amazing* job," Brian said.

They got up one by one and surrounded her in a massive group hug. Olivia started crying with relief. Melissa came out with a tray of drinks for another table, and Brian yelled, "Celebratory champagne over here, lass!" Melissa nodded and disappeared into the pub again. "Oh! You've paid for all our food and drink all week, Liv, and there's me ordering champagne."

"I'll pay for this one," Tel said, fishing out his wallet.

"No, no," Brian said, reaching for his, "This one's on me."

"It's on the house," Olivia insisted. "I can afford it, and it's a small price to pay for treating you like guinea pigs. Think of it as payment for your services, and … and for being my friends."

"Feels weird, celebrating with your own champagne though," Tel said.

"Champagne I ordered especially for you and which I expect you to drink, or I'll be offended."

"Thanks very much," Brian said, putting his wallet away.

Olivia stared at him. "You knew, didn't you."

"I … did."

"Brian!" Faye snapped, "Why didn't you tell me?"

"What, and ruin it for Liv?"

"I wouldn't have said anything!"

"Wasn't my news to tell."

"I'm your wife, you're supposed to tell me everything!"

"And how long would you have kept it a secret before the urge to splurge overcame you? Be honest now."

Faye lifted her chin and said, "A good hour, maybe two."

"What gave it away?" Mark asked.

"Oh, just little things, like Liv saying that she was having the gate lock fixed, not the pub, and some looks, some slips of the tongue. I wasn't certain, but I had an inkling. I'm big and loud, but I'm observant."

"And very secretive," Faye said. "The farmyard rescue, the race to the airport, Liv owning a pub and campsite. Is there anything else you're not telling me, Bri?"

"I was born a woman," he said, deadpan, and the whole table burst out laughing. Brian, still deadpan, said, "I was."

"Was you?" Tel gasped.

"No, you fool! Do I look like a woman trapped in a man's body, or," he frowned, "A man trapped in a woman's ...? I've confused myself now."

"Not as clever as you think, eh?" Faye said.

Brian leaned towards her and kissed her on the cheek, whispering, "I am." Sitting back down again he said, "And, of course, I looked at the website for The Woodsman, just to check if you'd put the pricing up or anything."

"I haven't."

"No, but what you did put up was pictures, and one of them has you in it?"

"Does it?" Tel said, tapping on his phone.

"Oh," Olivia said, "Bit of a faux pas. We had a web designer do our site. I guess Chelsea just sent him some photos to put on."

"Oh yeah!" Tel cried at his phone. "You and all the staff."

"I'd just hired the last one in that photo, Michael, the barman."

"Oh, the gorgeous one," Faye said.

"The one that *literally* has a lazy eye," Sophie laughed.

"A customer offered to take our photo."

"It's a good one of you."

"Thanks."

"Where did you learn to eject aggressive customers like that?" Sophie asked, "Did the brewery send you on a course or something?"

"No, it's a free house, it's all mine, no brewery involved. Mummy and I took some self-defence classes in ... I can't remember which country it was now, but it was good, taught us a lot and we weren't afraid of anything after that. Well, except for mummy's chronic fear of jellyfish, couldn't get her into the sea at all."

"Jellyfish," Tel said, still flicking through his phone, "Strange creatures, no brains, no hearts, no backbone."

"Bit like Jim then," Mark laughed.

"You really must stop picking on him, darling."

"I know." He patted her hand. "I'll try, but he's just so pick-onable."

"Where is he, anyway?"

"He went out back with Beth for some fresh air. Oh, talk of the devil."

Jim and Beth came sauntering out, holding hands. "You're always leaving me behind!" he cried.

"Did you not hear all the shouting and clapping as Liv manhandled a drunk out of the pub?"

"No, we were ..." he glanced at Beth and winked, "... a bit busy. Manhandled?"

"I put my self-defence classes to the test."

"She was magnificent," Mark said proudly.

Jim and Beth dragged a wooden bench over and sat down. Mark and Olivia plucked themselves from the scrum at their table and joined them. "Liv owns the pub," Mark said.

"Does she?" Jim's wide eyes looked at Olivia.

"And the campsite."

"Wow. Why didn't we know?"

"Because she's evil and scheming," Tel laughed.

"Oh don't, I already feel bad about it."

"Well done you," Jim said. "Nice place you've got."

"It's brilliant," Beth said, "S'got a really good vibe."

"Thanks, and thanks for testing it out for me."

"No, thank you for the free lodgings and food and booze!"

"Will you live here or in Bath?" Faye suddenly asked.

"We haven't actually talked about it yet," Mark said.

"I'll probably divide my time between both, although I imagine I'll be spending more time here." She snuggled up to Mark.

"And traveling the world," he said, "Don't forget the traveling."

"Oh, I've done all the traveling I want, darling. I want to settle down and make a new life now, with you."

They kissed. Tel leaned over and kissed Sophie's cheek. Faye, not wanting to be left out, threw her arms around Brian's neck and pulled his head down onto her lips. Jim said, "Sickening."

"Kiss me," Beth said.

He did, quite enthusiastically.

Sue came to the table with an open bottle in a bucket and some glasses. "Snogfest?" she asked.

"Love-in," said Brian. "We're all feeling very pleased with ourselves and want to share the *lurve*."

"Is Chelsea okay?" Olivia asked.

"She's fine, bragging about having a black eye tomorrow, said she might wear an eye patch and a pirate hat." She looked at Olivia with questioning eyes.

"I've told them," she said.

"Oh good!" she breathed. "It was killing me trying not to slip up or ask you anything." She poured the champagne, saying, "She's a brilliant boss, very fair, very lovely. She and Chelsea have the place running like a dream and it's doing *really* well. I've never enjoyed a job so much, and the pay's good too."

"Thank you, Sue, that's very kind of you to say."

"No problem, you can slip me the money later," she laughed, then rushed off.

Brian raised a glass and said, "To the new owner of The Woodsman pub and campsite."

"God bless her and all who drink in her."

"And all those who sleep in her, or on her," Faye said, frowning and quickly adding, "That didn't come out right."

"To Olivia."

"To the newly engaged."

"To us," Tel said, holding his glass up to everyone.

"Oh!" Sophie cried, "We've got you a present, Liv, from all of us." She pulled a small box from her bag and handed it to Olivia. They all watched her open it. She immediately burst into tears.

"It's a star for our little star," Sophie said, as Olivia pulled out a necklace. Mark dabbed at her eyes with a napkin. "It's to match the earrings we got for you last year." The earrings which had sparkled in her ears all week.

"From all of us," Faye said, "Because we love you."

"It's … it's beautiful. Thank you so, *so* much."

"And a card," Sophie said, handing it over.

Olivia opened it, sniffing, and burst into fresh tears. Mark took it from her and read out, "Friends are like stars, always there for you." Olivia was a blubbering mass, gasping, "Thank you, thank you."

"Oh, and I got something for you too, Bri," Faye said, pulling something from her bag. "Saw it at the market, my last purchase and the best."

She handed him a roll of material wrapped in cellophane. He let it drop open and burst out laughing. He turned to show it to the others and they laughed too.

"Perfect," Tel said.

It was a giant black t-shirt with 'the THE' printed on the front.

"It's a music band, apparently," Faye said. "I got it because, being Yorkshire, you never say the word."

"Thank you, my lovely wife!"

"You're welcome, lovely husband."

Tel threw his arms in the air and started singing about all you needed was love.

Sophie pulled his hands down, saying, "Too cheesy," just as both their phones beeped. Tel looked at his first and said, "Oh no!"

Sophie looked at hers and cried, "Yes!"

She pressed the play button on her phone and held it out for everyone to watch.

"Can't see," Jim whined, squinting.

"Too small for us oldies," said Faye.

"Sun's too bright to see anything."

"Take it inside," Olivia said excitedly, "We can play it on the TV."

"No!" Tel whined, as they all hurried inside.

He eventually plucked up the courage to follow them.

CHAPTER 16

A woman was just finishing a song at the mic when they poured back into the pub. Olivia went up to the bar and spoke to Chelsea, who nodded.

"Who would like to see our skydiving video from yesterday?" Sophie shouted to the crowd.

They all cheered. Tel sighed.

Chelsea turned on the TV with the remote and Sophie fiddled with the settings on her phone until her face appeared on the big screen. She was laughing and saying, "This is so exciting! Isn't it exciting, Tel? Oh, he's rushed off to the loo again."

Tel sat at their table and put his head in his hands. They settled around him. The pub was quiet except for Sophie's recorded voice.

"This is our plane," Sophie said to camera. "Not quite as big as I expected, I have to say."

"It was a shoebox," Tel breathed.

"Boring," said the real Sophie, "Let's skip to the good stuff."

Up on screen, Sophie raced to the plane, skimmed the faces of the other passengers, including a lingering shot of Tel, who looked like he was about to burst into tears at any moment, and then a view of her perched on the edge, about to jump. Tel peered through his fingers, then had to avert his eyes as she fell through the air, screaming with joy and smiling like a Cheshire Cat, her hair flying up from her head and the G-force emphasising her cheekbones and flapping her lips – and she still looked beautiful. She was talking and laughing, but you couldn't hear her through the sound of rushing wind.

"Worst sound in the world," Tel muttered.

The parachute opened and Sophie, still laughing hysterically, cried, "Oh my God, that was amazing! Bloody amazing! I'm so pumped up! Oh, look at the view! Stunning! Tel!" she shouted, "You can see our campsite from … Tel? Oh, he's fainted." The real Tel covered his face. "Is he okay?" she shouted over her shoulder to her instructor. "Are you sure? Oh, he's conscious again. Oh, he's … ugh. Are you okay, Tel? What? I can't hear you, will I what?"

In the background they heard the sound of a man screaming. Sophie looked into camera and, with a big smile, shouted, "This is amazing!" She turned her head and said to her instructor, "This is amazing!" Looking away from the camera she shouted, "You okay, Tel?"

The sound of soprano screaming continued.

Everyone watched, enthralled, until Sophie, bursting with excitement, landed on the camping field and started jumping up and down, saying how amazing it had been and could they do it again. Everyone in the pub applauded.

"Now yours, Tel."

"Oh no, no."

"Come on, don't be a spoilsport." Sophie pulled his phone from his pocket, and he wondered why he hadn't smashed it on the way in, destroying all evidence. "We want to see yours."

"No, you don't."

"We do," Brian grinned.

Sophie tapped his phone and Tel's sweaty, horror-filled face appeared. She skimmed through the first bit – Tel rushing to the toilet, looking pensively at the runway, rushing to the toilet again, and then lumbering reluctantly towards the airplane. She fast-forwarded to Tel sitting on the edge of the plane, screaming, "NO! I'VE CHANGED MY MIND! I DON'T WANT TO DO IT! I DON'T WANT TO DIE!" Then he was falling, his face moulded by the wind, his mouth open in a silent scream, his cheeks bulging with air. He went limp for quite a while, the rushing air moving his arms and legs and bobbing his head up and down.

"Kill me now," Tel mumbled at the table. "Oh, the shame, the shame."

"You've never looked more attractive," Sophie laughed. "Look, you can see the ring box in your pocket."

Up on screen, Tel made a choking noise as the parachute opened behind him. His eyes flickered open and he said, "Where -?" before his eyes focused and widened. It was then that the high-pitching screaming started, and Sophie was forced to lower the volume on Tel's phone. He clutched at the straps of his harness with his legs flailing, shrieking like a girl.

In the distance, Sophie's voice, "Tel! Tel! It's okay, Tel!"

"Okay?" he yelled, soprano. "We're thousands of miles above the – " He looked down. He vomited. The pub groaned. Mark heaved and rushed to the toilets with his hand over his mouth.

"Better?" came Sophie's voice, off-camera.

Tel started crying, really crying. Tears filled his eyes and rose up over his forehead. His lips quivered and flapped.

"It'll soon be over, Tel."

"Sophie! Sophie!" He reached out with his arms. ""Go ... after ... her! Don't let her ... get away! Sophie, will you -?"

"What?"

"Sophie, will you -?"

"I can't hear you, Tel."

Tel started breast stroking with his arms, yelling, "Get closer!"

The instructor's voice, saying, "This is as close as we can get without the parachutes tangling up."

"Tangling!" The camera caught him in close-up, hyperventilating. Someone at the next table said, "Isn't it exciting. Does he live or die in the end?"

"I don't know, I've never seen this before."

"Sophie!" Tel screamed from the TV, "Will you -?"

A sudden gust of wind shuddered the camera. Tel's mouth formed a perfect oval shape, before his eyes closed and his body hung limp in the harness, his head resting on his chest.

Sophie skimmed the video through the long minutes where Tel was flopped motionless in mid-air, and played the bit where he woke up, started screaming, and landed.

Mark, just coming out the pub toilet, glanced at the screen just as Tel was wiping tears and snot and vomit from his face, and dashed back through the door again.

"See!" Jim said, "Told you you'd wet yourself!"

Tel took the phone from Sophie and turned it off. He thought about going outside to wallow in his own misery for a while, maybe contemplate his manhood, his lack of bravery and the hitherto unknown streak of cowardice that obviously ran through him, when Sophie tenderly kissed the side of his face. "To think," she whispered in his ear, "That you'd still try and propose even when you were in the midst of pure terror, that takes courage."

"And love," he grinned.

Brian leaned over and said, "And some teeth-grinding, fist-clenching, gut-wrenching determination. Attributes for a perfect marriage, I'd say."

"Thanks, Bri."

A man from the crowd came rushing over and walloped Tel on the back. He thought he was maybe being mugged, until the man said, "I could never have done that in a million years. Bloody well done, mate."

"Yeah," someone else called over, "Takes guts, that, and to try and propose at the same time, take my hat off to you, I really do."

"Well done!"

"And well done on the fiancé," cried a man at the bar, raising his glass, "Bloody cracker, she is."

"Cracker or crackers?" Sophie said, laughing.

"Both," Tel told her, suddenly not feeling so bad anymore.

Chelsea came out of the kitchen carrying two plates,

just as a man at the bar asked her for a drink. "Be with you in a minute, love."

Olivia leapt up and hurried over. "Are you coping okay?"

"Yeah, just really busy, and I've got to take these out – "

"Oh, I'll do that." She took the plates from her. "Which table?"

"Seventeen."

Olivia made her way through the busy pub to the busy garden. Everyone seemed to be having a lovely time and she felt exhilarated by how well everything had gone. As she put the plates down on the table with a huge smile, the man asked, "Are you the manager?"

"No, I'm just the owner. The red-haired lady, Chelsea, is the manager, she does all the hard work."

"Really nice place you've got here," he said, and the woman with him nodded. "Good atmosphere. We've already booked our next holiday here."

"Oh, lovely!"

"And us," said a man at the next table. "I *would* say it's peaceful and relaxing, except for the midnight scramblers and motorised caravans running amok in the camping field."

"And some bloke who snores like a foghorn!" someone shouted over, and everyone laughed.

"Who is that, anyway?" asked a woman two tables away.

"My lips are sealed," Olivia said, "But we'll be giving away earplugs the next time he's booked in."

"Good."

"A really nice site, we'll be telling all our friends."

"We've had the best time."

"Little plots of happiness," a man shouted over, and everyone laughed again.

"Thank you."

Smiling like a mad thing, Olivia left them chatting and laughing with each other, feeling something warm and fuzzy growing inside her. The place was buzzing, the tills were ringing, and everybody seemed happy. It had gone better than she'd expected, all her hard work had paid off. A warm glow of satisfaction, and yes, a little pride, filled her as she passed lively groups of people. Inside the pub, Mark was at the bar, chatting to someone about clematis wilt. She gently touched his arm as she passed, and he turned and smiled at her.

At the other end of the bar, Brian and Faye were talking to another couple, who looked vaguely familiar. As she was trying to figure out where she'd seen them before, Sophie sidled up to her and said, "Doppelgangers."

"Oh yes!" Brian was talking to a bloke as tall and as wide as himself, with a big, bushy beard. Their deep baritone voices boomed over the bustling conversations all around them. Faye was talking to a woman who looked just like her. "How strange."

"Isn't it."

Tel was holding court in the middle of the pub, surrounded by men all holding pints of beer, regaling them with tales of terror in the skies. Sophie wandered over and joined in.

Jim and Beth were smooching at the table, Beth occasionally screeching with laughter.

Olivia took a moment to look around and savour all that she had achieved. Richard – Dick – said she'd never make it on her own without him, that she didn't have a head for figures and could 'never in a million years' be a businesswoman; had, in fact, laughed at the very idea when she once suggested opening a kitchen shop in Bath.

It was true, she didn't have a good head for figures, but she'd hired the best accountant she could find, who charged her for his services and didn't use her money as his own – win-win. She didn't have a good head for business either, but she'd been lucky enough to find Chelsea, who knew everything there was to know about running a pub – she couldn't have done this without her.

Chelsea passed her just at that moment, and she reached out to give her a hug.

"What was that for?" Chelsea grinned.

"Because you're brilliant."

"Good time to ask for a pay rise then?" she laughed. "Place is doing well, isn't it."

"It is, and it's all because of you."

Chelsea waved it off and went to serve the throng of customers at the bar.

And Mark, she'd found Mark. She looked at him across the crowded room, and he suddenly turned his head, as if he could sense her watching him, and smiled. This was what love was, comfortable, warm, easy. This was what happiness was, right here, right now, surrounded by happy people.

Hands drifted around her waist from behind. "You okay?" Mark rested his head on her shoulder.

"It's strange, isn't it," she said. "How much things can change in a year."

"It certainly is."

"It's like …" She struggled to find the words to describe how she was feeling, it was such a big feeling. "It's like I was living this tiny little life, restricted."

"Oppressed."

"And twelve months later I have all of this."

"And me."

"Yes, you're the cherry on the cake. I could never have imagined any of this in my wildest dreams."

"Happy?"

"So happy I could burst." She laughed. "Sometimes it feels like a dream, that I might wake up at any moment and find it all gone. Everything changed because of my friends, who made me realise that everyone has a right to be happy, even me."

Mark kissed her cheek. "My lovely, lovely Liv."

Behind the mic, a middle-aged woman with a Karen haircut and a long skirt started shushing and very sweetly singing about it being, oh, so quiet. Nobody paid any attention, until the big band section exploded from the speakers and the woman went a little bit wild with her vocals and her dancing.

Brian and Faye came over. "Funny how you always meet the nicest people just before you go home," Faye said.

"Nice chap," Brian said, "Scottish, have a lot in common."

"Deep pockets and short arms," Faye cackled

"Says the woman who's filled our caravan with unnecessary bric-a-brac."

"It'll all come in handy, you'll see."

A man in chef whites appeared behind the bar, his back half turned to the crowds.

"Oh!" Olivia cried, rushing over to him, "Can I have everyone's attention please?" she said in her tiny voice. "Can I just say a few words about -?"

"QUIET!" Brian bellowed, and the pub was stunned into silence.

"I'd like to introduce you to the jewel in the Woodsman crown, my chef, Tony."

A cheer went up and Tony instantly turned puce.

"He's the one responsible for the delicious meals you've been eating all week."

"Your beef bourguignon was amazing," Mark shouted, pinching his fingers between his lips.

"Best food I've ever had," someone else yelled.

"Your chicken, spinach and potato curry was to die for," Brian yelled. Then, leaning into Faye, he whispered, "He's twelve years old, tops."

"Does his muvva know he's out this late?" Beth cackled.

Olivia leaned towards them and said, "He's thirty-two, with two children."

"Ask him what moisturiser he uses," Faye quickly asked.

"Cooking oil," Tel laughed.

"Sirloin steak jus, surely," said Sophie.

A rousing rendition of *He's a Jolly Good Fellow* followed a still red-faced Tony as he fought his way through the crowd with his head down and exited.

"Whatever you're paying him," Tel said, "It's not enough."

"I know," Olivia grinned, "We were very lucky to get him."

Chelsea was talking to the karaoke man. "We have a winner," he announced. "Worst singer of the night ..." He conferred with Chelsea again whilst the crowded pub waited expectantly. "Sophie Forbes!"

"Oh, surely not," Sophie sighed, "There were *much* worst singers than me."

"There weren't," Tel laughed. "Don't give up your day job is my best advice."

Sophie made her way, eyeballs rolling, up to the karaoke man to collect her 'prize', a bottle of wine. "Liebfraumilch?" she said, showing it to Tel, "What even is that?"

"It's cheap pleb plonk," Jim laughed. "I'll have it if you don't want it."

Sophie clutched the bottle tightly in her arms. "No, it's mine, I won it."

"We can display it in the toilet," Tel said.

"Which toilet, yours or mine?"

"Well, I was rather hoping, now that we're engaged, that we could ... maybe ... share a toilet?"

"Your place or mine?"

"Up to you."

"Mine, I have more wardrobe space."

"And the best singer of the night." The karaoke man paused for effect, slowly looking around the room full of eager faces. "Adele."

Everyone turned to stare at Beth, already clapping and cheering.

"Who?" Beth cried.

"You, love!"

"Oh!" She sauntered up to receive her prize with people congratulating her on all sides. She took it all in her stride and graciously accepted her bottle of champagne. Holding it up in front of her, she approached the mic and said, "Thank you, everyone, I'm thrilled to bits. I'd just like to thank me mom and dad, and Jim, me 'usband." She glanced over at Melissa behind the bar, who suddenly took an intense interest in the bottles of spirits on the back wall.

"We've got time for one more from our winner before I shut up shop," the karaoke man said.

"Oh, have you got …?" Beth quickly scooted over to him, shared a few words, a couple of nods, and came back to the mic. "I've picked a good one to end the night wiv and I fink you'll all enjoy, once you've figured out what it is." In her sonorous, mezzo-soprano voice, she began to sing *Happy Days Are Here Again*.

By the end, everyone had joined in and were singing their hearts out.

Olivia cried.

* * *

"I think I'm a bit drunk," Faye said, staggering across the car park towards the camping field.

"More than a bit," Brian laughed, "You're talking to a tree, lass."

Faye looked up at the tree she'd mistaken for Brian and started to turn around to face the others, but fell against the gate and hung there like an abandoned rag doll. Brian pulled her off and hauled her over his enormous shoulder. "Race ya!" he cried to the others.

Sophie screamed as Tel bent his knees and reversed into her. She jumped onto his back, piggy-back style, and Tel started running. Mark, slightly drunk himself, tried to do the same, but missed Olivia and fell onto his back. Olivia wavered on the spot, looking around and saying, "Mark? Where have you gone?"

"I'm down here."

She looked at the ground. "Are we sleeping here?" She gave a beaming smile as she crouched down next to him, saying, "I'd sleep anywhere with you, you're so lovely."

"Get up, you two," Tel cried, as he gave chase after Brian, who was now galloping down the driveway with Faye screaming, "Bri! Bri! Help me, I'm being kidnapped!"

Mark and Olivia struggled to their feet. Beth looked at Jim, who was gauging his best approach on her body with wavering eyes, and said, "It's okay, darlin', I don't want you to do yourself an injury."

"No," he said, "I got this." He gripped her waist while she stood there with her arms up. He pressed a shoulder into her chest and tried to grab her bottom, then stood behind her with his hands under her armpits.

Beth walked off, leaving him in mid-lifting pose, and cried, "Come on, babes, lead me to our little love nest." Jim chased after her, still trying to figure out a way to pick her up, darting from one side to the other with his arms striking different poses.

"Let me down!" Sophie screamed, "I'm going to throw up!"

Mark, jogging behind them with Olivia at his side, dry-wretched and shouted, "Don't you dare!"

Brian reached their caravan first and flung Faye off his shoulder so quickly she staggered back and fell into a chair. "That'll be £4.50, madam."

Tel, puffing wildly, and Sophie, elegantly slipping off his back, came to a stop in the driveway, followed by Mark and Olivia, with Jim and Beth in the rear. "Can't win everyfink," Beth shrugged. "Right, 'usband, where's the boudoir?"

"Boudoir?"

"Place we're sleeping at."

Jim held out a hand. Beth turned to follow it, looked at the shepherd's hut, and said, "A shed?"

"It's a shepherd's hut."

"A wooden box on wheels? Can we both even fit in

315

there?"

"You can have my caravan, if you like?" Mark said, "I'm not using it."

Olivia giggled and placed a hand against her hot face.

"That yours?" Beth asked, nodding at the caravan in the corner. "No offence, darlin', but it'll be full of man dust and belly fluff, I fink I'd rather take me chances with the spiders in the shed."

"There's rooms upstairs at the pub," Olivia suggested. "You're more than welcome to – "

"Cheers, but I ain't no posh bird, tiny wooden cabin will do me fine. You want to carry me over the threshold, Jim?" She burst out laughing as Jim eyed up the best way to pick her up. "Don't look so horrified, I'm only kiddin'."

Olivia grabbed hold of Mark's hand, pulling him towards the motorhome. "I'm so tired," she cried, trying to yawn but hiccoughing instead, "Come and sleep with me."

"Now there's an offer I can't refuse." He let her drag him off, just as Jim and Beth were squeezing through the doors of the shepherd's hut and falling onto the airbed, and Tel and Sophie were quietly sloping off to their caravan.

"Wife?"

"What?"

"Time for bed, said Zebedee, hopefully."

Faye, lounging askew in a chair, quietly burping, said, "Is Zebedee here?"

"No, just a big Yorkshireman."

"I like Yorkshiremen."

"I've noticed. You coming to bed, or would you prefer to sleep out here with the rats and the bats and the things that scream *argh!* in the night?"

"Coming!" she cried, heaving herself up and crashing into the unopened caravan door.

* * *

At first, they couldn't get to sleep because of Beth's shrieking laughter coming from the shepherd's hut.

Then they couldn't get to sleep because of Brian's loud snoring.

And then because of the screaming of a woman coming from the trees all around them.

* * *

"Our last night," Sophie sighed.

"I know, it's been good, hasn't it."

"Very memorable, as Brian would say."

"Yes, very."

"Our very last night," Sophie sighed again. "Maybe time for one last memory-making event?"

"Intrigued. Elaborate."

She leaned up on one elbow next to him in bed. "Well, do you remember when you mentioned outdoor pursuits?"

"Yes," he drawled.

"It's our last night. There's a forest just outside. Do you fancy a bit of … outdoor sport?"

It had seemed like a good idea at the time. Exciting. Slightly naughty.

The reality was something completely different.

* * *

"Here?" Tel asked.

"We're still too close to the campsite."

They walked on, off the pathway, in the pitch dark, through the endless shadow of trees and ferns.

"Bit spooky, isn't it," Sophie whispered.

"Are there still wolves in Middle England?"

"Oh don't!"

"No, I was genuinely wondering."

"There's no bears in England, that's for sure." Sophie

said this just as a loud crack sounded from the shadows to their left. In a slightly higher pitch she breathed, "Are there?"

"No, I'm pretty sure there aren't."

"For highly educated people we're a bit lax in the old wildlife department."

"I'll take a Ray Mears course at the earliest possible opportunity, and if he's not available, a Bear Grylls survival course."

"Is there a course on how to make love in the woods without –" A heavy rustling in the undergrowth to their right, and again her voice went up a couple of octaves, " – being scared to death?"

"If only you could have sung that high earlier," Tel laughed quietly. "How about here?"

"Too many trees."

"Hard to find a place without too many trees in a forest, Soph."

"Yes, okay, fine. I don't want to be too far from the campsite anyway."

"Not too close, not too far."

"Like Goldilocks with the porridge."

"At least we know our fairy tales."

"Having heard so many of them in court," Sophie laughed softly. "I feel quite like a child myself at the moment, I can't remember the last time I felt this scared."

"I do," Tel said.

He laid the blanket on the forest floor and helped her down onto it. "OW!" she said.

"What?"

"Ground's prickly."

"It's a forest floor, what did you expect, memory foam and Egyptian cotton sheets?"

"We should have brought the duvet. And pillows."

He lay down next to her. She fidgeted. He tried to kiss her and she said, "I can't get comfortable."

"Are you sure you want to do this?"

Her voice said yes, but her darting eyes said, 'I'm definitely going to die.'

He tried to kiss her again and she froze. "Did you hear that?"

"No."

She sat up, frantically looking around and saying, "I think there's somebody out there."

"There's nobody."

"There is! Listen!"

A rustling of dry leaves, followed by the crack of a branch.

"Somebody must have followed us," Sophie hissed, "A psychopath with a loathing for lawyers."

"You should put that imagination to good use and write a book. Come here." He tried to pull her down next to him again but she pushed him away, her eyes scanning the area. He said, "We could stand up, against a tree, perhaps?"

"Yes, let's try that."

Sophie put a hand down to stand up, and something ran across it.

That's when the screaming started.

* * *

"What's that?" Faye shot bolt upright in bed. Brian already had the window blind up and was peering outside.

They heard another scream, high-pitched and terrified, echoing over the campsite. Brian leapt out of bed and hurled himself out the door. He snatched his power torch off the table, turned it on and unzipped the awning. They both stood outside, listening.

The scream came again, even more terrified than before. Jim burst out of the shepherd's hut with Beth right behind him, and said, "What the hell is that? Are these woods haunted?"

Mark hurried over with Olivia, who was wrapping

the belt around her dressing gown. "Is somebody being murdered?" he asked.

"Is someone in trouble?" asked Olivia.

Brian held up a finger for silence and stared off into the trees.

The scream again, closer this time, followed by a man's holler. Brian moved towards the perimeter fence, his torch illuminating the way. The others followed a few steps behind, the women clinging to each other and Jim clinging to Beth, saying, "I heard they have witches' covens in these – "

"Where's Sophie?" Faye suddenly cried.

"Is that Sophie screaming?"

"SHHH!"

They heard hurried, heavy footsteps racing through the forest towards them. Brian swung his torch around, casting shadows of trees onto trees. The women and Jim took a step back. Brian and Mark hurried through the gate. A woman in the darkness shrieked, "THEY'RE FOLLOWING US! THEY'RE RIGHT BEHIND US!"

Brian and Mark were about to race up the embankment and onto the footpath when two shadows appeared above them and frantically began scrambling down. Brian swung his torch around, just in time to see Sophie hurtling towards him, with Tel hot on her heels.

"THERE'S SOMEBODY CHASING US!" she yelled, crashing into him as Brian threw the torch beam into the trees.

Sophie clung onto Brian, stifling hysteria. Tel spun round and followed the beam of light, panting heavily.

A deer pranced along the path.

"Oh," said Sophie.

"Joking!" Tel gasped, "A deer? It was a deer, Soph!"

"Well I know that *now*!"

"Sophie!" Olivia cried, "Are you alright?"

"I'm fine." She hauled herself off Brian and straightened out her dressing gown.

Faye came through the gate and hugged her. "What

were you doing out ...? Oh."

"Oh?" said Mark.

"Nothing, it's nothing."

"'Oh' usually means something.   Oh!" he gasped, catching on.

"Oh?" said Olivia.

Tel feigned confusion and rubbed at his forehead. "We must have been sleepwalking!"

"Both of you, together?" Brian drawled.

"Badger spotting," Sophie said, jutting out her chin and walking through the gate. "We just thought we'd do a bit of midnight badger spotting."

"Yeah," said Tel, following her. "We're quite keen on ... badgers."

"Are you?" Mark asked, "What's a badger sett called then?"

"A ... a den."

Olivia giggled and reached up to Sophie as she passed. "You've got some ... foliage in your hair, darling."

Jim started laughing. "You dirty buggers!"

Sophie struggled to maintain her composure as she hurried towards their caravan, followed by the sound of muted laughter.

Tel just smiled awkwardly and hurried after her.

"Everything alright?" someone shouted from a small group milling about outside their tents.

"Yeah," Jim shouted back, "Just someone enjoying a spot of *outdoors activity*, if you get what I mean."

Sophie gasped out loud and broke into a run.

"Good torch," Mark said, as they ambled back to the caravans.

"700 lumens," Brian said proudly. "Look, it can reach the sky." He shone the torch up at the clouds, where it formed a perfect bright circle. Somebody from the tents screamed, "WHAT'S THAT IN THE SKY?"

"ALIENS!" someone else cried, "WE'RE BEING INVADED

BY ALIENS!"
Brian turned the torch off.

CHAPTER 17

Day 8 – Friday

They each woke up at different times the following morning and sauntered over to the pub for breakfast. Brian and Faye were first, Brian proudly wearing his 'the THE' t-shirt, joined by Mark and Olivia a short while after.

"I thought champagne wasn't supposed to give you hangovers," Olivia said, delicately sitting down.

"Not mixed with rum, Liv."

"I don't drink rum, darling, only pirates drink rum."

"Ay, Jim lad," Mark laughed, then stopped to hold his head. "Ugh, I'm never drinking again."

"Famous last words."

"It was the whisky that got me," Brian groaned, glaring at his full breakfast. "Ewan, that's the Scottish bloke – "

"Figured."

" – gave me a tour of Scotland via the medium of whisky. Sampled entire country. Seemed like a good idea at the time. Not so much now, of course."

"I just stuck to champagne," Faye grinned brightly.

"Gallons of the stuff, as I recall."

"Had no effect on me at all."

Brian looked at her sharply, then mimicked her high voice, "Oh hello, tree, how long have you been there? Save me, Brian, I'm being kidnapped!"

They laughed, gently, whilst clutching their heads, except for Faye, who tucked into her sausage and bacon. "I think I'm only drinking champagne from now on," she said.

"Then you should find a better paid job or a richer husband, my love."

"Whatcha!" Jim beamed, putting his and Beth's plates down on the table and jumping into the seat.

Beth slowly perched sideways on the edge of the bench. "Nobody get up or your breakfasts will end up flying through the air."

"Who is this woman?" Brian asked Jim.

"I know!" Beth cried, squirting tomato sauce all over her breakfast, "I look different without me makeup, don't I."

"You look younger," Faye said, "Very fresh."

"'Ard to look fresh when you've drunk your own body weight in alcohol, which is a lot for me," she cackled, "And then spent the night in a shed. Good laugh, though."

"Yes, we heard."

"Oh? Surprised you could 'ear us above the *thunder* of your snoring! Never 'eard nothing like it in me life. You wanna get that sorted, mate."

"We could have the caravan soundproofed," Faye laughed, "Or order industrial earplugs, the kind they use in really loud factories."

"You'd still hear him," Mark laughed.

Tel ambled up with a plate containing one egg and a slice of unbuttered toast.

"Morning, action man. Where's Sophie?"

"In the caravan, where she assures me she'll be staying until we get back to London. She's beyond embarrassed."

"Know the feeling well," Faye said.

"It's not as if we caught you in flagrante," Brian said.

"In where?" Jim asked.

"Flagrante, it's a nice little village just off the west coast of Ireland."

Jim looked at Tel and said, "Is there a place called Ireland round here?"

"Please," Tel said, holding up a hand, "It's way too early for Jim-isms."

Brian burst out laughing. Jim looked confused, then shrugged and lay into his breakfast.

"I'm only eating this to soak up the alcohol," Tel said, nibbling on the corner of his dry toast and chewing distastefully. "I actually drank Sophie's Liebfraumilch last night, straight from the bottle. It tasted like diesel."

"That's why most folk fondly refer to it as Liebfraumuck."

"Made from the sour dregs of …?" Tel burped, then said, "I can't even talk about it, I can still taste it."

"Takes a day or two before the tastebuds go back to normal."

Tel put his toast down and grimaced at the tables around them. "All I can smell is greasy food."

"Quite common in a restaurant at breakfast, apparently."

"I'm on sensory overload." Tel stood up. "I'll see you back at the vans."

"Okay." Brian looked at his breakfast, then pushed his plate away.

"You not eating that?" Jim said, already spearing the bacon with his fork.

* * *

"Sophie!"

"I'm not coming out."

"Come on, Soph," cried Brian. "Faye's going to counsel you through the first fifteen seconds of excruciating humiliation, you'll be fine after that."

"It's true," Faye shouted, shaking her head and mouthing 'It's not' to everyone. "We don't care, anyway."

"Bit jealous, actually," Olivia giggled.

"Later," winked Mark.

"You've got ten seconds to get out here," Brian shouted, "Or we're coming in to get you."

The caravan door swung open and Sophie stiffly came down the steps, marching over to them with her face set firmly to one side. "I can't even look at you," she said, "I'm too embarrassed." She threw herself into a seat, her face still averted.

"How's your 'angover?" Beth asked.

"Hard to tell over the shame and humiliation."

"Nothing to be embarrassed about," Mark soothed.

"We didn't even do anything," said Tel.

Sophie gasped, "You don't have to tell them that!"

"What were you doing in the woods in the middle of the night then?" Jim asked.

"Screaming, mostly," Tel said.

"Screaming and running," Sophie added, with a frightened look in her eye. "Never again." She turned to Tel. "Having no electric light is just not natural, is it!"

"It kind of is, Soph."

"Soft city dwellers," Jim laughed.

"How did stone-age man ever manage to procreate?"

"They just clubbed their women over the head," Brian said, "Women weren't much bothered about the dark and rampaging deer after that. Maybe you should take a club with you next time, Tel?"

"There won't be a next time," Sophie shuddered. "I might need therapy to recover, and I'm definitely not watching another horror film ever again. Let's talk about something else."

"When can we get together again?" Jim asked.

Faye ran into the caravan, crying, "I'll get my calendar."

"You can pop in any time for a stay, no charge," Olivia said.

"No, we'll pay the going rate, like normal people," Tel said.

"Normal?" Beth cackled. "Never met such a bunch of reprobates, and I'm speaking as Jim's unfortunate wife. You're totally my type, normal is uber boring."

"Business is doing well," Olivia said, "I can treat my friends to freebies if I want to and there's nothing you can do about it." She stuck her tongue out. "Honestly, any time you're passing, any time you need a break, you're more than welcome."

"Very kind of you, Liv."

"You'll have to pay for your own food and drinks though," she added, "You lot can knock it back a bit."

"Says the woman who was drinking rum straight from the bottle last night!" Brian laughed.

"I wasn't!"

"You were. Photographs were taken, you look like a mad woman in every one of them."

Faye flicked through her calendar. "I just need to give a week's notice at work, and Brian needs two."

Sophie and Tel opened their online diaries. "Got the Pilkington case coming up next month," Sophie said.

"I've got a corporate shareholder fraud next week, that'll take a while."

"August?"

"Can maybe fit in a long weekend?"

"I could possibly do the beginning of – "

"Why don't we just text each other when we're free?" Brian suggested.

"I'm free and easy any time," Olivia giggled.

"So we've heard," Jim laughed.

A car pulled up on the caravan area next to theirs. The door opened and a familiar voice cried, "Coo-ee! I'm back!"

Flo burst through the hedge with her arms outstretched. "Oh, Faye, my little cat is fan*tas*tic, absolutely fan*tas*tic. I nearly brought her to meet you all but she needs time to settle in first, but I've already got her a harness so I can take her out for walks." Tel glanced at Sophie, who shrugged. "How are you all? You all look … well, a little hungover, to be honest, but it's fan*tas*tic to see you again, have you missed me?"

Before anyone had a chance to speak, Flo continued, "We've just come back to collect the caravan, haven't we, Bill."

Bill appeared through the hedge and raised a hand in greeting, since he couldn't actually get a word in, and didn't seem that bothered about it. "He's going to put it back into storage and then we're going to have our own little holiday together in Birmingham, which will be fan*tas*tic, we can go and see all the sites. I mean, I've seen them all before, obviously, but we thought it would be fan*tas*tic to revisit them together and still be home at night for Kitty-Kat."

"Kitty-Kat?" Faye managed to ask.

"Yes, that's what I'm calling her. I can't wait for you to meet her, she's just the most adorable cat you've ever seen, very friendly, likes a lot of fuss. Anyway, no time to chat, want to get back to Kitty-Kat before she notices I've gone and starts pining, but it's been fan*tas*tic to meet you all, we'll have to do it again sometime. Come on, Bill, let's pack up and hitch up."

Bill raised a farewell hand as Flo dragged him back through the hedge.

"Poor Bill," Brian said, "I don't know how he puts up with it."

"People say the same about you," Faye said.

"What, how do I put up with you?"

She eyeballed him. "They seem happy enough though."

"Until the PTSD sets in."

"And on that note," Tel said, standing up, "We'd better get this show on the road."

"Oh, there's no rush," Olivia said, "Management are very flexible about leaving times, although we do have new arrivals coming after lunch."

"It's nearly lunch now," Brian said, glancing at his watch. "Let's get packing."

Mark relaxed back in his chair with his arm across Olivia's shoulders and said, "Not me, I think I might stick around for a bit."

"Me too," Olivia giggled.

"And we'd best be off," Jim said, as he and Beth stood up. "Enjoyed it, it was … nice."

"It was," Beth said, leaning down to hug them all. "I 'ope you'll invite me again."

"Oh we will," Brian said, "Most definitely."

"Do you want us to put the shepherd's hut back," Jim asked Olivia.

"Us?" said Mark.

"No, I quite like it where it is, I might leave it there."

"Okay. Well, see ya, reprobates."

He waved, Beth waved, they all waved, and then they were gone, ambling through the hedge towards the pub with their arms around each other.

"Nice couple," said Faye.

"They actually are," Mark said, watching them. "Who'd have thought it, eh?"

"Right, let the packing commence," Brian said, standing up.

Tel looked at Mark and said, "So, you're just going to sit there and watch us, sweating, in the heat?"

Mark laughed and got up to help them pack away. The deconstruction of Brian's awning passed without incident. Olivia provided them with copious amounts of orange juice with ice to stave off dehydration.

Flo and Bill came back. "We're all packed and hitched," she said, hugging Faye. "We're going to have a bite to eat in the pub first, and then go home on the A roads, but just wanted to say bye and to thank you for having me."

"It's been a – "

"See ya, Bri." She jumped up to hang around his neck, planting a big quick kiss on his cheek. "Thanks for putting up with me, I know I got on your nerves and I'm sorry about that." She jumped down. "I will try and curb my talking a bit when I'm round yours, but I can't make any promises, I can only say I'll do my best."

"That's very – "

"Are you ready, Bill? I'm starving, and I don't want to leave Kitty-Kat on her own for too long."

Bill pumped Brian's hand. "Lovely to – "

"We'll pop round for lunch on Sunday, if you like, so you can get to know Bill a bit better."

Bill gave Faye a hug, saying, "It's been – "

Flo grabbed his hand and pulled him back through the hedge, saying, "Absolutely famished, I am. See ya, Faye. See ya, Bri."

And then they were gone.

Brian laughed, shaking his head. He glanced across the driveway and noticed Tel winding his jockey wheel up and down, muttering to himself. He wandered over, bent down, and whispered, "You might find it better if you raise the legs on the caravan before attempting to lower the wheel, Tel."

He wandered back, chuckling to himself, and was about to get into his car to hitch up, when Ewan, the Scotsman, came over with his wife, Isla. "Yer off then?"

"We are."

"Brought ye a farewell gift." He held out a bottle of whisky, and Brian felt a little sick after the previous night's overindulgence. "It's okay," Ewan said, "It's a breakfast whisky."

Brian grinned and took it from him.

"Not before five o'clock," Faye said, taking it from him. To Ewan and Isla she said, "We'll have to get together again soon."

"Aye, that we will."

"It's been lovely to meet you both." She hugged Isla, then reached up to hug Ewan. Brian gave him a hearty handshake and Isla a delicate kiss on the cheek.

"Have a safe journey," they said, wandering off.

"Nice people," Faye said.

Brian snatched the whisky from her. "Mine."

"If you start putting it on your cornflakes I'm pouring it down the sink."

Brian gasped dramatically and hugged the bottle to his chest. "Never!"

He put it safely in the boot of his car and looked over at Tel, who was furiously driving his car backwards and forwards in front of his caravan. He wandered over again. "Soph?"

"Yes, Bri?"

"Come and stand over here by the hitch."

"The hitch?"

"Yeah, this bit here, where the caravan attaches to the car."

She came and stood next to it, looking down. "Does it do something?"

"No, but you do. Watch me." Brian had to wave his arms around a bit to get Tel's attention in the rear-view mirror, he was staring determinedly at his dashboard. He signalled for Tel to reverse, indicating a little left or a little right, until the towball was centred and touching the hitch.

"See?" Brian said.

"I do see," Sophie said, grinning. "Tel can also see using the reverse camera on the back of his car, but if technology ever fails and we need to escape rampaging zombies in a hurry I'll know exactly what to do."

Brian bent down to peer into the tiny camera, and Tel yelped in the car. "Scared the living daylights out of me!" he cried.

Chuckling, Brian made his way back across the driveway. The cute little boy he'd met at the barbecue and who waved at him every time he saw him came running over to him. "Are you going home?" he said.

"I am."

Hayden lifted up his arms, wanting to be picked up. Brian obliged. The little boy covered the side of his mouth and whispered in Brian's ear, "Can you tell your brother that I'd like a remote-controlled car for Christmas, a red one?"

Brian smiled. "Yes, I will."

"Can I touch your beard?"

"You can."

Brian jutted out his chin and Hayden gently stroked it,

saying, "Does it turn white at Christmas?"

"Only if the sister-in-law outstays her welcome."

"I heard that." Faye came and stood next to them. "You have a nice holiday, little man."

"I will." He wriggled to be put down again and ran off to where his mom and dad were peering over the hedge. "Cute kid you've got there," Brian called over to them.

"Thanks." They both waved. Dad lifted Hayden up so he could wave too.

Mark stood on the gravel driveway with his arms outstretched. "Group hug!" he cried, and they converged into a rugby scrum.

"It's been brilliant"

"Yeah, it's been really good."

"Different."

"Exhausting."

"I need a week to recover."

"I love you guys."

"Love you more."

They broke apart.

"I hate this bit," Olivia said.

"It's not goodbye," Sophie said, "It's a 'see you soon'."

"I like that. Thanks, Sophie, for everything."

"You're more than welcome, Liv."

Mark pumped Brian's giant hand. "Always good to spend time with you, big man."

"Same here. I'll pop down for a pint and a chin-wag soon."

"I'll cook," Olivia grinned.

The departing couples clambered into their cars.

"Do you want to follow us to the M40?" Tel yelled.

"What, and end up stuck in some farmyard? You follow me."

"Okay."

"Start your engines!" he hollered, raising an arm out of the window. "Wagons roll! Me first, Tel, you big plonk!"

"Bye!"

"Drive safe."

"Call me."

"Miss you already."

"Miss you more."

Mark and Olivia stood on the driveway, waving at them until the cars and the caravans slowly trundled out of sight.

Olivia's phoned pinged almost immediately. "Oh, it's a message from Sophie. 'Have fun, but don't bother with any midnight adventures, ghastly. S x'."

"I think we'll be the judge of that," Mark winked, holding the motorhome door open for her. "Cup of tea and a snog?"

"Lovely."

If you enjoyed this book please leave a rating or, better still, an actual review (I love those) on Amazon. I thank you.

OTHER BOOKS BY DEBORAH AUBREY

PITCHING UP! (Book 1)
PITCHING UP AGAIN! (Book 2)
PITCHING UP IN STYLE! (Book 3)
PITCHING UP IN AMERICA! (Book 4)

TIPPING POINT

Contact Me - I'd be thrilled to hear from you!
Email: deborahaubrey01@gmail.com
Facebook: AuthorDebbieAubrey
Amazon Author Page: Deborah Aubrey

Until next time, ta ta. Dx

Printed in Great Britain
by Amazon

31302062R00188